THE DEFINITIVE GUIDE TO

PASSING THE POLICE RECRUITMENT PROCESS

Visit our How To website at www.howto.co.uk

At **www.howto.co.uk** you can engage in conversation with our authors – all of whom have 'been there and done that' in their specialist fields. You can get access to special offers and additional content but most importantly you will be able to engage with, and become a part of, a wide and growing community of people just like yourself.

At **www.howto.co.uk** you'll be able to talk and share tips with people who have similar interests and are facing similar challenges in their lives. People who, just like you, have the desire to change their lives for the better – be it through moving to a new country, starting a new business, growing their own vegetables, or writing a novel.

At **www.howto.co.uk** you'll find the support and encouragement you need to help make your aspirations a reality.

You can go direct to **www.the-definitive-guide-to-passing-the-police-recruitment-tests.co.uk** which is part of the main How To site.

How To Books strives to present authentic, inspiring, practical information in their books. Now, when you buy a title from **How To Books,** you get even more than just words on a page.

THE DEFINITIVE GUIDE TO

PASSING THE POLICE RECRUITMENT PROCESS

A HANDBOOK FOR
PROSPECTIVE POLICE OFFICERS,
SPECIAL CONSTABLES AND
POLICE COMMUNITY SUPPORT OFFICERS

JOHN McTAGGART

howtobooks

Published by How To Books Ltd,
Spring Hill House, Spring Hill Road,
Begbroke, Oxford OX5 1RX, United Kingdom
Tel: (01865) 375794 Fax: (01865) 379162
info@howtobooks.co.uk
www.howtobooks.co.uk

How To Books greatly reduce the carbon footprint of their books by sourcing their typesetting and printing in the UK.

British Library Cataloguing in Publication Data.
A catalogue record for this book is available from the British Library.

ISBN 978 1 84528 435 0

Produced for How To Books by Deer Park Productions, Tavistock
Typeset by PDQ Typesetting, Newcastle-under-Lyme, Staffordshire
Printed and bound in Great Britain by Bell & Bain Ltd, Glasgow

Contents

Introduction **1**
What is this book about? 1
Why is this book different? 1
What do the police think of this approach? 2
Using the skills you have and preparing effectively 3
Summary of this approach 5
Understanding the background of the assessment process 6
What if they change the format of the assessment centre from that described in this book? 7
Should I complete a police preparation course as well? 8
How to use this book 9

1 A brief outline of the application process **10**
The application process 10
Do assessment centres work? 12
Why do people fail assessment centres? 17
Summary 22
The police and inappropriate behaviour 23

2 The core competencies **26**
Explaining the core competencies 26
The behavioural statements 28
How the competencies relate to your application 36

3 Application forms **41**
The application form explained 41
The competency questions in detail 44
The diversity and respect question 46
The team-working question 48
The 'working under pressure' question 49
The communication question 51
Summary on competency questions 52
The motivation and perception type questions 53
Summary on the motivation and perception type questions 57

4 The national assessment centre 58

The thinking behind assessment centres 58

A typical assessment centre 59

Inappropriate behaviour in the general context of the assessment centre 61

The welcome pack 63

5 An introduction to role plays 69

Role plays 69

Signposts, hooks and blocks 83

Problems when dealing with inappropriate behaviour 101

Summary 102

6 The role play planning and preparation phase 103

The preparation phase 103

The CAR system: how to plan properly 107

Exercise: Abbot 110

What happens if you fail to plan? 122

Recognising, confronting and dealing with inappropriate behaviour 129

Common mistakes in the planning phase 130

Summary 134

7 The role-play interactive phase 136

What is the interactive phase? 136

The principles of role-playing: what are assessors looking for? 137

Inside knowledge about role plays 138

The techniques of the interactive phase 145

What makes a good solution? 151

The role play and inappropriate behaviour 155

Scalars: it's not what you do it's the way that you do it 161

Common mistakes in the interactive phase 162

What if it all goes wrong? 168

Some home truths about role actors 171

Final insider tips 174

How to practise role plays 175

Summary 176

8 Interviews 177

The two types of interview: national and local 177

The national recruitment model interview 177

Preparing your answers 184

What is evidence? 186

Using the CAR system and the competencies to develop answers 189

General advice 213

Summary 214
The local interview 215
The most common themes 216
Typical questions asked at local interviews 222
Summary 224

9 The written exercises: reports and proposals 226
What are written reports? 226
Recognising and dealing with inappropriate conduct 231
The principles of written responses 232
Common mistakes in written reports 238
Exercise 1: Complaints of potential inappropriate conduct 241
Exercise 2: The parking problem 246
Exercise 3: Health and safety inspection of the centre kitchen 251
Some general points on this type of exercise 252
Summary of written reports 255

10 Preparing for the assessment centre 256
Preparation techniques 256

11 The marking guide 264
Explaining the marking guide 264

12 The final word: IQ and fitness tests 267
The IQ test 267
The fitness tests 268

13 Example role-play exercises 270
General instructions 270
Abbot 271
Byrnes 274
Charles 277
Deane 280

14 Role-play specimen plans, role actor's instructions and marking guides 283
Abbot 284
Byrnes 287
Charles 290
Deane 293

Index 296

This book is dedicated to all those officers I had the privilege of serving with in Merseyside and Cheshire Police. In particular I would mention the Crime Car, the Warrington Early Intervention Team, and my team when I was an Inspector at Warrington, but to all of you street warriors, it was a pleasure to work with you.

Thank you also to my editorial guide (you know who you are!).

Finally, thanks are due to everyone involved in Operation Dramas, without whom Talking Blues would not exist.

Introduction

WHAT IS THIS BOOK ABOUT?

This book has been written with one very specific objective in mind. It aims to give you, the reader, an in-depth appreciation of the skills and abilities required to pass the police national recruitment tests, including the process for applying to be a Police Community Support Officer (PCSO). As you read through this book, you will see the approach is to explain in detail the reasoning and rationale behind each exercise, the mechanics of how each exercise works, and the various limitations that exist within the exercise itself – from the perspective of those who designed it. It is not about making you a better person, although if you follow the principles contained throughout, you may just end up that way!

In essence, this book is a 'how to' guide to passing the police recruitment system. It aims to give you the best chance of passing through the process successfully. It cannot guarantee a pass, but I believe that it is fair to say that it will give you a huge advantage over an unprepared candidate.

WHY IS THIS BOOK DIFFERENT?

There are a number of books in existence aiming to explain assessment centres. These are invariably written from a 'developmental' perspective. The authors tend to have come through the police assessment centre hierarchy themselves. They therefore tend to argue that the assessment centre itself is a model of good practice and integrity, and that candidates should not be told the 'inner workings' of assessment processes. Such books therefore adhere to the official police line that the centres are completely objective, and that the whole system is fair and transparent.

Taking a pragmatic approach

Whilst this approach is entirely praiseworthy, this book takes a much more pragmatic approach. I have no interest in commenting on whether the system is fair or not. I have no interest in keeping on the right side of the police establishment. Instead, the whole purpose of this book is to get you, the reader and the *candidate*, through the police recruitment system. Clearly, I do not wish the police service I love to recruit racist, sexist or homophobic people. However, whilst there are undoubtedly those in the establishment who would accuse me of aiding this very thing, they would do well to remember that if reading a book, or indeed attending a privately-run recruitment training course, can completely subvert their recruitment process, they ought to thank individuals such as myself! If it is so easy to subvert the national recruitment process, this should be a huge wake-up call to those responsible for assessment centre design that they need to do something positive to come up with a more robust system.

This book is written to get you through the assessment centre. If the police are unhappy at this, then regrettably they will need to come up with a better system. That is their problem, not the candidate's, nor indeed mine.

WHAT DO THE POLICE THINK OF THIS APPROACH?

Equality of all candidates

As far as the police are concerned, they would much prefer every candidate to turn up at the assessment centre with an equal level of prior knowledge of the assessment process and the exercises it contains. Ideally, this knowledge would be zero. Their argument is that this gives each candidate an equal chance of passing. Consequently, it would be fair to say that the police have no interest whatsoever in assisting privately-run preparation training courses. Indeed, at one stage the Home Office complained about statements made by my company's advertising when we stated that the course provided an advantage to candidates at assessment centres. The Home Office felt that providing this 'advantage' went against the whole ethos of the recruitment system. As a training provider I regard this as a compliment! Why else would students come on a course?

The official police line therefore is that the assessment centre is merely testing your potential to be a police officer. There is a definite suggestion from the service that the best way to prepare for this process is simply to be yourself.

The reality of life: how this book can help you

As with many things to do with police policies and aims, the reality of life is completely ignored in the assessment process. Assume there are two candidates attending the assessment centre on the same day. One is a taxi driver, who spends his or her working day driving around a large city in a black cab, having numerous short conversations with people they are unlikely to meet again. They have never found themselves in a situation where they have had to take part in a role play which has been marked and assessed. The second candidate is a sales person for a photocopying company. Any professional sales company will subject its employees to numerous training courses, a fundamental part of which will almost invariably involve role-playing. They will have been taught how to ask questions, they will know about the principles of time management, they will be aware of the principles of finding solutions. It is clearly foolish to suggest that both candidates go into the assessment centre on an equal footing. Consequently, to suggest that every candidate would go to the assessment centre with an equal level of knowledge is simply naïve. Special Constables, for example, are a group of volunteer police officers who are not paid, but clearly have exposure to the police organisation and culture that non-police staff will not have. Therefore, they must have an advantage over, say, a taxi driver. Having said that, many special constables and members of support staff actually fail the assessments as they treat the role-play scenarios as they know they would be dealt with in reality (i.e. poorly), and subsequently get low marks.

USING THE SKILLS YOU HAVE AND PREPARING EFFECTIVELY

The assessment centre process is supposed to assess a candidate's ability to be a police officer or PCSO. It basically requires candidates to perform a certain number of tasks. If they display the skills and abilities desired to the required standard, they will pass. On the face of it from the police perspective, every candidate should enter the assessment with an identical level of knowledge. As illustrated above, though, there is a huge flaw in this argument. If your life experiences – your background, education, employment or any of the dozens of factors that make you an individual – have made you particularly good at some of the skills being assessed, then clearly you will have an advantage over somebody who has not been so fortunate. The notion therefore that all candidates walk through the door at the assessment centre with the same opportunity to pass is clearly flawed. No matter how much the police recruitment system may wish otherwise, preparation is a huge factor in passing.

Gaining an advantage through books and training courses

Of course, it is obvious that *any* book or training course that seeks to provide information about the assessment centre process will state that preparation is the key. However, I truly do believe this – and this is why. The police assessment system is based on the national police promotion examinations to the rank of sergeant and inspector. These began in 1991. For the next 10 years, the national police training organisation actively promoted two national companies who provided training and development courses in preparation for the examinations. The reason the police service stepped away from these training providers was due to concerns that candidates using those companies may be perceived to have an advantage over those who did not use them. It was not because they were ineffective in preparing people. The vast majority of candidates for the police promotion examinations, which include role plays, still undertake preparation courses, most at their own expense. Many forces actually pay companies to run courses for their officers. It is nonsensical for the police to then argue that training courses for recruits are worthless, when forces are actively providing (and funding) courses covering the same principles for promotion examinations.

Taking the opportunity to prepare

Another factor to be considered is that when the police say they are against preparation training courses, what they really mean is that they do not like the average candidate being given preparation and coaching advice for the assessment. Yet the police service is in favour of providing the same support to people who are under-represented in the service. If you are from certain minority groups, the chances are you will be offered the opportunity as a candidate to go on some form of assessment centre preparation course run by the police themselves. My view therefore is this: if one group of people is to be allowed the opportunity to prepare in advance, so should any other. It makes a mockery of any police claims that there is no need for preparation. If preparation is of no value, then why do the police themselves run preparation courses for minority candidates?

SUMMARY OF THIS APPROACH

To summarise, and to answer the question posed in the title of this section, the police are ambivalent about privately provided assessment centre training. You, as the candidate, need to ask why this is the case. The police argument is that preparation training serves no purpose and will not help you to pass. Whilst they will not admit this, the real view is that they want to see you, the candidate, as you really are. They want to see you in the assessment centre, warts and all.

If you fail, it doesn't really matter to the police, because they have another 60,000 people to assess. It's the candidate who misses out. Aside from this, it is not in the police service's interest to have even more successful candidates. It just makes it harder for the police to select people if everyone is good. Also, from a political perspective, if the standard of candidate goes up, it makes it even harder for the police to recruit from disadvantaged communities or groups.

None of this of course should really be the candidate's problem. If you have the ability to prepare, and the determination, then there is no reason why you should not be allowed to do so.

A final thought on effective preparation

One final thought on the value of preparation. Candidates have the choice of preparing by using a book or attending a training course, such as the one provided by Talking Blues. So if the candidate pays to attend a course, or buys a book, and that preparation will do them no good whatsoever, why should the police be bothered? If reading this book is a complete waste of time, why would the police care? If the ideas contained within it, along with the information and techniques, were of no value, why would this trouble the police? Are they that concerned about you wasting your money? I suspect not.

Even if you're a cynic, and to be honest I like cynicism in a police officer, the only logical conclusion is that the police service will try to play down the value of such preparation because they do not want you, the candidate, to do it. Ask yourself this final thing. Are they really concerned about you wasting your money on a course or a book? Or is it more likely they are concerned that having prepared thoroughly you will fly through your assessment centre? Think about it!

UNDERSTANDING THE BACKGROUND OF THE ASSESSMENT PROCESS

Why was police assessment framework developed?

Before examining the assessment centre process in detail, it is worthwhile gaining a brief understanding of how the current system developed. There are 43 police forces in England and Wales. Over time each of these forces developed their own selection process. Whilst there were often common elements in these, there was no consistency nationally. For example, some forces just had an interview. Some had an interview and a letter writing exercise. Others ran formal assessment days, consisting of role plays, group discussions and written exercises. In some forces, candidates attended an assessment centre and were then called back for a final interview. There was no structure in place to provide national standards. It was entirely possible to apply to one force that had a full assessment centre process, fail and be told to come back in a year. Having just failed, you could then apply to a neighbouring force whose recruitment process consisted of different assessment criteria and pass. This was clearly nonsensical. The skills required of a police officer in Weymouth are no different from those required of a police officer in Warrington. There are numerous examples of potential police officers who, upon being rejected from one force, immediately applied to a neighbouring force and were successful. Just to make things even more farcical, a candidate rejected by their first choice force might be accepted by another force, successfully complete their two-year probation, and then transfer over to their first choice force having completely bypassed that force's recruitment system!

A system lacking credibility

So, the situation was that there were widely varying standards and the system lacked credibility. Candidates rejected from one force could become highly successful recruits in another. There was no doubt that potentially great candidates were being turned away for reasons that were not readily explainable or justifiable, and conversely some candidates were getting in who should never have been able to do so.

The development of a national system

It made sense therefore to develop a national system whereby the same standards applied to all forces. If a candidate does not have the skills to be accepted by one force, they should not be able to get into another one. The responsibility for the development of a new national system was undertaken through the Home Office by the National Policing Improvement Agency (NPIA), a non-departmental government body. Whilst NPIA are financed by the Home Office and the police service, they are technically independent of them. NPIA developed a national package which has now been implemented by all 43 forces. As with many things, whilst the theory behind it is laudable, the practical reality is arguably something else.

WHAT IF THEY CHANGE THE FORMAT OF THE ASSESSMENT CENTRE FROM THAT DESCRIBED IN THIS BOOK?

Since the national system was introduced, NPIA have made only a few minor changes to the format of the examination. For example, the written exercises were originally in the form of letters. This format only lasted a year, though, before the exercises were redesigned in the form of proposals.

However, there are limitations on what can be changed. The basic set up of the role plays, for example, is a building block of the whole police assessment process. It is unlikely that a replacement can be found for this. The principles of a role play remain the same, irrespective of the content. It is feasible, for example, that NPIA may do away with the five-minute planning phase. If they do, it just means that all of the factors described in the relevant chapter will need to be kept in mind in the first few moments of the new format.

It is possible that written exercises in the form of letters could make reappearance. However, again the fact remains that the basic principles involved are the same.

Remember that for ease of explanation, I have simplified many of the concepts discussed in this book. This will have no impact, however, on the relevance of the advice or techniques provided for each exercise.

Interview questions and format can be changed easily. However, as the assessors are looking for certain key qualities, there are always going to be key issues that the candidate will be asked about.

The competencies could change slightly but again this is irrelevant. The description of the desired qualities may change, but the qualities themselves remain the same. It is therefore certainly possible that the format of the assessment centre may change slightly; however, the underlying principles and techniques will always remain the same.

SHOULD I COMPLETE A POLICE PREPARATION COURSE AS WELL?

The simple answer to this question is 'it depends'. People have been getting into the police service for a very long time with no book like this nor any preparation courses to attend. On the other hand, for every one person who gets into the service, *seven* others fail.

It is the amount of preparation you prefer to undertake which is really the issue. Some people will always fly through any assessment with no preparation. Others will have to work their hearts out. Whether through natural ability or luck, this is just a fact of life. This book tries to explain the concepts involved in as simple a manner as possible. The advantage of a classroom-based course is that such concepts are more easily explained face to face, and on the day you'll be able to complete a number of role plays in real life circumstances, in front of an expert, and gain immediate honest feedback.

Ultimately, whether you attend a course or not will be for you to decide, based upon how confident you feel about the process, how fully you wish to prepare, the cost and your determination to avoid failing.

You can find out more about my own course at **www.talkingblues.co.uk**. The final choice about attending or not depends entirely upon your circumstances.

HOW TO USE THIS BOOK

In the following pages, you will find explanations of the thinking behind and the mechanics of each of the stages of the recruitment process. Approach the explanation aspects with an open mind. Understanding the background to the process and gaining an insight into the assessors' thinking will give you a definite advantage. You can then attempt the specimen exercises. These are representative in every way of the type of exercise you will get on the day.

You will find that key points are repeated. This repetition is deliberate and reinforces the learning points. Remember, if some of the concepts used seem a little hard to understand, your chances of success are directly related to the amount of preparation you undertake!

1

A brief outline of the application process

THE APPLICATION PROCESS

The assessment centre process will be identical irrespective of what part of the country you apply to. However, the elements of the PCSO system will be slightly different to the police system due to the role requirements. This next section describes the overall system. The national system consists of three main elements.

Completing an application form

Firstly, applicants are required to complete an in-depth application form. Obviously, this contains the normal basic information you'd expect. However, as police officers need to be security vetted, there are also a number of security questions involved. For example, candidates have to provide names and addresses of close family members, because they too will be security vetted. If your father was an international drug smuggler, clearly the service will want to examine your motivation for joining more thoroughly than the average candidate! All this is fairly straightforward, however, although many applicants underestimate the thinking behind asking for such information. This is why many candidates fall at the first hurdle. A more common source of failure can be found in the 'competency' questions. This section consists of a number of questions asking for specific examples from your own background of when you have displayed certain key qualities. The remaining parts of the form normally consist of such things as medical declarations and a few other pieces of administration.

Attending an assessment centre

When you have passed the application phase, you will be invited to attend an assessment centre. This assessment centre consists of the same exercises for every single force. If you are taking the assessment next Saturday in Milton Keynes, you'll be doing exactly the same assessment as someone taking it the same day in Wales – and I mean word for word. The North Wales candidate will undertake exactly the same role plays, the same interview questions and the same written exercises. This has to be done in the interests of fairness otherwise there could be allegations that candidates in one region had an easier assessment than those in another region.

Taking a medical and physical fitness assessment

If you pass the assessment centre, you will then be invited for medical and physical fitness assessment. Once passed, your references will be taken up and you will then be offered a starting date. The whole process can take anything between six and 18 months.

Regional differences

The procedure described so far is the theoretical national system; however, individual police forces have started to tinker with it. The centralised training agency for the police is very unhappy with this. After all, they have designed a national system and are not keen to see individual forces tampering with it. However, some forces continue to do their own thing. A minority of forces put candidates through a further interview once they have passed the national system. A few forces have 'screening interviews' prior to candidates attending the national assessment day. Forces may alter the positioning of the medical and physical tests to before or after the national assessment day, mainly in order to suit themselves and their own administrative procedures.

Additional interviews

The actual order of events is irrelevant to a large extent. It really doesn't matter if you do your physical assessment before or after your assessment day.

One thing that can catch people out, however, is the additional interview – that is if you happen to apply to one of the small number of forces that hold them. The easiest way to check this out is to simply ring the police recruiting department of your force and ask if you will be called to an interview other than the assessment day. If they will not tell you, and some forces (for no apparent reason) will not, there are ways to find out. One of the easiest is to use one of the police forums that can be found on Google. As far as this book is concerned, whilst the majority of candidates will not need it, a separate section has been included on this 'local' interview. Even if you do not need it, then it is there for interest. If you do require it, then it will form a further basis for your preparation. With regard to PCSO applicants, the assessment will simply be a 'cut down' version of the standard one.

Whilst there may be slight differences in what happens either side of the assessment day, it should be stressed the actual assessment day itself is the same nationally.

DO ASSESSMENT CENTRES WORK?

To be fair to the police service, there is no foolproof way in the world today to guarantee that a person selected using any available criteria will be able to perform in the role required of them. The best an organisation can do is to utilise a method of selection that offers the highest chance of successful candidates being able to do the job. Assessment centres in general have been proved time and time again to provide the highest probability of a successful candidate being able to do the job. In general, assessment centres are currently the best way to assess a candidate's potential.

Flaws in the assessment system

Having said that, the police have inadvertently built several flaws into the assessment system which can impact very heavily on whether or not the right candidates are selected. The qualities required of a police officer are many and varied. The person who makes a good detective may make a terrible public order officer. A great traffic officer may be a dreadful custody officer. That is one of the interesting things about the service. However, the new national system tests people in a comfortable (relatively speaking!) environment, where, for example, the people they meet in role plays may be rude, but never obnoxious, verbally but never physically threatening, and the situations themselves have a huge dollop of 'ideal' as opposed to 'real' world about them.

The reality of the role of the Police Officer

Although it would be denied by the police service, the system can be said to not sufficiently test strength of character. Anyone can act 'assertive' in a role play lasting five minutes, or challenge an inappropriate comment. Whether they can do so to an aggressive drunk on the street outside a nightclub at 3am is a different matter. Conversely, any trace of 'political incorrectness' will result in an automatic fail. Whilst that is all well and good, sometimes in the real world of policing, you need people whose idea of political correctness is less important than their ability to act decisively in the face of danger. One of the best police officers I know is an ex-army man and totally politically incorrect. He does not believe in force strategy, or the wider implications of issues such as sanction detections or corporate development (if you are not sure what these are, have a look at your local force's website). All he is interested in is arresting the bad guys. He is also extremely capable in defending himself in a physical encounter (or to put it the old fashioned way, he is a 'hard man'!). This officer is the one that I as a supervisor and operational officer was always glad to turn to when either a prisoner became violent, or we were dealing with a nasty public order situation. By way of example, at one incident, the officer responded alone one night to an assault in progress on a pub car park. On arrival, he found two offenders hiding, who upon realising he was on his own, attempted to assault him. By the time other colleagues arrived to assist the officer, suffice it to say he had already put both offenders on the floor, and they were begging him to let them surrender. Whilst I am not suggesting that every officer should be like this one (as that would be a supervisory nightmare!), some officers like him are needed in the police. The new system would never have allowed such a character to get in.

So, do assessment centres work? Maybe. Ultimately though, for you the candidate, it does not matter. They are a fact of life, and if you want to join the police, you need to accept their rules and play by them.

Are they fair and objective?

This is another interesting question. Assessment centres are designed to be fair and objective, and it is intended that every single candidate will be marked in exactly the same way. This is easy to achieve in the likes of a multiple choice examination. For example, the sergeant and inspector promotion examination is currently in two sections. The first part is a three-hour multiple-choice examination. Candidates mark the answers on to a printed marking sheet. They tick one box out of five options, selecting the answer they believe is right. The sheets are then inserted into a computer, which marks questions either right or wrong. There is no human marking element. For each question, there is only one box out of the five which will indicate to the computer that the answer is correct. Simply put, if the candidate ticks the correct box they get a mark. If they tick the wrong box they don't. The computer does not care. The computer does not make mistakes, and is not biased in the way people are. The computer does not find you attractive, and give you more marks, nor does it ever feel ill, or get into a bad mood. The marking of that exam is therefore completely fair and objective.

Marking the assessment

With regard to the actual assessment itself, things are slightly different. It can be argued that it is fair and objective in that every single person taking it takes the same exam. Therefore, everyone has the same theoretical opportunity to pass it. There are of course arguments about whether or not people from different backgrounds will fully understand the questions or ideology, but that is beyond the scope of this book. I am only interested in how such things are marked as I cannot influence how they are written. The police service would have candidates believe that this system is completely fair and objective. Having said that, of course, wherever there is any human element whatsoever, there will always be an element of subjectivity. This is unavoidable. Consider the type of exercises involved in the assessment process. There are four main elements to be considered. These are the IQ tests, the written exercises, the role plays and the interview.

The IQ test

The IQ test, of which there are two, one verbal and one numerical, involves a tick box marking system similar to the one described above. The answer therefore is either right or wrong. There is no debate and can be no argument about this. You ticked the correct box or you didn't. Therefore, the marking for this is clearly fair and objective.

The interview, role play and written exercises

Now consider the interview, role play and written exercises. For any interview answer that the candidate provides, how can anyone be sure that the answer will be marked in the same way by different assessors? Imagine a candidate is asked a question in relation to when they have experienced inappropriate behaviour. One assessor may listen to the answer, and think what a fantastic example of assertive behaviour the candidate has provided. Conversely, another assessor could be thinking the candidate did not go far enough in their actions, and should have taken the matter further. The police service would argue that these variations are all but eliminated by an intensive training course which explains to assessors how they should evaluate answers. The reality of this is that the actual training course for assessors consists of 10 working days, during which they cover the principles of the entire assessment process. It is therefore foolish to suggest that every assessor marks every single answer in the same way. In short, the personality and personal outlook of your assessor will directly affect your mark. People have always liked people that fit in with their own ideas, and always will do.

Attaining consistency in markers

Of course, to attain consistency is very, very difficult. The police service doesn't help itself by the fact that many of the people involved in the assessment centre process are not human resource professionals. The likely background of the assessors is described in the separate section on page 172, but their work and life experiences will be completely different. Even if the entire 10-day assessor training course was devoted to eliminating these differences, it would still be an impossible task. The reality of the situation is that only a few hours of that 10-day course will be devoted to marking students equally. To try to ensure consistency of marking, individual assessment centres, along with individual assessors, are compared in some cases. Realistically, however, this will not show up individual assessors making value judgements based on their own perceptions, which may be to the candidate's detriment.

Several years ago, for example, there was a noticeable trend in the national sergeant and inspector promotion examinations which indicated that some male assessors were marking attractive female candidates more highly than would be expected. It was also noted that where male role actors (more on them later) were supposed to be playing an 'aggressive' part, they tended to be less confrontational with attractive female candidates than with male candidates taking the examination.

Objectivity in the recruitment process

Objectivity is not as easily obtainable as the service would suggest. If the service were completely confident that the marking of candidates for examinations and assessment, both internally and externally, was as fair as it could be, they would allow candidates to be filmed during their performance. Therefore, if anyone felt they had been discriminated against, the matter could be easily resolved by having an independent panel of assessors view their performance. There would not be a huge cost implication either – all that would be needed would be a video camera in each room and for each candidate to bring a videotape. The service will not do this. I suggest this is because if a tribunal somewhere started comparing the videotapes of successful candidates in one location with videos from disputed performances by other candidates, huge discrepancies would be shown. In the absence of such videotape evidence, it is very hard for candidates to prove that their performance was in fact to the required standard.

However, as stated previously, the candidate cannot influence the make-up or design of the assessment centre. All you can do is fully understand the rules and limitations which exist at the centre and play by them.

Observing political correctness

The system is now extremely politically correct, and some would argue by too much. Clearly, nobody wants to recruit racists, sexists or homophobes, and it is only right that any system seeks to filter such individuals out of the process. However, on assessment you'll be marked down if, for example, during a role play, you are talking about a senior manager who has written a letter, and you accidentally keep referring to the writer as male, when in fact no gender has been specified. Whether this makes you sexist or not is I believe debatable, but it can result in a candidate failing for not respecting diversity. I have had examples of people allegedly failing to consider diversity under the following circumstances. In a role play where the discussion centred on an issue concerning a group of immigrants living in a certain area, the candidate tried to defend the actions of the group over something, and used the phrase 'these people', which I would argue is simply an impassioned way of referring to a group. It is used most days in the media. In the eyes of some police assessors, however (and more on them later), such a phrase is 'exclusionary', as it is singling out a certain group. The candidate therefore failed the assessment for failing to consider diversity.

WHY DO PEOPLE FAIL ASSESSMENT CENTRES?

There are two main types of candidates who fail assessments. The first of these are those who for one reason or another are in fact completely unsuited to a career as a police officer. Hopefully, anyone who is racist, sexist or homophobic will fall immediately into this category. Nobody wants these types of people to join the police service, and a police assessment system should be able to screen them out. Less harmful, but equally undesirable in other ways, are those who are simply not suited in terms of character to be police officers or PCSOs. This may be either in terms of their mental capacity, personal standards, or simply the natural make-up of their character. For example, on my candidate training course, the first half-hour consists of an outline of the techniques involved in role plays. On one particular course in Newcastle, we told the students that after a short break we intended to give them a role play to do. We then had a coffee break, and upon resuming class found one student had just left without saying a word to anyone. They had been unable to mentally face the prospect of being involved in a role play with the rest of the class. The student would no doubt consider that they were just highly nervous on the day of the course, and that it was no big deal. However, looking at their inability to face a role play provides a bigger insight into their character. Whilst no doubt putting the candidate under some pressure, a role play is a controlled environment. From an assessor's perspective, if somebody cannot face the prospect of doing a role play how on earth can the assessor then consider that such an individual would be able to deal with a fight outside a nightclub on a Saturday night as a police officer? Whilst assessment centres have their flaws, it is very difficult to fault this particular piece of logic.

People unsuited to being police officers

The first type of people who fail assessments are those completely unsuited to being a police officer or PCSO. This book, along with its associated training courses, is not designed or intended to help these people get into the police. Not having the kind of personality required to be a police officer does not make you a bad person of course, but if somebody is of a nervous disposition or not very decisive or self confident, and managed somehow to get through the recruitment system, they would discover that being a police officer can be a very miserable occupation. Not everyone can deal with physical confrontation for example. I'm not suggesting that everyone needs to be able to go five rounds with some knife-wielding assailant (that is what radios, batons, CS incapacitant, your colleagues and police dogs are for) but inevitably, a part of the job is facing situations which at their best involve having to assert yourself, and at the highest level involve you in activity which represents real physical risk to yourself. Not everyone has the character traits to do this – thankfully, or what a world we would live in.

People failing to display the correct skills for being a police officer

This brings us neatly on to the second group of people who fail. This is by far the bigger group. This band of people would probably make excellent police officers. However, they have failed to display the skills required to the correct level. This in itself can be for a number of reasons. Some candidates simply do not understand the mechanics or rules of the assessment centre.

Consider this analogy. Imagine a good rugby union player attempting to play rugby league without being told there was a difference in the rules. Without taking anything away from their playing abilities, they would still lose because they did not understand the differences in what the rules allowed them to do.

Those candidates whose background, skills or education has simply not allowed them to develop the sort of skills that are tested at assessment centres are at a real disadvantage. Additionally, those who perhaps doubt their own ability, either in terms of them being able to do the job or in terms of confidence levels, will also struggle.

With the right kind of coaching and preparation, these people are able to perform much better throughout the assessment. Again, that is the purpose of this book.

Why some fantastic applicants fail assessment centres

Having helped thousands of people join the police service, it never ceases to amaze and disappoint me that some candidates, who would have made excellent police officers and should have flown through the assessment process, somehow fail. There are a number of reasons for this. Firstly, it has to be accepted that anyone can have an off-day. Any one of us can get up in the morning and simply not be on top form, and if that day happens to be your assessment centre, you are at a disadvantage from the start. On the day of the assessment centre – for whatever reason, whether it be stress, nervousness or numerous other reasons – some people do not perform to their full potential and therefore do not pass.

Then again, internal factors within the assessment centre can also come into play. Although the police service would deny it, sometimes the role actors in a particular exercise will not be particularly good on the day, and will adversely affect someone's performance. Sometimes an interviewer will be having a bad day, and not be inclined to give somebody the marks they really deserve. Sometimes the assessor misinterprets or forgets what has been said, or not said, by the candidate, and marks accordingly.

Being unprepared

However, the most common reason why excellent candidates fail is simply lack of preparation. You will find throughout this book that great emphasis is placed on dealing with inappropriate behaviour. Many readers will struggle with the concept of inappropriate behaviour as defined in this book. However, I assure you that the emphasis placed on dealing with inappropriate conduct could not be higher in the assessment centre environment. On every training session I have ever run, I advise people about the need to confront any form of potentially racist, sexist or homophobic comment immediately, firmly and fairly. On occasion some of these students will contact me saying they have failed. When we speak, it will emerge that they were given a comment in a role play for example, which they realised contained some form of unacceptable view. Nonetheless, under the pressure of the exercise, their in-built reluctance to challenge a 'mild' inappropriate comment, for want of a better expression, has meant they did not take positive action and therefore failed. This is one of the most common reasons why good candidates who should succeed do not.

Being aware of development needs

Conversely, one of the best candidates I ever saw on a course was an army captain. This man had worked his way up to officer level from the ranks, which is a great achievement in itself. However, on the police recruitment training course with me, he constantly reverted back to his army background when dealing with situations. For example, when being briefed on an issue, he would ask a few basic questions, and then immediately move on to solving the problem. This of course is what army officers are trained to do, and was the reason why he had risen so high. In the police context what he failed to do was to ask enough questions to be able to fully ascertain the situation before acting. This is a great example of someone's background and experience actively damaging their potential performance at assessment centre. A few weeks after the course, this student contacted me and told me he had failed his assessment. Before I could say anything, he stated that he knew why this had happened and explained that he had reverted back to military methods when dealing with the role plays –

which I had specifically warned him about. He therefore failed. This is what I mean when I refer to a fantastic candidate failing. To his credit, however, this student recognised his own development need and successfully reapplied.

Attitude to failure

There is one further thing to be said about a failure. There is no shame whatsoever in failing this type of assessment. Candidates often feel that they have been unfairly marked, and in quite a few cases this is probably true. The bottom line, however, is that if someone does fail, they need to decide what they are going to do about it. I have spoken to people who have said to me that they intended to have one more try to pass the police assessment process and if they fail it, they had no intention of trying again. We will speak about competencies shortly; however, such an attitude clearly shows that the candidate has no real desire to be a police officer. If someone is willing to give up after one attempt, whether they deserved to pass or not, do they really possess the self-determination and motivation to patrol alone at night on a difficult housing estate? I would suggest the answer is no, and this attitude probably contributed to their failure. In any event, such an attitude meant they did not deserve to pass.

Why do some fantastically inept applicants pass?

Another interesting point that often arises is when a number of people who know one another apply to join the service together. Again, I have had numerous conversations with people who simply cannot understand how somebody else has managed to get into the service when they themselves have failed. One classic example of this occurred when I was speaking to a man who was in his 40s, with a large amount of life experience behind him and a responsible job as a manager. This particular individual was certain that he possessed the right kind of skills to be a police officer. He was astounded when he failed the assessment centre. He was enraged, however, when a 21 year-old from the same company then took the same assessment centre and passed. The older man simply did not understand how his life experience could be considered unsuitable when somebody who was 21 could be taken on. The simple truth behind this is as follows. Your actual life experience is of no use if you do not articulate this properly throughout the assessment centre. In the particular case described, it was the interview that the older male had failed and the younger one had passed. The 21 year-old had probably fully researched what was expected of him on the day and had fully prepared examples of the types of questions that would be asked of him. The older candidate was so confident that he could handle anything put to him, he failed to prepare. As with most things in life, failing to prepare for something equates to preparing to fail. If there is a moral to this story, it is never to assume anything, and prepare accordingly.

SUMMARY

To summarise, there are several points to consider about failure. Firstly, one must be honest. The assessment centre certainly has its faults, but if someone were to fail it simply because they were unable to contain their nerves on the day, to the extent perhaps that they started to cry or were physically ill, then in all truthfulness I would have to question their suitability to be a police officer. However, if someone realises that they have failed because they did not fully 'play the game' as per the assessment centre rules, that in itself is an achievement. Frustrating as it seems, it gives the candidate the opportunity to improve and learn to avoid that issue next time around. It is only human to be angry upon getting a rejection letter, and tempting to decide not to re-apply. However, once the anger and disappointment have faded, a good candidate will recover and the determination to join will drive them to apply again.

Playing the game

In answer to the question why some people pass the assessment who will never make effective police officers in a million years, it is because they play the game. No matter how much the police service may argue against it, if you know how to play the game, you can pass the assessment. Superficially at least, every candidate takes the same assessment centre, and is examined against the same set of skills criteria. In general the reason one candidate fails and another passes is that the successful candidate has prepared and practised, and implicitly understood the theory and practices of the assessment centre process. Practice, as with most things in life, is the key to success.

THE POLICE AND INAPPROPRIATE BEHAVIOUR

Throughout the book, as each exercise within the assessment centre is explained, I have added an accompanying explanation of the issues surrounding diversity specific to that particular exercise. However, it is appropriate at this stage to stress the importance at assessment centre of demonstrating your 'respect for diversity'. Any candidate for the police service must be aware of the emphasis placed by the service on weeding out any behaviour whatsoever that can be termed as racist, sexist or homophobic. No right-thinking person would disagree with this. It is certainly not the purpose of this book to allow such people to bypass the system. Having said that of course, if the reading of a book enabled any in-built safeguards at assessment centre to be bypassed, it shows there was a huge fault with the centre and that it needs to be addressed!

Defining inappropriate behaviour

What most people find difficult to believe is the very wide-ranging definition of 'inappropriate behaviour' and 'respect for diversity' that the police service professes to believe in. Clearly, any candidate who uses insulting words, phrases or behaviour at assessment centre should be failed. Difficulties arise for many candidates because they do not realise what the police define as inappropriate conduct. For example, the use of a phrase such as 'these foreigners' when dealing with an issue in a role play could well be considered as displaying a racist attitude and therefore result in an automatic fail.

Jumping to conclusions

Candidates may find, for example that in some of the documents they are given to read before a role play, a senior manager is referred to by the name 'Sam'. If the candidate then enters the role play, meets someone other than 'Sam' and constantly refers to this manager's gender as being male, they will be marked down. This is of course because the name can also be used by a female. It will be argued therefore that by assuming that the manager is male, the candidate is biased towards sexist behaviour. It is not the purpose of this book to debate whether this is going too far or not but such issues need to be borne in mind by candidates.

Inappropriate language

There are numerous other examples. In the north of England it is normal for people to address others as 'love' or 'duck'. Visit Liverpool or Manchester for example and the chances are you will be addressed by one of these two terms several times within the space of an hour. Using them in an assessment centre, however, will be seen as patronising and potentially sexist. Therefore they could be the cause of a failure. To be fair, of course, I know a lot of females who really resent a complete stranger calling them 'love'. I can completely accept that they view the term as being patronising. This is the reasoning behind it being deemed sexist.

The need to challenge inappropriate behaviour

When I speak about these issues on a course, I can see the looks of disbelief on candidates' faces. I have a theory that the average candidate still believes that the last thing the police want is people who will challenge such 'minor' issues. There are those who still believe the police service 'looks after its own' and would not wish anyone to join who was going to start criticising people for using such phrases as the ones above. I can assure you, after 16 years in the police, that these beliefs are completely false. Candidates need to accept that any comments that can in any way be construed as being sexist, racist or homophobic will result in failure. If you do not subscribe to this belief, and actively follow it at the assessment centre, then you will fail.

As far as the police service is concerned, respect for diversity is the single most important core competency being assessed. Consider this. There are seven core competencies, which will be described in detail in the next chapter. Each competency is assessed a number of times throughout the assessment day. In six of these competencies, a candidate's marks are taken throughout all of the exercises, and then averaged out. If the average mark in these six areas is above the required level, then the candidate will pass that competency. In other words, if you get a grade D in one exercise, you can make it up by getting higher grades in the other exercises for that competency. In the area of diversity, however, a single grade D will result in an automatic fail even if every other grade achieved on the day by the candidate is a grade A.

I cannot stress strongly enough that if you are not prepared to act on this essential piece of information, you have dramatically reduced your chances of passing the assessment centre.

I would also suggest that if this is the only piece of information you actually remember from this book, then your investment in reading it was totally worth while.

2

The core competencies

EXPLAINING THE CORE COMPETENCIES

One thing I promise you to be true, believe it or not: *this is the most important section of this book*. The framework that I will now describe is the thing that underpins the whole assessment centre. However tempting it may be simply to glance at these phrases and ignore them, remember that they form the basis of the marking guide and it is vital therefore that you understand them.

If you ignore this section, and do not gain a firm grasp of these behaviours, then you place yourself at a great disadvantage.

How the competencies were developed

In essence, the competencies were developed by analysing the role of a police officer and defining certain characteristics or behaviours (known as competencies) that a successful police officer would require to perform effectively. These competencies are broken down into seven main headings. When you receive your application information, a copy of these characteristics (competencies) should be included. You can download them from most police force recruitment websites. The competencies described in this book are different from the official ones supplied for your assessment as those are subject to copyright. However, the essence of each one and the meaning of the description given is the same. These seven headings are as follows:

1. *The ability to respect other people's cultures, values and beliefs*
   This is effectively the ability to take into account other people's feelings, irrespective of such irrelevant factors as gender, sexuality, personal circumstances or background.

2. *The ability to work as a team*
   Team working is based on the ability to work together with other people for the benefit of the organisation, involving people in the work of that team, and the decisions taken in order for the team to work properly.

3. *Being aware of the needs of the customer and the community*
   An awareness of community and customer needs is essential to ensure high service levels for the people that the police service deal with.

4. *The ability to communicate*
   A police officer clearly needs to be able to communicate. Communication is more than just telling people things, however; it is just as much about listening, and checking people actually understand what is being said. Communication is meant to be an exchange of ideas.

5. *The ability to overcome problem issues*
   Police officers are expected to be able to solve problems, rather than just deal with the symptoms. Theoretically at least, the days of a police officer just turning up and moving a group of youths on from a street corner and doing nothing else have gone. The organisation now expects the officer to look at why the youths actually gather at that particular place, and come up with a solution that will stop them gathering there again.

6. *The ability to take responsibility*
   Police officers and PCSOs are expected to take responsibility for their actions. They are expected to use initiative and to take pride in themselves and the organisation. They are also expected to take responsibility for their own self-development.

7. *The ability to react well to pressure*
   Resilience is the ability to effectively show moral and ethical courage, and make difficult decisions when necessary. Basically, it comes down to being able to do the right thing under pressure.

THE BEHAVIOURAL STATEMENTS

The seven competencies described in the previous paragraph are the kind of characteristics that a police officer requires. However, the service would clearly require more detailed 'behaviour descriptions' in order to be able to base an assessment centre on them. Consequently, each of the seven main competencies has been examined in much greater depth. Each competency has been broken down into between 8 and 15 'desired characteristics' or, to give them their technical name, 'behavioural statements'. Each competency has both positive and negative statements. For each given competency, the assessment team will be looking for all positive indicators. In simplistic terms, the more positive statements you provide or 'evidence' as a candidate, the more marks you will receive. Conversely, if as a candidate you provide evidence of negative characteristics, then you will lose marks. If your overall mark does not reach the required standard, you will fail on that competency.

Possessing all the competencies

It is also important to remember the following. It has been decided by the police service that to be a successful police officer you need to possess every one of these seven competencies to the required standard. Therefore, a candidate can get great marks in six of the competencies, yet fall below the required standard in the seventh. The candidate will fail because they have only reached the necessary standard in six of the required seven competencies. The marking guide is discussed in Chapter 11, but in essence this is the reason why people can gain very high percentages in excess of the overall centre pass mark, and yet fail the assessment. This is logical if you think about it. Having six out of seven skills will mean that what you are very good in certain areas, but will be unable to fulfil your role as a police officer. This also means that you have to have a good solid performance in all seven of the competency areas in order to pass.

Are the competencies relevant to the role of Police Officer?

For the moment, consider the seven core headings in Figure 1.

Fig. 1. The seven core competencies.

By themselves they perhaps do not mean much. But have a look at Figure 2 below, where I have changed the technical names of the competencies to a more practical set of headings. Imagine these as the skills the assessors are looking for you to display throughout the assessment process.

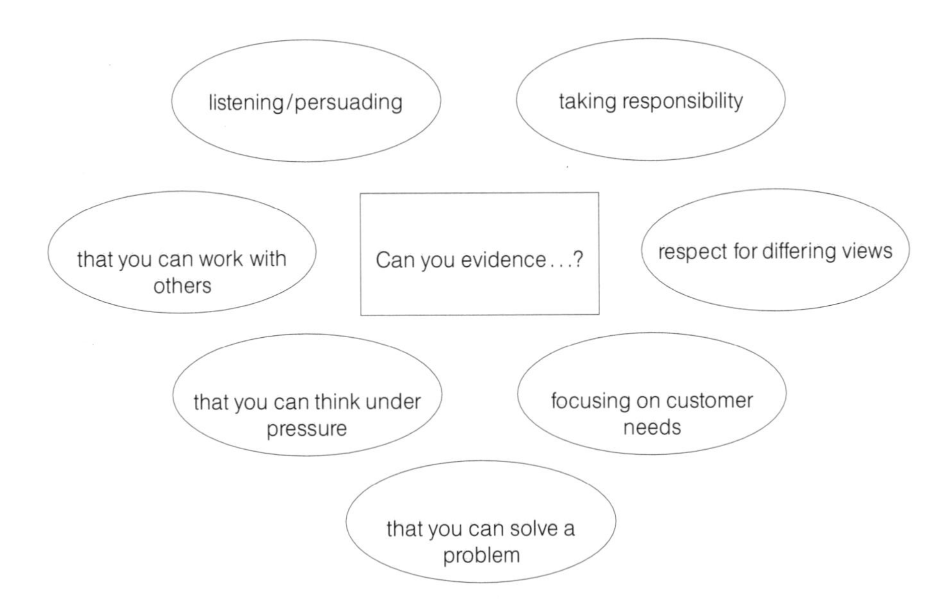

Fig. 2. Another way of looking at the core competencies.

Ensuring you understand the competencies

The following pages contain my version of the competencies required (Tables 1–7). Again, the official version will be sent to you with your application, or can be downloaded from official police websites. For our purposes, however, although the wording is different, the qualities described are the same as at assessment. You will see that for each competency area, the list of 'behaviours' a candidate may provide is split into two lists: 'desirable' and 'undesirable'. Many candidates make the mistake of viewing the information that follows as just a list of phrases of no real consequence. As we will see later, in effect these lists of key characteristics form the marking guide and they are a tremendous source of information and guidance once you understand them. Most candidates, however, ignore them.

Table 1. Competency 1: The ability to respect other people's cultures, values and beliefs.

Desirable factors regarding other people's cultures, values and beliefs	
1.1	Is able to see the other person's perspective
1.2	Respects everyone's beliefs and sense of dignity
1.3	Is always polite and patient with people
1.4	When sorting out conflicts, realises everybody's needs
1.5	Realises that everyone has their own issues, weaknesses and requirements
1.6	Listens and supports people to make them feel involved
1.7	Is conscious that the things one says can affect people in different ways
1.8	Realises different people have different beliefs and is able to value these
1.9	Is able to recognise things that may cause potential offence
1.10	Is able to hold a confidence when required
1.11	Is able to communicate difficult issues with sensitivity and honesty
1.12	Is honest and open with colleagues and the public
Undesirable factors regarding other people's cultures and values and beliefs	
1.13	Shows favouritism towards one side
1.14	Uses humour at the wrong time

1.15 Is overly assertive or controlling
1.16 Stresses power more than actually required
1.17 Cannot maintain confidentiality
1.18 Impatient with others or takes no account of their thoughts or ideas
1.19 Has no sense of tact
1.20 Whether deliberately or not, uses inappropriate conduct so making situations worse
1.21 Takes no account of the feelings of others when criticising them
1.22 Has no interest in helping other people to talk about important personal issues
1.23 Takes no account of how other people feel

Table 2. Competency 2: The ability to work as a team.

Desirable factors regarding team working

2.1 Realises as a team member that teams change in their structure and membership
2.2 Is a team player whether or not they gain personally
2.3 Is happy to take on mundane or less popular jobs
2.4 Works to develop confidence and trust between team members
2.5 Accepts team working involves both giving and receiving help when required
2.6 Is always willing to help other colleagues
2.7 Is always willing to help and co-operate with other people
2.8 Makes efforts to get to know other team members, has approachable personality and is open to ideas of others
2.9 Enthusiastically assists with team tasks at work
2.10 Comprehends that they have a particular role in the team

Undesirable factors regarding team working

2.11 Does not work to stop arguments
2.12 Will not give or take advice
2.13 Is not interested in hearing what other people think
2.14 Is unwilling to share information
2.15 Makes colleagues work against each other
2.16 Allows cliques to form

2.17 Is less interested in the team than in their own set of goals
2.18 Does not share credit where appropriate
2.19 Is only interested in glory seeking
2.20 Will not assist other members of the team

Table 3. Competency 3: Being aware of the needs of the customer and the community.

Desirable factors regarding the needs of the customer and the community
3.1 Balances needs of the organisation with those of the customer
3.2 Always keeps customers up-to-date on what is happening
3.4 Ensures customer has realistic expectations of results
3.4 Works to keep customer happy with level of service provided
3.5 Meets customer demands as quickly as possible
3.6 Is willing to apologise for mistakes and put them right
3.7 Works to put customers' difficulties right as quickly as possible
3.8 Recognises that the customer is important in everything
3.9 Realises certain things may cause offence, and changes behaviour appropriately
3.10 Supports plans to make the organisation reflect the community
3.11 Understands there are a broad range of cultures and lifestyles
3.12 Always presents a professional image

Undesirable factors regarding the needs of the customer and the community
3.13 Has no interest in recognising diversity
3.14 Has no sympathy with other people's beliefs
3.15 Does not understand other people's beliefs
3.16 Does not make an effort to talk to people in the community
3.17 Is more interested in the organisation than the customer
3.18 Is not interested in the needs of local people
3.19 Is interested in dealing only with problems, not the customer
3.20 Is unable to see the customer's perspective
3.21 Acts in an unprofessional way towards customers
3.22 Fails to communicate with customers
3.23 Fails to consider the needs of individual customers

Table 4. Competency 4: The ability to communicate.

Desirable factors regarding the ability to communicate	
4.1	Is able to produce well-written documents and summaries
4.2	Can argue their case effectively in writing
4.3	Clarifies that people have understood information by summarising
4.4	Can manage a discussion between groups effectively
4.5	Recognises different people require different communication styles
4.6	Is able to speak confidently and with authority
4.7	Speaks person to person if possible and appropriate
4.8	Explains the decision and reasoning for decisions clearly
4.9	Explains requirements and commands
4.10	Addresses issues directly
Undesirable factors regarding the ability to communicate	
4.11	Interrupts and refuses to listen
4.12	Presumes what is meant without clarifying this
4.13	Is unable to spell or uses incorrect punctuation or grammar
4.14	Writes reports in an illogical manner
4.15	Fails to consider the people they are speaking to
4.16	Uses words or phrases the audience may not understand or consider appropriate
4.17	Fails to think through what they want to say before speaking
4.18	Shows lack of confidence when speaking to audience
4.19	Dodges questions they believe are hard

Table 5. Competency 5: The ability to overcome problem issues.

Desirable factors regarding the ability to overcome problem issues	
5.1	Makes decisions taking account of the whole picture
5.2	Checks policy before acting or making decisions if required
5.3	Remains open-minded and does not take sides
5.4	Deals with issues in a logical manner
5.5	Understands some things can be changed and others cannot
5.6	Recognises not just the symptoms of a problem but also the causes
5.7	Makes reasoned conclusions after having gathered all necessary information

5.8 Speedily takes in information after ensuring it is correct
5.9 Has the ability to sift important facts from those which are not important
5.10 Gains as much information as possible before solving a problem as is appropriate
5.11 Recognises different sources of information and news exist and can be used

Undesirable factors regarding the ability to overcome problem issues

5.12 Leaves problems to others
5.13 Gets too caught up in small points of no consequence
5.14 Does not fully consider all factors before acting
5.15 Loses sight of the main problem by getting bogged down in details
5.16 Fails to see problems developing
5.17 Makes assumptions about situations instead of judging the reality
5.18 Fails to consider other evidence affecting a decision
5.19 Does not go to the trouble of obtaining or using information already known about the problem
5.20 Does not research the situation
5.21 Fails to consider speaking to other people who may have further information that will be helpful
5.22 Makes decision before gaining as much information as appropriate
5.23 Only scratches the surface of the problem and fails to identify real cause

Table 6. Competency 6: The ability to take responsibility.

Desirable factors regarding the ability to take responsibility

6.1 Is willing to do the (ethically and morally) right thing, and is always truthful, open and honest
6.2 Takes responsibility for keeping their own professional knowledge current
6.3 Will perform routine tasks to the best of their ability
6.4 Is always enthusiastic in their part of a task
6.5 Always brings each task to a close
6.6 Makes sure work is completed by agreed deadlines
6.7 Takes pride in their own work
6.8 Does not let colleagues or customers down
6.9 Will take responsibility for dealing with issues

6.10	Is willing to work on their own initiative when appropriate
6.11	Volunteers for tasks without having to be told
6.12	Takes responsibility for the actions they themselves have taken

Undesirable factors regarding the ability to take responsibility	
6.13	Is not interested in keeping knowledge up to date
6.14	Fails to recognise that they have their own areas for improvement
6.15	Surrenders easily when faced with difficulty
6.16	Has negative attitudes towards the service and their role
6.17	Has little interest in work
6.18	Is destructive and critical in their attitude
6.19	Does the minimum amount of work
6.20	Will not take on responsibility for tasks
6.21	Will not admit mistakes and is reluctant to ask for assistance; will blame others for errors
6.22	Fails to deal with problems in the hope that they will simply go away
6.23	Is not bothered if they let other people down
6.24	Will defer decisions to supervision when it is not necessary

Table 7. Competency 7: The ability to react well to pressure.

Desirable factors regarding the ability to react well to pressure	
7.1	Even when under pressure will maintain their point of view when correct to do so
7.2	If appropriate, will make decisions that they know will be unpopular or difficult
7.3	Stays calm in difficult situations
7.4	Realises the role requires the ability to make difficult decisions
7.5	When necessary, will not give in to pressure to make decisions when more thought is required
7.6	Is able to deal with lack of certainty, and frustration
7.7	Even when under pressure will maintain their high ethical standards
7.8	Is able to deal with conflicting demands and viewpoints
7.9	Deals with emotional issues and is able to put them behind them as appropriate
7.10	Deals with difficult issues in a logical manner, without using inappropriate emotion

7.11 Remains calm and has the ability to deal with conflict and hostility
7.12 Keeps a clear head in a crisis

Undesirable factors regarding the ability to react well to pressure

7.13 Avoids difficult situations in case they make a mistake
7.14 When under pressure immediately gives in
7.15 Complains about issues rather than dealing with them
7.16 Is overly aggressive when dealing with problems
7.17 Over-reacts when faced with conflict or aggression
7.18 Becomes too emotionally involved
7.19 Uses excessive force
7.20 Requires excessive amounts of reassurance from colleagues and supervision
7.21 Is afraid to become involved in confrontation
7.22 Cannot cope when difficulties arise
7.23 Easily becomes angry, upset or frustrated

HOW THE COMPETENCIES RELATE TO YOUR APPLICATION

The entire recruitment process, from application form to final interview, revolves around the seven competencies. At every stage of the process the assessors will examine the 'evidence' you have provided, whether it be in an example on your application form or something you have said in interview, and they will compare it against the competency lists. If the evidence can be classed as being a positive factor, you will receive a mark. If it is on the negative list, you will lose a mark. This is a crucially important fact to realise. For example, literally thousands of candidates will somehow try to include in their application form or assessment the fact that they believe they have a good sense of humour, which will therefore in their opinion help to make them a good police officer. If you read through the list of positive characteristics, humour is not mentioned once. Therefore this answer is merely a waste of ink or breath and will not score you any marks.

The importance of an error-free application form

As a further illustration, consider this. Sixty thousand or so applications are received each year by the police service and thousands contain spelling mistakes, or poor use of grammar and punctuation. These applicants would no doubt try to argue that missing out the odd full stop in no way reflects on their ability to be a police officer or PCSO. However, if you were to look at the list of characteristics under 'Communication', you would see the following on the list of undesirable behaviours:

4.13 Is unable to spell or uses incorrect punctuation or grammar

This is clearly a negative indicator, and so would lose the candidate marks. Let's take another example. If the candidate was asked to fill out the form in black ink, and instead used blue, how might the assessors view the application? The following undesirable behaviours might apply:

6.17 Has little interest in work
6.19 Does the minimum amount of work
6.20 Will not take on responsibility for tasks
6.23 Is not bothered if they let other people down

It could be said that as the candidate has used blue ink when specifically asked to use black, they are not interested in their work (so evidencing undesirable behaviour 6.17), which will have an impact when they are asked to complete reports as a police officer. Also, the candidate did not bother finding a black pen, which suggests that they will look to do the minimum amount of work (so evidencing 6.19).

The candidate was asked to do a simple task, and in this case has failed miserably (again evidencing 6.19). If they were asked to do something more meaningful, would they be likely to do it? And finally, having ignored a direct request, they have let themselves and the organisation down by not doing the best they can (so evidencing 6.23).

The candidate would probably just say they did not have a black pen handy. The assessment criteria, however, will suggest that the candidate already has four negative characteristics, and that is without reading what they actually wrote!

Remember, it does not matter whether you as an individual consider this fair or right. The point is that this is the system. You either play by its rules or accept you are likely to fail.

The role-play exercises

Think about the role-play exercises for a moment. The candidate may be a bit nervous, or jump to a conclusion about the situation they are dealing with. In any event, they fail to ask a few important questions or at least questions that the assessment team considered important enough to put on to the marking guide. In missing out the questions, the candidate may have been said to show negative indicators taken from the competency of problem solving:

5.14 Does not fully consider all factors before acting
5.17 Makes assumptions about situations instead of judging the reality
5.18 Fails to consider other evidence affecting a decision
5.19 Does not go to the trouble of obtaining or using information already known about the problem
5.20 Does not research the situation
5.21 Fails to consider speaking to other people who may have further information that will be helpful
5.22 Makes decision before gaining as much information as appropriate
5.23 Only scratches the surface of the problem and fails to identify real cause

By failing to ask questions, the candidate has potentially shown that they do not take everything into account (so evidencing 5.14), may be making assumptions about the situation (evidencing 5.17), that they have not looked at all of the evidence (evidencing 5.18) and so on.

Whether they actually solve the problem in the role play may well be irrelevant, as this candidate will now have a huge problem to overcome in terms of the negative marks they may have picked up.

The key therefore to gaining good marks is to understand the competency system. A candidate must aim to 'hit' as many of the positive competencies as possible, whilst avoiding all of the 'negative' ones.

Telling anecdotes at the interview

In the interview, for example, a common mistake many candidates make is to basically tell an anecdote or story from their life, which they think fits in with the question being asked. Because they have failed to consider how their answer fits in with the positive competencies, they put themselves into a lottery as to whether that particular anecdote will give them a worthwhile number of positive characteristics. The same lottery applies as to whether they will include negative characteristics without realising it. For example, when asked the question about how they dealt with a situation whilst under pressure, many candidates are under the impression that the assessor is looking for some example of physical conflict. The inevitable example trotted out by poor candidates is how they somehow got involved in some kind of altercation inside a pub, and how they stepped in to break up and defuse the situation. If you compare this with the competencies contained within the heading of 'reacting well under pressure', you will see that this kind of story is unlikely to score many points. What it is quite likely to do, however, is introduce a few negative points that the candidate has not even considered.

Do you need to know the competencies off by heart?

Thankfully, the simple answer to this is no. No assessor is going to ask you to recite a list of competencies. If you did so voluntarily you would not gain any extra marks. The assessment centre is not a test of memory. However, it is vitally important to understand them and their concepts. For example, within the context of the role-play exercise, the good candidate will understand that it is essential to ask questions. Not just because of the information that those questions will hopefully gain them, but simply because they will be given marks for asking the question.

Having a good working knowledge of the competencies is also extremely useful when it comes to answering the interview questions. As you will see later, techniques recommended in terms of preparing interview answers involve tailoring your life experiences into an answer that will hit as many competencies as possible. Clearly, in order to hit the competencies, you must be familiar with them.

One final thought about competencies

Nobody would argue that lists of behavioural statements are particularly exciting things to read. However, I hope that by now you understand that in essence they form the marking guide. With regards to the interview, the competency framework provides a blueprint on which to base your answer (which you will clearly be doing months ahead of your assessment!). In respect of the rest of the exercises, competencies give you an outline of the kind of things and the type of behaviour the assessors are looking for. The vast majority of candidates skim read through the competency lists, see no apparent relevance in them, and move on. You do this at your peril!

3

Application forms

THE APPLICATION FORM EXPLAINED

The purpose of the application forms

Sixty thousand people a year apply to be police officers. The number of potential police community support officers is probably similar. Be under no illusion therefore that the application form is anything other than a way of taking people out of the system. In other words, if the service can find a way to filter out your application, it will do so. It is essential therefore to treat the forms with the utmost respect.

Taking care with the forms

Complete all of the forms with the same amount of care. You will probably need to complete additional forms such as medical questionnaires and background check information. Ensure that you complete every form you are given, missing nothing out. Read the completion notes and instructions carefully. If you are asked to supply a photograph, signed on the back by a responsible member of the community, make sure you do. If you fail to do so, you are immediately providing doubts to the recruitment team about your ability to follow simple instructions, and your attention to detail. These are not desirable qualities in a prospective member of the police service.

The principles of selection

I have already discussed competencies and their application in the previous chapter. These are just as relevant to the application form as to the rest of the assessment centre. The forms you complete will be judged against the competencies, and if you have not provided enough evidence of your suitability for the next stage, you will be sifted out of it.

The structure of the form

The main application form can be split into three distinct sections. The first requires basic information about you and your family. The second part requires you to give examples from your life experience of times you have displayed certain key competencies. The third part of the main form explores the reasons why you are joining the police, and what you think the job entails.

The 'general information' section

The general information section carries everything from parents' details to employment and medical history. These are all fairly straightforward, although time-consuming. Do not underestimate this section though. If you complete the form incorrectly, using for example the wrong colour ink, or send it back in an untidy condition, you are evidencing your inability to understand basic instructions. Answer as fully as you can. If you have the opportunity to put down the fact that you have a full driving licence, or are familiar with Microsoft Office, try to put these in. These are all good indications of your general self-motivation.

The 'competency' section

The competencies are by far the hardest section of the form. In this part, you'll be asked to provide examples of when you have dealt with certain situations, or displayed specific characteristics. These questions are seeking evidence that directly links to the qualities listed in the behaviour statements. Quite simply, if you fail to provide this evidence, you will not succeed in your application.

Failure to provide evidence of competence

I have spoken to many people who complain that they have not been afforded the opportunity to gather such evidence, because of their background, education, employment and so on. To begin with, these are simply not valid excuses. From the police perspective, if you are unable to evidence diversity for example, then it is doubtful that the service would wish to take a chance and recruit you – how could they post you to a place where you would have to deal with people different to yourself and be confident you would manage? The service would quite rightly suggest you needed further life experience. Generally speaking, however, most of us can find examples in our past of such skills. The trick is in recognising them. To help you with this, in the following sections I will shortly provide a number of example answers to give you some ideas (see pages 47–52).

The 'motivational' section

The third part of the form concerning your motivation for joining the service is perhaps not quite as hard as the competencies section, but again requires respect. The last thing that the police service wants to do is to recruit people who think the job is about rushing around in fast cars and having a desire to tangle with violent criminals. The service requires its recruits to be very heavily community focused. It wants candidates who have taken a thoughtful approach to joining the service, and who show a certain amount of maturity. These questions allow some insight into why the candidate is applying.

Basic do's and don'ts in completing the forms

Surprisingly, people do make some real blunders on the application forms. Here are some basic guidelines to consider before putting pen to paper.

- Photocopy all of the forms and practise completing the copy first. Make sure what you intend to say will fit on the page and aim to fill all the available space.
- Don't get the original forms dog-eared or dirty.

- Read the form fully, and comply with all instructions. If told to enclose certain documents, make sure you do. If you don't, you are making the assessor's life harder and making it more likely you will fail.
- Before starting to complete each competency question, have a look at the competency areas that the question is examining. Make sure you understand exactly what the question is actually asking.

Using your own experiences

Remember that the examples I have given here are intended simply to give you a flavour of the level required. Do not simply copy these or change a few words and expect to pass. You should use your own truthful examples – as after all, integrity is one of the key issues of a police officer. Be advised that you are potentially going to find yourself being asked about the examples you give at interview. If you get caught out, clearly you have proven yourself to be a liar and are unsuitable to be a police officer! Having said that, the police do not have the resources to check every example that you give is completely accurate. No one is going to check with your boss to see if you really did challenge the managing director's sexist comments at the last board meeting! Everyone exaggerates a little bit after all.

THE COMPETENCY QUESTIONS IN DETAIL

There are usually four main competency questions on the application form. Broadly speaking, these cover the areas of:

- Diversity and respect
- Team working
- Working under pressure
- Communication.

Each of these competencies is broken down on the form into a number of specific segments. Each segment asks the candidate for certain specific parts of the example. Photocopying the pages and practising your answers before you write anything on to the real form will pay huge dividends. The best way to go about completing these questions is to consider each one separately. Without worrying too much about the specifics of the example, compile a list of potential examples for each question. Once you have some examples in mind for a given competency, you can then start comparing each one with the specific parts of the question.

Your examples must be about you, in terms of showing 'you' in the best possible light as being the one who has contributed to the scenario. They should not be instances where you merely observed something happening, or were just a minor player. Anyone can watch a film – the police service are looking for people to work in front of the camera!

Use 'I' not 'we'

This is a common failing by candidates both on application forms and interviews. Most of us play down our involvement in situations due to modesty. In this recruitment process though, the form is looking for specifically what *you* did. Therefore, your answers must always include the word 'I'. It is you who is being assessed and your actions, not the person you happened to be with at the time the incident occurred. Using the word 'we' often suggests that in the reality of the situation you're describing, you simply happened to be there and the other person whom you are speaking about actually did all the work. This is a particular problem with special constables and police support staff applicants. The application form is no place for modesty.

What if you can't think of any examples?

This is a common cry from candidates. However, it is unacceptable as an excuse. If you have no evidence of a certain skill area, then quite simply you will fail. One student on one of my courses lived in a small village in rural South Wales. There were only 30 or so residents, all from the same ethnic background and religion as the student. She was only 19 and had never lived or gone to school outside the village. She therefore made the point, and it is not an unreasonable one, that she had had no opportunity to gain experience of diverse communities. However, from a police perspective, this would be unacceptable. Quite simply, the police would consider that this candidate has no evidence to convince an assessor that she would be able to deal with a diverse policing environment. No one is saying that she could not do it, just that she has not evidenced it. There are 60,000 other applicants to choose from. There will be more than enough of those people who do evidence such qualities. If you were the police service, would you choose the candidate who cannot produce any evidence, or the one that can?

How to ensure you can demonstrate competency

Over the following pages, I have provided example answers along with explanations of how you can find your own examples. I do accept that in a few circumstances, such as the rural Welsh village student, there will be certain areas where you cannot produce any evidence. However, there is always a solution. If you were to find yourself in a similar predicament to her for example, I would suggest you enrol yourself in some form of community course which will give you an insight into other cultures. These are easily accessible on the internet, relatively cheap, and provide excellent evidence of your self-motivation and determination to respect the needs and beliefs of all communities.

Note that for each example question, I have broken the answer down into a similar format to the original application form.

THE DIVERSITY AND RESPECT QUESTION

Where might examples come from?

This question is basically about dealing with unacceptable behaviour. Ideally, your answer would be about challenging racist, sexist or homophobic behaviour, but you're not limited exclusively to these kinds of examples. Any experience you may have had of someone making allegedly humorous remarks about, for example, the way people dress, speak, act or look may provide evidence. These could include age, weight or disability. In essence, you just require an example where someone has been doing something that would offend somebody else. It does not matter if that person was offended or not. As the question itself states, the assessors are looking for evidence that you did something positive to resolve the situation, whatever it was.

Everybody has seen someone at some time doing something that would make another person uncomfortable. Those candidates who say that they have not either live in some amazingly perfect part of the country, or are admitting that they do not recognise inappropriate behaviour.

An example diversity answer

Background

A new female colleague transferred into my office at work. She was quite young, and had only been out of college for a few months. A few days after she started, I was in the staff canteen sitting with her, when a male member of staff began to make inappropriate sexist comments about her. These attentions were clearly unwelcome, and she appeared embarrassed and upset by them.

What did you do?

I immediately challenged the comments in front of the rest of the group, pointing out that he was causing embarrassment, and showing a complete lack of respect. I also told him that I found his conduct personally offensive, and that I intended to bring it to the attention of management due to its seriousness.

Why do you think the offender acted inappropriately?

I do not think my male colleague had stopped to consider the effect of his actions. He regarded himself as being a bit of a joker, and was shocked when I pointed out the effect his thoughtless actions were having. He simply had not realised the effect his actions had on the new staff member, and was immediately sorry.

What would have happened if you hadn't intervened?

Had I not intervened, I believe the female colleague would have either left, or had no alternative but to make a formal complaint to management. In any event, she would have been miserable at work, and the inappropriate comments from my colleague may well have got worse if left unchallenged.

THE TEAM WORKING QUESTION

Where might examples come from?

Clearly, the working environment is a good source of team working situations. However, if you participate in some form of social group, that may be sufficient. Sport examples can be considered to be a bit weak, unless you play at a very high standard. College projects will suffice if you have no stronger examples, but try and avoid them if possible. Your example can be quite basic. It simply needs to be a time when you've worked closely with other people to achieve a specific task.

One course student once told me that she worked as a switchboard operator for a large company, and therefore did not consider herself part of the team. I explained to her that being part of a team does not just mean having an important job, with a big desk in an office full of people. In her case, if she did not answer the phone correctly, and routed the call to the wrong person, the business would have been unable to function. If she was inefficient when placing outgoing calls, the firm could lose business. Logically therefore, if she did not do her job, then the office could not function. In actual fact she was a vital part of the team.

An example team working answer

What were you required to do?

Recently at my workplace, a very large customer order of goods had to be assembled at short notice. Only one loading bay member of staff was available, as the others were working on another important order, and it was obvious that they would be unable to process this new order on time by themselves.

How did the situation arise?

I was delivering some files to the loading bay, when I saw the five people in the warehouse team looking worried. When I spoke to them, they explained the situation to me, and I realised that as a company we needed to meet this target. I therefore volunteered to help them achieve this.

What actions did you take?
I suggested that we borrow another two members of staff. I then held a quick briefing conference, and suggested that we split the work between us. For example, one person called out the items required, another got them from the shelves, and the others loaded the vehicle. I explained to the others why I thought we ought to do this, and listened to their suggestions.

How were the plans made?
I used to be a loading bay supervisor, so I proposed the main ideas because I was the most experienced, although each member of staff made a suggestion which we adopted to improve the actual time it took to load the lorry. For example one person suggested borrowing a forklift truck, which I arranged.

How did you ensure that you reached your target?
I made all of the team members aware of the time and quality target, and explained the standards required. Working in a quality control capacity, whilst sure to do my share of carrying, I ensured the team worked together to get the job done quickly and on time.

What did you gain by this personally?
I realised that by all working together, and being willing to take on personal responsibility, we got the work done much more quickly to the benefit of the company and also my own self-development. This has made me more willing to get involved in working with others to achieve results.

THE 'WORKING UNDER PRESSURE' QUESTION

Where might examples come from?

Candidates wrongly believe that the best examples to working under pressure should evolve some earth-shattering situation. This is simply not correct. The assessors are just looking for examples of occasions when you have been required to carry on whilst under moderately unusual or difficult circumstances. Simple examples may include:

- working to a deadline;
- being under pressure to get something done;
- dealing with difficult work or life pressures such as illness or personal problems;
- having too much work to handle comfortably.

Ideally, from a marking perspective, somewhere within your example there will be an individual who disagreed with your proposed course of action, which will allow the assessor to judge how you handled the resulting minor conflict.

An example working under pressure answer

Describe the situation and why it was awkward

A few months ago I was working in a call centre within a credit control department. One of my customers contacted my desk regarding the fact she had received a letter telling her that her gas supply was about to be cut off. She could not understand why she was in arrears. Winter was approaching, and I was concerned that the lady would suffer health problems if we went ahead and cut off her gas supply. I wanted to keep her connected for the time being, and send out a Customer Service Officer to her. My manager thought this view was wrong.

Who thought your view was wrong?

My supervisor was adamant that company policy should be followed, and the customer should be disconnected. They said they would move me to another team if I did not comply with this regulation. I felt under pressure in that if I followed what I felt to be right, I would be moved off the team.

What did you do?

I asked the supervisor to allow me to speak to the customer on the phone, and if there were no good reason to do otherwise, I would comply with policy and disconnect the customer. Because the supervisor could see my concern, they agreed. I rang the lady concerned, and discovered her husband had recently died, and that he had handled all of her finances. She did not understand how the direct debit system worked. I sorted out some financial details over the phone, and there was therefore no need to disconnect her.

How did you feel at the start of the situation?
Initially, I was in a dilemma between my conscience and staying on the team. I felt under pressure to give in and disconnect the lady even though I did not feel it was right to do so.

How did you feel at the end of the situation?
I was pleased I followed my conscience, and negotiated the chance to speak to the lady and sort out the problem. I felt that I acted morally and ethically correctly.

THE COMMUNICATION QUESTION

Where might examples come from?

This is an interesting question as this really combines two competencies in some ways: the candidate's ability to convey a message, and being able to do so under challenging circumstances. Good examples can often be found in situations we have dealt with at work. Perhaps you have had to tell someone their work is not up to the required standard, or that a friend has been hurt or injured, or else that someone has done something which they simply should not have done. A good measure of the challenging circumstances should be that at the end of the conversation you have had with an individual, they have been unhappy or concerned about what you have told them (but not obviously at you!).

An example communication answer

Who were you dealing with?
I run a local Cub Scout group for young people. About a year ago I was at a meeting, and was contacted by a parent to say that their child had been badly injured in a road accident, and was critically ill. She asked me to tell the group that the child would not be coming back soon, if it all.

What did you see as the difficulties?
The group was only young, and the child concerned was very popular. I knew the news would be very upsetting, and was aware I had to be honest about his condition without creating unnecessary distress.

What did you say?
I decided I had to be honest with the group, but phrase my words in such a way as to avoid increasing the upset. I decided the best time to inform them would be at the end of the session, but before the group were collected by their parents. This was in order that parents would be able to offer support if required. I gathered the group together, with some other group helpers, in the main hall. I started talking of bad news in general, and how it affected us all. Then, I gently told them about the Scout who had been hurt, and that he needed to be in our thoughts. I made no reference to death as such, but every one realised how serious he was, and the potential for such an eventuality.

What factors did you consider before speaking?
I was concerned about the effect the news would have on the young group, whether or not it would be better for them to stay together as a group for support, or whether the Scouts would be better off with their parents. I clearly did not want to cause alarm unnecessarily, or create the fear of death. I was also conscious of not undermining the trust of the group or patronising them by concealing the truth.

SUMMARY ON COMPETENCY QUESTIONS

Any poor answers you provide to the competency questions will be the ones most likely to lead to your application being rejected. You must give a great deal of thought to the examples you use. By completing a short list of examples before you begin, you will be able to see which ones best fit the requirements of each question. Where the questions asked are split into segments, again consider how your proposed example will fit into each particular segment.

Ensuring the example is about you

Your examples should be based around *you*. The questions will all ask what you did, not your team, friend or whoever else was there. Ensure you do not make the basic mistake of simply putting down plain statements, such as 'I communicated the message taking into account the needs of everyone'. This is not evidence. It is just a collection of nice things you are saying about yourself and will be marked down accordingly.

Using examples from all aspects of your life

You do not have to use a work-based environment for all your examples, and in fact it is probably ideal if you can mix in some social examples as well. At the end of the day, however, you must use the best example to fit the criteria. The examples I provide are simply a guide. They are meant merely to give you the idea of how to evidence your answers. There are a million different examples, and clearly you should only use ones from your own life experience.

THE MOTIVATIONAL AND PERCEPTION TYPE QUESTIONS

In relation to the competency questions, there is a further part of the form that you will now have to deal with. This basically covers questions as to why you wish to join the service, along with examining your level of commitment and self-motivation. Broadly speaking, this section can include questions such as:

- Why do you want to become a police community support officer or police officer?
- Why you want to join this particular force?
- What impact you think your role will have on your personal life?
- What preparation have you undertaken for the role?
- If previously unsuccessful how have you developed since your last application?

Again, this type of question also needs to be treated with respect.

Why do you want to become a police community support officer or a police officer?

Even if it's true, do not even contemplate mentioning here that you want to fight crime, tackle injustice and arrest bad guys. The service wants recruits who are community focused (they have even made a competency based around it), so ensure your answer revolves around this. The service likes people to consider a police career for reasons such as:

- you want to give something back to the community;
- you want to help people in the community;
- you want to develop yourself;
- you want to face new challenges.

The fact that a candidate might want to become a firearms officer, or drive a Volvo down the motorway at 130mph, are not considered good reasons for wishing to join. Nor should you consider mentioning the wage or job security. Remember, this question is really asking for reasons that the police may want to employ you. You should be joining because you want to help your community.

Why apply to this particular force?

This is a particularly foolish question in many ways. If you live in Manchester, the chances are you're going to apply to Greater Manchester Police as it is simply the force covering the area in which you live. The chances of you applying to Devon and Cornwall are pretty remote. However, the better answer will be to explain how you are part of the local community, that you are aware of local issues and therefore want to be involved in helping your local community be a safer place.

Thinking about the opportunities within the force

If the force is a large one, consider referring to the fact that you would have the ability to experience a wide range of diverse police work within the force area. If it is a small force, consider the fact that perhaps there is more of a team spirit, whilst the organisation will still offer a diverse range of policing experiences. Consider what type of force you are applying to. If you're looking to join the City of London Police, it would be foolish to talk about the desire to experience rural policing. If you are joining North Wales, don't express a desire to police big cities.

What kind of things do you think you would do as a police officer or PCSO?

Do not over dramatise the job here, or give the impression that you think the role will be a constant conveyor belt of pub fights and car chases. Consider routine police tasks, crime reports, missing from home reports, minor crime investigation, and most importantly of all, any kind of work you think will help your local community feel safer. Key to this will be visible patrol, tackling any problem issues affecting the community on your particular beat. Read your local force website to find out about community-based initiatives their teams are running, and that will give you some idea of the kind of tasks you will be expected to perform.

What about the impact on your personal life?

It is naïve to think that joining the service will have no impact on you and your personal life. The service will involve shift work, and place you in demanding and sometimes unpleasant situations. This must impact on your family and friends. You will also be subject to some severe restrictions on your personal life, so consider how you will cope with these realities in your answer.

What preparation have you undertaken?

This question is testing your self-motivation. The service will spend a lot of money on your training, so wants to know that you've done more than simply read the information on the website of your chosen force. Consider doing research tasks such as:

- visiting a local police station and asking for a tour;
- going to a community meeting;
- researching the force's aims and objectives;
- reading a copy of the Chief Constable's Annual Report;
- joining the Special Constabulary;
- improving your spelling and grammar by going to night school if necessary.

Fitness preparation

A word about fitness. I suspect in excess of 80 per cent of candidates say they are going to the gym to get fit in terms of job preparation. It's boring and obvious, so use some other example that is more interesting and therefore more likely to gain you marks.

If you have been unsuccessful in the past, how have you developed yourself?

This question only applies if you have previously been unsuccessful. If this is the case, irrespective of whether you feel you should have passed last time or not, swallow your pride and come up with some way in which you have developed yourself. Perhaps last time around your questioning or self-motivation let you down, and you worked hard to improve it. Specify clearly what you have done to achieve this. Improvement and development is good. It shows you have a willingness to listen, to learn, and to be self-motivated enough to move on from disappointment and still have the will to succeed.

SUMMARY ON THE MOTIVATIONAL AND PERCEPTION TYPE QUESTIONS

I have deliberately not given specimen answers to these questions. Instead I have provided a number of ideas to get you thinking along the right lines. Please do not simply copy my suggestions. If you do, remember that many assessors will read this book too!

Why should the service want you?

Carefully consider not just your reasons for joining the service, but also why the service should want you. The questions are really asking you to display qualities that the service will find desirable. Give good, clear community-based reasons, and evidence them if you can. Simply stating that you have always wanted to be a police officer is just not good enough.

A final thought

A good application form can take you a week or more to complete so allow yourself plenty of time. Before you go anywhere near the competency questions, have a good think about your life experience in order to come up with relevant examples. Remember, if you get this form wrong, you effectively bar yourself from the application process for a minimum of six months. That assumes that the force is recruiting again by then, which would be unlikely. Rushing your form is more likely to lose you a year or more!

4

The national assessment centre

THE THINKING BEHIND ASSESSMENT CENTRES

Up to this point, we have examined the type of skills that the police service is looking for in terms of competencies, with particular reference to the application stage. Having gained an understanding of this, it is now possible to look at the ways that the assessment centre itself works.

In a perfect world your abilities might be assessed by simply placing you in a blue uniform, sending you out on patrol in your local area and observing your performance. If you made a mess of it, the service would know that you weren't cut out for the role. This method, whilst probably fairly accurate in terms of defining future performance, would be extremely expensive both financially and perhaps more importantly in terms of public relations.

Using an artificial environment to test you

The thinking behind 'on the job' assessment may still be attractive to some but the next best thing is making someone do the job they are being recruited for by putting them into an artificial environment and giving them some tasks to do. The elements of these tasks can be made similar to the kinds of things they would expect to do if they were performing the real job. Having said that, if the assessment designers were to make the tasks too police oriented, then groups such as special constables and existing civilian police staff would have an advantage.

Using a fictional job

The most practical way to assess somebody's behaviour, but avoid any favouritism towards those in the police service in some other capacity, is to create a fictional job. The candidate is then effectively given this fictional job on their assessment day and asked to perform tasks in their new 'role'. The tasks they are asked to perform are theoretically directly related to those a police officer would need to carry out. More specifically, the skills needed to solve the problems in the assessment are the same skills that should hopefully indicate that the candidate will make a good police officer.

The context of the national assessment centre

For the purposes of your assessment day, the national police assessment centre therefore takes the following format. You will effectively be given a job, the title which is that of a customer service officer, (not to be confused with the role of Community Support Officer). You will work in a fictional leisure complex in a fictional town. For our purposes from now on, we will call this fictional leisure complex the East Ham Centre.

On your first (and only!) working day at the East Ham Centre, you will be given a number of exercises to perform. Most, but not all of these, will require you to work in the role of a customer service officer. Before the assessment centre, you will be sent a 'welcome pack' to help you. The contents of this, and the importance of it to the candidate, are covered on pages 63–68.

A TYPICAL ASSESSMENT CENTRE

The assessment centre consists of the following four main elements:

- a competency based interview;
- a number of role-play exercises;
- a number of written exercises;
- verbal and numerical IQ tests.

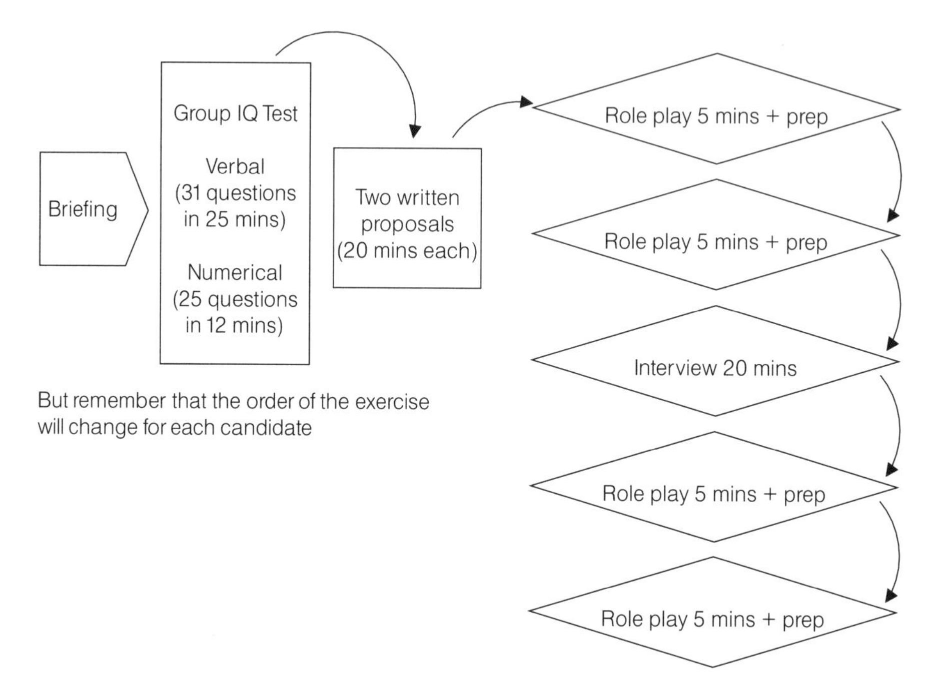

Fig. 3. A typical assessment centre.

You may be asked to complete the elements in any order, so do not assume you will be doing your interview first on the day. Note that the centre for PCSO recruitment is effectively a cut-down version of this. Each element is the subject of a separate section of this book. However, by way of introduction, I will now briefly explain what each element involves.

A competency based interview

This interview may be unlike anything you have experienced before. It is not a touchy-feely, getting to know you type of interview. It is seeking particular information, concerning specific competency areas. Your answers will either provide evidence which matches the positive competencies, or they will not. If your answer provides enough specific evidence which can be related by the assessor to the desired competency, then you will pass. If this is not the case then you will fail the interview.

A number of role-play exercises

Police candidates undertake four role-play exercises, whilst PCSOs may only need to take two. Each individual role play consists of a five-minute preparation phase, followed by five minutes with a role actor. The information you will be allowed to read in the five-minute preparation phase will have a direct impact upon the meeting you are about to have with the role actor. Again, in your performance the assessors will be looking for you to provide evidence of the desired competencies required for that exercise.

A number of written exercises

You will undertake two written exercises. You will be provided with certain information and asked to provide some form of proposal or written response to a particular individual or group, which should contain your recommendations to resolve the issue described in the documentation.

Both the role plays and written exercises will require you to take the role of a customer services officer in our fictional leisure complex.

Verbal and numerical IQ tests

You will undertake two IQ tests, one on verbal reasoning and one on numerical reasoning. The scores from all these exercises will be collated, and your total scores in each of the seven competencies calculated. You have to pass all seven individual competency areas in order to be successful. If you fail one, you fail the entire assessment centre.

INAPPROPRIATE BEHAVIOUR IN THE GENERAL CONTEXT OF THE ASSESSMENT CENTRE

I have already touched on inappropriate behaviour in terms of the exercises, and will return to it in more depth in later chapters. However, it is vitally important to realise the extent to which your behaviour will be monitored on the day. It is also important to remember that you're not just being assessed inside the rooms where the exercises take place. It is not so much that your behaviour outside the rooms is being monitored or marked, but if you are overheard making any form of inappropriate comment, then the rules allow the assessment centre staff to fail you immediately on the basis that you have shown a lack of diversity. The theory behind this assessment centre rule is based on that of the national police promotion examinations for the rank of sergeant and inspector.

How inappropriate behaviour standards were developed

There is a story about how standards concerning inappropriate behaviour developed. Several years ago, one of the exercises concerned a scenario whereby the candidate met a traffic warden who had some particular issue they were unhappy with. The role actor's script required them to be quite argumentative and negative about this particular issue. According to the story, one candidate finished the exercise and left the assessment room heading for the next exercise. As he did so, he turned around to another candidate and said, 'If that bitch worked for me in real life, I would soon sort her out'. This remark was overheard by a visiting Assistant Chief Constable observing the examination. This senior officer, who either had no sense of humour or was particularly good at keeping their own feelings in check when under pressure, immediately demanded to see the head assessor and stated that they wanted this candidate failed. (Remember that the comment was made outside the assessment room and was effectively a private conversation.) For that particular candidate there were no rules in existence at the time which allowed such a failure to take place. However, this rule has now been introduced for both promotion and recruitment training.

Remaining conscious of your actions whilst at the centre

The moral of the story is to be very conscious of what you say throughout your entire time inside the assessment centre building. Do not make any comment that could in any way be considered inappropriate. If you find a fellow candidate is particularly attractive, appears grotesquely ugly, or would appear to be as dumb as a box of frogs, keep this opinion to yourself. If you make any kind of comment and this is overheard, the chances are you will gain an automatic grade D for diversity. A single grade D in diversity means an automatic fail.

THE WELCOME PACK

It has already been explained that the assessment day revolves around providing the candidate with the fictional role of a customer service officer inside a fictional leisure complex. The police realise, however, that in order to make the assessment as fair as possible for everyone, there need to be some guidelines, or advance information, as to the roles and duties required of a customer service officer. This is quite logical in many ways. If your experience of working life since school has been in the army, you would be at a definite disadvantage in terms of dealing with a customer service issue compared with somebody already working in that sector. Personally, I'm not quite convinced that the provisions the service make to try to equalise the situation are adequate, but at least they try.

The make-up of the welcome pack

The welcome pack is designed to help the candidate to understand the role expected of them on the day. Between two and six weeks before your assessment date, you will be provided with your 'welcome pack'. This should be treated as being a set of guidelines provided to you upon starting your new 'job' as a customer service officer. It contains a number of documents, although candidates should be aware that they do change from time to time. The pack generally contains the following materials.

Information about the centre itself

This documents will provide such information as centre opening hours, disabled access, car park arrangements and general facts about the centre. You will be told that on your assessment day you will be working at a fictional leisure complex. (For our purposes I will refer to this from now on as the East Ham Centre.)

There is a description of the Operations Department, which outlines the staffing levels and functions of such teams as housekeeping, security and customer services.

There is a job description for a customer services officer. This describes the range of duties expected from such a person, who is of course you, the candidate.

Additional information provided

You will almost certainly find some form of equal opportunities policy in the pack. This is a particularly crucial document worthy of considerable attention.

There will be some kind of set of rules to be followed by all people inside the centre, both visiting members of the public and staff.

You may also find that policies appear or disappear with each new issue of the pack. The significance of this will be explained later.

The typical candidate will read through this documentation and fail to attach any real significance to it. They often fail to consider some basic facts about the welcome pack. It is essential that candidates realise that every single word you are provided with in terms of advance notification or data given to you on the assessment day has a purpose. The same applies to the information you are given in the role play for example. All of this has been written or is being imparted with a purpose in mind. The welcome pack was not written to give the assessor something to do on a rainy day. It contains a series of prompts which, if you understand what they are, will positively affect your performance on the day. Just as importantly, it also contains guidelines that should enable you to avoid making stupid mistakes in issues such as diversity.

The information it really contains

I have described above the type of information contained within the welcome pack. A fully prepared candidate, however, will also understand the significance of each of those pieces of information.

To begin with, details about the East Ham Centre are meant to give the candidate key background information about the centre. It is likely that the centre information will impact to some extent on the role plays and written exercises. For example, the centre information may contain facts about disabled access. It is not therefore inconceivable that one of your scenarios could deal at some point with somebody complaining about access to a centre facility for a disabled person. Knowing the background to the centre will enable the prepared candidate to deal with customer complaints more easily.

Complaint scenarios

Imagine you're dealing with somebody complaining about lack of disabled car park spaces. They may well accuse you, as the representative of the centre, of not being interested in the needs of disabled people. If you are able to state that the centre is concerned and evidence that by reeling off the fact that a certain number of places are reserved for the disabled, you are much more likely to score a better mark.

If you find yourself faced with somebody who is complaining about the cleaning standards in the centre, it may help to know how many cleaners work in the centre, and what their chain of command is. If you're dealing with somebody who's complaining to you about gangs of youths roaming around the centre, it may be useful to know how many security guards are on duty at any one time, along with the fact that there are a number of CCTV cameras inside the centre.

The duties and responsibilities of the role

Whether you are fortunate enough to be a customer services officer in your normal job, or whether you have never experienced working in customer services before, the fact that the police provide a copy of the main duties and responsibilities for your new role is useful. You may well find that within the role play or written exercises there exists a problem which needs to be taken in hand by someone. Many candidates will be wondering throughout the exercise who the correct person for dealing with that problem should be.

For example, many candidates when confronted with a problem in an exercise will try to pass it on to a manager. However, the description of the customer service officer main duties and responsibilities clearly states that customer problems are to be dealt with and solved by customer services officers. The significance of this is that if in a role play the candidate tries to duck responsibility for the problem by passing it on to somebody else, then clearly they are failing to comply with their own job description. Of course, if you are familiar by now with the competencies, you will also recognise that this sort of action would be in direct contravention of the points concerning taking responsibility for solving problems.

Addressing the equality statement

The equality statement is almost invariably ignored by most candidates. Many people will read through the equal opportunities policy provided, and think that this is just political correctness, and has been put in for the sake of being included. This could not be further from the truth. In the case of the assessment centre, the inclusion of the equal opportunities policy is significant for two reasons. Firstly, it is designed to explain and emphasise the kind of behaviour the police themselves will consider totally unacceptable. Secondly, it goes on to provide three distinct steps that should be taken by staff if such a complaint of inappropriate conduct is received by them. Although the vast majority of candidates never even realise it, this document even goes on to stress that if somebody at the centre feels that they have been subject to discrimination, they should seek advice from a customer service officer. This is another subtle way of the assessment centre planners telling you, the candidate, that if you encounter such inappropriate behaviour, *you* must deal with it. Failure to deal with it means you will probably fail the centre.

The importance of policies and information

There can also be important clues contained in the welcome pack about the scenarios. Knowing these policies in advance of the assessment day by studying the welcome pack makes your life a lot easier. Such knowledge should also start you thinking well in advance of the centre as to what ways such a scenario could develop.

Getting hold of a welcome pack

You will get a copy of the welcome pack somewhere between two and six weeks before the exam. This will relate directly to the individual assessment you will take, so this is the one to study fully.

However, copies can be obtained of older welcome packs by searching the internet. The locations of these, usually provided by individual police forces or NPIA themselves, change from time to time. It should be stressed that these will be old copies and, whilst the majority of information will remain the same, it is vital you remember that the only pack to rely on is the one sent to you before your assessment.

Comparisons of old and new welcome packs

An extremely useful technique used by most police promotion candidates is to try to get hold of the previous welcome pack to your exam. Having done so (and having made certain it is the one before, not two before!) it is worthwhile comparing the previous and current one and seeing what differences there are, if any. For example, in one year a policy may appear on smoking inside the centre. There may be a list of conditions attached as to when smoking is allowed. Working on the basis that nothing is done without a reason, an astute candidate could reasonably come to the conclusion that somewhere in the assessment there will be an exercise requiring candidates to make a decision to do with someone who is contravening that policy! It may therefore be wise to make sure you learn that document.

There is no guarantee of this of course. It may be that the policy was inserted into the pack, then a problem was found with the exercise it related to, and the exercise was dropped. However, it is always better to prepare for something that does not happen, than not prepare for something that does!

Learning the pack

One common question I am asked is whether or not it is worthwhile leaning the welcome pack off by heart. The simple answer is no. You will not get any extra marks for quoting it word for word.

You will probably be given extracts from it on the day, so remember, if these are selected extracts, they should act as a heads up. Ask yourself why this particular extract has been given to you. The answer is probably because whatever is coming up in the exercise relates in some way to that extract.

Familiarity with the pack

However, being familiar with the welcome pack itself can be extremely helpful. Each of the documents in the pack is about an A4 page of medium sized font. Let's say it takes the average person 60 seconds to read it. In a five-minute preparation time therefore, a poor candidate can waste 60 seconds of that time studying a document that had been sent to them weeks before. This is foolish.

You should be familiar enough with the pack so that as you read through the actual exercises, you are able to make any links between the problem you have to face, and the policies you have read in the welcome pack. Then, if you have to, you only need to glance at the extract you will be provided with to check your recollection is correct.

5

An introduction to role plays

ROLE PLAYS

What are role plays or the 'interactive exercises'?

The role-play exercise is designed to see how the candidate will react to certain situations in the presence of another individual with whom they will interact. In this section I will discuss role plays as a whole with regard to the police system. The two component parts of the role-play exercise will then be explained separately.

Preparing for the role plays

In the police assessment centre, candidates are currently required to undertake four role-play exercises. Each one of these exercises is in two distinct, but interrelated, parts. Firstly, there is a five-minute preparation phase. Typically, the candidate will be placed in a room, or be required to sit outside a doorway at a desk, and is then given a number of documents to read. They have five minutes to read this documentation and use it to prepare for the second part of the exercise. This preparation phase is not marked in any way. If the candidate chooses to sit down and do nothing, they will not gain or lose any marks whatsoever. Well, not at this stage anyway. The next phase would be a challenge for them though!

Taking part in the role plays

At the end of the five-minute preparation phase, a buzzer will sound, and two people will enter the room. (Depending on the layout of the assessment centre, it is possible that the two people are actually inside the room, and the candidate will be required to enter upon the buzzer sounding.) In this second part, the candidate will be expected to deal with issues that have been raised either in the preparation documents, or else use the information from those documents to deal with an issue that is about to be revealed to them.

The role actor will feature in some way in the preparation documentation. It may well be, for example, that the preparation documents contain a letter written by this individual complaining about something.

There are a number of ways in which the preparation documentation may be linked to the role actor. Typical kinds of scenarios include:

- The preparation documentation contains a letter written by the person (role actor) you are about to meet.
- The preparation document makes reference to the person you're about to meet, but it may be a report by somebody else, such as a staff appraisal, and a memo from your manager requesting you meet this person and so on.

The role-play actor

The person (i.e. role actor) you are about to meet may or may not know the reason for the meeting. They may wish to complain to you, or they may need your help. The person you are meeting could be somebody who is a member of your staff. They could be a customer from the centre, or a concerned resident. They could even be some local celebrity or politician.

Whichever is the case, there will be issues raised in the documentation, or by the individual you are seeing, which you, the candidate, must resolve. This is the whole purpose of the role play.

Evaluating you through role plays

Role plays provide a great opportunity for assessors to evaluate how the candidate performs in a 'real life' meeting with somebody. Imagine for a moment a typical role-play scenario. The preparation document may be set up as follows. Your manager at the leisure complex has sent you an internal memo which they wish you to deal with in your role as a customer service officer. This memo concerns a letter of complaint from a member of the public called Jones. The complaint concerns a problem Jones had parking at the centre. Also included in the documentation is a report from a member of the centre staff, who perhaps was involved, witnessed, or is the actual subject of the complaint that Jones wishes to make.

The preparation phase

In the preparation phase of the exercise, you will have five minutes to go through the documents and decide how you are going to deal with the role play. At the completion of the preparation phase, Jones will enter the room and interact with you. How you deal with this interaction as a candidate allows the assessors to evaluate how you behave under a wide range of conditions. For example, they will assess how well you are able to use the information you are given in a written format, and how you cope with summarising the issue to Jones. The exam writers could make Jones confrontational and aggressive, in which case they can see whether you can be assertive. They can see if you can question Jones effectively on the accuracy of the information provided. They can evaluate your ability to generate options to deal with the problem. The assessors can see whether or not you can decide which one of the options you suggest should actually be implemented. Finally, they can see how interested you are in Jones as a customer by the way in which you involve and consult Jones in the final decision. When looked at in this context, role plays are a very useful predictor of future performance.

How are role plays developed?

The basic outline of a role play can come from a number of sources. It may be that the exam writers will hear a story about a real customer-service incident that has taken place and feel it interesting enough to turn into a role play. Alternatively, they may decide that there are certain issues they want to put to candidates. So, they may write a role play which reflects those issues. Exam writers make a great play about the extent to which scenarios are tested and developed. Simplistically, however, they are developed as follows. An assessment writer will come up with an idea of an outline role play. They will build into it certain elements that they wish to assess. So, for example, they could write the scenario in such a way that the candidate is required to ask a number of questions, so the assessor can test the candidate's ability to gather information. The writers will probably include a number of 'clues' as to what options may or may not be available to solve the problem. Although they will deny it, they will often throw one or two red herrings into the script to trip up unwary candidates. A secondary issue may also be thrown into the scenario, for example the use of an inappropriate phrase, or the introduction of some form of welfare need. In this way, the candidate's flexibility and ability to react under pressure can be measured. Finally, the candidate's ability to make a decision and explain it to the person they are meeting can also be included for marking purposes.

The drafted role play

The draft role play will then be reviewed to see whether or not it contains the competency areas that the assessors wish to mark. Remember they are looking for the full range of the seven competencies across the assessment centre. If they have realised that the other exercises do not contain as much questioning as they may like, then individual role plays can be 'tweaked' in order to make the candidate ask more questions. Once the exam writers are happy with the draft format, they will then 'pilot' it. The exercise can be piloted by having a number of probationary constables take the exercise in a controlled examination setting, to see how they deal with it. If nobody passes it within the allocated time frame, then it is rewritten to make it easier. If everybody passes it, it is rewritten to make it harder. This process will go on until the exam writers are satisfied that compared with the average successful candidate, the required percentage of candidates will actually pass it.

Completing the role play in the allotted time

People have often said to me that they were unable to finish the exercise within the time allowed. My reply is that they cannot have been doing it properly. By the time the real candidate sits the role-play exercise, scores and scores of individuals will have sat it in the piloting stage. The average successful candidate will be able to complete it within the time frame allowed.

To be fair to the assessment centre staff and exam writers, each role play is designed and tested to ensure that the average candidate of the required standard can complete it within five minutes. In short, if they can do it, you, the potentially successful candidate, must be able to!

Are the role plays realistic?

I am often asked whether the scenarios used are actually realistic or not. The answer really depends on your perspective. As a customer service officer you'd expect to deal with somebody who felt disappointed by the level of service that they have received. Nor is it unrealistic for you to have to deal with a member of staff who is underperforming.

It is without doubt, however, that you would most certainly not be expected to deal with such meetings inside a tight five-minute schedule. It is a long-standing complaint about the role-play elements of the national sergeant and inspector examinations that this time-frame is unrealistic. Indeed, recruitment professionals in the real world have long since moved to much longer role plays, of up to 50 minutes in some cases. However, the bottom line is that whether the scenarios are realistic or not does not matter. What is important is that candidates fully understand how role plays are constructed, the limitations placed upon the exercises by the design process, and understand how to perform in such a manner as to attract the most marks.

Whether or not people actually behave in the way depicted in the role plays is also irrelevant. I will describe some techniques which in the real world would make our customer service officer sound foolish. However, in the context of the assessment centre they will allow the role play to move forward and score marks. This of course is the whole purpose of the exercise and this book.

Developing rapport with the role actor

It must be remembered therefore that the interaction between the candidate and the role actor will not mirror that of a normal conversation. In most meetings in real life, the people involved will take a while to familiarise themselves with one another ('small talk'). The person making the complaint can probably be relied upon to explain their case fully, and to explain to the customer service officer exactly what they want. This will not happen in a role play. Candidates must remember that the whole purpose of the exercise from the marker's perspective is to see how many competencies the candidate scores in the five-minute period. It is not about how nice a person you appear to be, nor whether you are able to make the assessor like you or not in your role as a customer service officer. The role actor's presence in the room is merely a mechanism for the candidate to show to the assessor that they can display certain abilities. No more, no less. The role actor is exactly that, an actor, so do not fall into the trap of trying to establish some kind of rapport with them.

So do I need to behave the same way as I would in real life?

The exercises are based on situations that could have happened, and then are adjusted to suit the needs of the assessment centre. So, the police argue that they are therefore as realistic as possible. Of course, the reality is that it is highly unlikely that you will ever deal with a situation where, in addition to the fact that you only have precisely five minutes to deal with an issue, the person you are meeting

- is pretending to play a part;
- will deliberately try to catch you out by effectively withholding key pieces of information just to see if you will ask key questions;
- will dodge the issue when you ask them what they want from the meeting;

- effectively refuses to say which of the options you offer them they actually want.

So, the role play may be realistic in that it describes a potentially realistic situation, but the manner in which it is dealt with in the assessment is completely unrealistic.

Remembering to abide by the rules

Remember though that it is simply an examination, nothing more and nothing less. Therefore, you have to abide by the rules, and the key to that is to understand them. You may not agree with nor understand the offside rule in football, but if you want to play a proper game you have to follow it. The same principle applies.

So, despite what the police would say, forget real life and play the game. The same basic principles of the real world do need to be followed but adjusted to compensate for the artificial nature of the exercises.

Can candidates prepare for the role plays?

The police service takes every opportunity to stress that candidates cannot really prepare as such for this particular phase of the assessment centre. The very bland advice given by recruitment departments is usually along the lines of 'act naturally and try not to worry about the situation'. This is in my view complete and utter rubbish. Over the following pages I will describe techniques commonly used in industry for dealing with role plays. These techniques have been customised to deal specifically with the police recruitment system. There are three types of people who pass role plays. Firstly, there are those whose life experience has already trained or prepared them to deal with similar situations. Secondly, there is a very small minority of people who just happen to be lucky and possess naturally the approach to deal with problems. The third category are those who thoroughly plan and prepare their approach to role plays, and fully understand the mechanics, aims and techniques of the exercise.

The wider use of assessment centres

A search of the web, particularly of sites such as those of colleges and universities, will show that most run some form of assessment centre training for their students. Many police forces run training to help people pass the promotion examinations – on which parts of the assessment centre are based. It is laughable for the police to suggest therefore that you cannot prepare for them. The reality is that, as stated before, they wish to see candidates in their unprepared state.

It is probably fair to say that it is role plays which catch most people out. As there are four of them, they count for a proportionately large section of the marks. They therefore deserve a large amount of consideration when it comes to the preparation undertaken by the candidate.

The importance of time management

Like all the exercises contained in the assessment centre, the role plays are very strictly timed. The preparation phase lasts exactly five minutes, followed immediately by the further five-minute interaction phase. This amounts to a total of 300 seconds per phase. These 300 seconds will absolutely fly by on the day. In both phases, you, the candidate, cannot afford to be indecisive. In the interactive stage, you cannot spend two and a half minutes making small talk with the role actor in a pointless attempt to get the character to like you. Neither can you spend four minutes asking questions. The whole role play is a timed event. Mentally you must be able to divide your time, not necessarily into equal segments, and deal with all the points you believe could be on the marking guide within this 300 second period.

Keeping track of time during the role plays

You will be told in the briefing phase of the assessment centre that you're not allowed to have any kind of timing device that makes a noise. However, you should be able to get away with a digital watch or timer even if it has a small beeper attached. Whilst it may take some practice, it is essential for you keep track of time throughout your role play. This requirement applies equally to both phases. For example, the overall purpose of the role play is to see whether or not the candidate can actually solve a problem. If you are in your interactive phase, and the time has reached four minutes out of your allocated time of five minutes, then you should be able to realise that you have only 60 seconds left to make your decision, explain it, and check how the role actor views it. This is where being able to look at some form of digital timer can be useful, if not essential. If you have no time reference, it is easy to get carried away with asking questions, or explaining options, and so discover that the buzzer has gone ending your performance before you come anywhere near solving the problem. Whilst this will not mean an automatic fail, it certainly creates an uphill struggle for the candidate. Time management is everything.

Limitations and mechanisms of the role play written preparation phase

Before moving on to the techniques for dealing with role plays, it is extremely useful to understand the limitations such exercises place upon the assessment centre designers.

Time limits

The first limitation is that of time. The exam writer has to provide the candidate with some form of initial information to start the role play off. This is the purpose of providing the documentation to be read in the initial five-minute preparation phase. Five minutes, however, is not a long time. Therefore, the effect of this short period is a guarantee that every piece of paper given to you to read in the preparation phase is directly relevant to the role play you are about to do. So, for example, if you're given a copy of the policy concerning car park access, it is a safe bet that at some point in the following role play you will need to discuss that policy with the role actor. So, an astute candidate will be aware before they read the first line of the document that there will be all manner of clues inside that document as to what the role play is actually going to be about. The prepared candidate will therefore be reading that document trying to work out where the role play is likely to go.

The context of the role play

The second limitation is that of context. Within the documentation, the exam writer has to remind you which role you, the candidate, are fulfilling. They have to provide you with some form of background to the problem you are about to face and with some form of information you will be able to use to solve the problem. The following is a typical example.

The candidate opens up the preparation document when the buzzer sounds, and has five minutes to read it. There are three sheets of paper in total. The first will often be some kind of covering memo, from someone that works at the centre, possibly a manager, which is addressed to the candidate in their role as a customer service officer. This memo will often go along the lines of explaining that the person the candidate is about to meet has perhaps written in to make a complaint about something that has happened in the centre. Perhaps it may involve some service they have received or the attitude of a member of staff. The memo may ask you, the customer service officer, to deal with the situation and may refer to a copy of the original letter also enclosed to help you solve the problem. In addition, often there will be some form of extract of an official policy or guidance forming the third page of the preparation papers. Remember, every single word provided to the candidate is there for a purpose.

Taking personal responsibility during the role play

For example, the fact that the memo may ask for the customer service officer (i.e. you) to deal with the matter is a way of telling you to take personal responsibility for the issue and deal with it – that's if you wish to pass the centre!

Providing a copy of the letter the role actor has written also provides the candidate with the background for the meeting. If the role actor is complaining about something, the document may set out key information, such as times, dates, names of people involved and so on, with which to take the matter forward. Providing a policy should highlight to the candidate what standards of behaviour or actions should have been taken by the organisation. So, if the member of the public (the role actor) is complaining about the actions (or lack of them) from a member of staff, the policy may enable the candidate to explain and defend those actions, if appropriate. If such actions did not comply with policy, then appropriate action can be taken. If you think about it, the examination writer has to give the candidate some guidelines to work to, in terms of what is acceptable and what is not. Failure to do so would mean the exercise would not work.

Inability to use contradictions

In real life, most meetings between people of opposing views, whether they be complaints, staff appraisals, staff development meetings or whatever, will result in two versions of events that may well contradict one another. For example, a member of the public may say that they were parked in a disabled bay for only five minutes. The traffic warden who has issued a ticket to that motorist may say that in actual fact they were parked there for 20 minutes. If this particular example were taken to court, witnesses would be required who would give their version of events supporting one party, and it would be the job of the magistrate to actually decide who was telling the truth.

As each role-play interactive stage is limited in length to five minutes, exam writers are not able to use such contradictory accounts of events. Using the above example of the dispute over a parking ticket, imagine you are the candidate in that role play. You have been given a letter to deal with which contains a complaint from a member of the public that they have been given a parking ticket for over-staying their time in a parking bay. You see from the company memo that you are about to meet the traffic warden who issued the ticket. In the interactive phase, you will naturally (hopefully) ask the traffic warden how long that person was in the parking bay for. If the parking warden states the person was there for 20 minutes, yet the other party states in their letter they were only there for five, how could you solve the issue? Within the confines of a five-minute role play, when you are only speaking to one party with no evidence to go on other than a letter and no access to anybody else, it would be impossible for you to decide who was telling the truth and therefore impossible for you to solve the problem.

The 'opposing' parties involved in a role play, whether you either physically meet them as you do the role actor, or have been provided with written information without meeting them, cannot give you any form of conflicting information. If they did, you would simply be unable to solve the role play, which would defeat the entire purpose of the exercise.

The differing perspectives within role plays

What characters in a role play can have, however, is different perspectives on the same thing. Consider this example. In your preparation phase, you are given documentation which includes a report from a member of staff that they have overheard the cleaner in the leisure complex making some form of inappropriate comment. The comment would probably be quoted to you. Being a smart candidate, you will by now realise that when you go into the interactive phase, you will have to point out this alleged (and it is important to remember the word alleged) inappropriate comment to the cleaner. From the cleaner's perspective, however, they may not feel that the comments they made were in fact inappropriate. So, if you say to the cleaner 'Have you made any inappropriate comments about immigrants?', they may well say no. As far as they are concerned, the comments were not inappropriate and are therefore answering your question truthfully. If you were to ask them if they made the comment quoted, they would have to say 'yes'. This may appear to be a contradiction, but in actual fact is not. What the cleaner is saying in this instance is, 'Yes I made the comment, but I do not think it was inappropriate'. It would then be for you as the candidate to deal with those reasons, and to decide whether they are valid or not.

Moving the role play forward

The importance of this is that the cleaner cannot simply deny that the specific comments were made. If they were to do so, it would be impossible for the candidate to move the role play forward. Therefore, the cleaner must admit that the comments were made if the question is phrased in the correct way. What they may well do, however, is to state that the context that these comments were made is in fact completely different from that originally thought.

Imagine the issue had been this. A member of the security staff has been accused of ignoring a request for help by a member of the public, instead apparently preferring to carry on walking wherever they were going and failing to take any action whatsoever to help the person concerned. This has been reported to you by some form of written report in the preparation phase. When you speak to the security guard, because of the set-up of the examination, they will have to admit to you that yes, on reflection, they did walk past a person asking for help. Whilst on the face of it this may be a gross dereliction of duty, a good candidate will then start digging into the reasons why the security guard failed to help the individual. Consequently, you may find that the security guard's actions were due to the fact that they were on their way to give first aid to somebody who was seriously injured in an accident around the corner. So, this is another example of how, if you are told as a candidate that an incident has occurred, the person you then see in a role play simply cannot deny that incident ever took place. They will always agree (perhaps with a little bit of probing) that the event did take place, but they may have a completely different perspective on it. Our security guard, therefore, if accused of dereliction of duty by failing to help the complainant, may completely deny it. If, however, they are asked if they ignored the original request for help, they will have to agree that they did. They may have a completely valid reason for it, or not, as the case may be, but ultimately they will probably have some reason as to why they did what they did. Again, it is then up to you, the candidate, to decide whether this reason is good enough, or whether further action is warranted.

The need to provide alternative points of view

I have previously explained that the role actor cannot give contradictory information, in other words, they cannot lie to the candidate. This is simply because the candidate has no way of checking out the information to find the truth within the limits of a five-minute time frame. To get around this, the following technique is often used by examination writers. In the preparation phase, they will set up the documents so that two opposing views, or perceptions, of an incident, policy or whatever, are included. These will not be totally contradictory positions, however. If you look closely, the reports are invariably simply opposing sides of the same coin.

Content of preparation packs

Imagine in your next role play, you are given a preparation pack that firstly contains a memo stating you are about to see a member of the public who has written to complain that juveniles convicted of minor crimes and disorder are to be given free access to the children's amusement area. The letter writer is arguing that this is unfair as children who have not been in trouble with the authorities have to pay full price. The second document provided may well be a copy of this letter. It may contain various (usually unsubstantiated or inaccurate) allegations or anecdotes which the letter writer used as an argument for you not to take the action that the centre is proposing to take. The third document in this kind of scenario may well provide a breakdown of statistics showing that where similar schemes have been introduced in similar environments to the leisure complex, there have been no increases in crime whatsoever (and therefore no cause for concern for the public), and in actual fact, crime rates in the local area have fallen because youngsters have been kept actively occupied. The letter writer's opinions are therefore based on incorrect information, or unsubstantiated bias. This does not make them a bad person of course; perhaps they just need the facts gently explaining to them, or some reassurance.

Conflicting sources of information

In this type of scenario, the candidate is being tested on their ability to deal with conflicting sources of information, to maintain a balanced and impartial view, and to be able to persuade others who may have a different viewpoint. At the same time, of course, candidates will be expected to show respect for the other person's point of view, as all such complaints will be a genuine community concern.

There are numerous permutations in terms of setting up differing viewpoints. The key to dealing with them is to be on the lookout when initially reading the document, and to be aware of the kind of issues that may well arise. Ultimately though, as a candidate you should remember that these differences will be in there. There is no point in the examination writer creating a role play in which all parties are in total agreement. This would not give you, the candidate, any chance whatsoever to display competencies. It would therefore be a waste of time. The key point to remember is that, as you know these differences will be contained within the role play, if you fail to see them, you are probably missing something.

SIGNPOSTS, HOOKS AND BLOCKS

This section covers three elements which together make up the most important set of design criteria in the construction of role plays. Signposts, hooks and blocks are built in by the examination writers in order to ensure that a candidate has a realistic prospect of completing the exercise within the given time period. The skill for the candidate is in recognising these for what they are.

Signposts

Signposts is the term given to specific phrases or pieces of information that are designed to enable the candidate to move the scenario on. For example, you may find that your role play deals with a centre employee who appears to have an unacceptable attitude to their work. Perhaps their motivation has gone down, and you are given some documentation in the preparation phase that suggests they are lazy. Also in the documentation pack may be the centre's policy on dealing with unacceptable performance by staff members. The policy is meant to be the signpost to the candidate to ensure they take some positive action regarding the behaviour of the staff member. Another example could be along the lines of a customer writing a letter of complaint demanding that the centre takes a certain course of action. This is a signpost to the candidate to deal with that particular issue.

Signposts can also be found in the script given to the role actors. For example, if the member of staff described above suddenly tells you the reason for their underperformance is that they are having domestic problems, this is an indication that the assessors want you to deal with this particular welfare problem. You, as the candidate, may not be able to solve the role actor's marital difficulties, but you probably will be able to make life easier for them perhaps by adjusting their personal circumstances at work. So, for example, if they're struggling with working shifts, perhaps you could arrange to move them on to a normal daytime office job.

Hooks

Hooks are pieces of information, either given in the written preparation phase, or more commonly by the role actor themselves, which are deliberately designed to elicit a response from the candidate. There are a number of ways in which hooks can be introduced. The good candidate should be able to recognise them by the fact that they often invite further questioning. Remember that every word in the role actor script is included for a reason. For example, staying with our example of the person whose performance has dropped, consider the following exchange:

> **Candidate:** *'I notice from your staff appraisal that your performance at work has fallen. Can I ask you why this is?'*
> **Role Actor:** *'I have just got a lot of things on the go, you know how it is.'*

At this point, a poor candidate will now go on to explain that the behaviour by the person concerned is unacceptable. What they have failed to consider is that there may be reasons behind the fall in performance. The 'hook' is in the fact that the reply from the role actor invites follow-up questioning. A good candidate on the other hand would carry on the conversation as follows:

> **Candidate:** *'You say a lot of things on the go, what do you mean by that?'*

Remember, every word the role actor says is for a reason. The fact that they have given you a vague answer here probably means that your questioning ability is being tested and you're meant to ask further questions. In this case, the candidate is probing further for information. The role actor's script will now allow them to deliver further information to the candidate. So, you may find that the role actor's reply is something along the following lines:

> **Role Actor:** *'I just have one or two things going on at home. It's nothing I can't handle and I will sort out the problems at work. It won't happen again, sorry.'*

This is an example of the hook. The role actor is again being very vague, but is offering the suggestion that there is further information to be had. What the reply also does, however, is tempt weaker candidates into thinking to themselves that they do not want to push the role actor into giving information, and that they can now move on. The strong candidate on the other hand will follow up the hook given by asking:

> **Candidate:** *'You say you have one or two things going on at home, can I ask what you mean by that?'*

At this stage, you will probably find that the role actor decides that they have made you work hard enough for the information and may well then say something such as:

> **Role Actor:** *'My partner has just got a new job working away, and I am finding it difficult looking after my two children and working at the same time.'*

Immediately, therefore, this changes the scenario from one involving a poor performer, which may have required disciplinary action, into a welfare issue. There are now two issues to address: the poor performance, which still needs to be dealt with (although the candidate now knows the reasons for it) and the welfare issue itself.

Spotting the hooks

The role actor's lines therefore have been used to 'hook' the candidate down a certain path. Naturally, if you miss the hook or, more commonly, ignore it, then you will not get the extra information, and therefore you will never be able to solve the problem. Relating this back to the competencies, candidates who missed the 'hooks' would have failed to evidence the ability to ask probing questions. In addition, they have shown they are unable to realise that just because there are some symptoms of an issue visible, it does not mean that there is not an underlying cause. It would also show very poor listening skills.

Failing to identify the hooks

Students on my courses frequently ask me what happens if they miss hooks. Regrettably, the most common answer is that they fail. However, the examination writers recognise that we can all miss an occasional line under pressure. So, within the briefing given to the role actors, there is normally the provision for them to repeat a key line. In general terms, if a candidate misses a hook, the role actor will often repeat it once for them. Although they shouldn't really, if the role actor likes you, you may find you are really lucky and have it repeated twice. However, if you haven't got it by this time, that's your lot. The candidate unaware of its significance will have missed the line. This means that there will be little chance of passing in this scenario.

Lessons to be learnt

There are two vital lessons to be learnt here. Firstly, remember that every single word spoken by the role actor, or every single line contained in the preparation stage, has been inserted for a reason. Pay very careful attention to them, and if they seem slightly odd, or if a small question mark is raised in your mind, follow it up. It is not a slip of the tongue or a line of text the writer just felt like putting in, it is more than likely a hook.

The second lesson is that if you ever find the same line being repeated back to you, stop talking, calm yourself down for a moment, and consider why the role actor has just said the same thing twice to you. The reality is they are probably saying, *'Listen stupid, you missed the significance of this line the first time round, have a listen to this because you need to ask me more questions about it, and you need to move the role play forward based on what I will then tell you!'*

Blocks

The third element of the interactive stage design criteria is 'blocks'. I have discussed how hooks are used to steer the candidate down a certain route. Blocks are designed to do just the opposite and stop the candidate going down a path that they do not need to go down. A common example will go along the following lines. You are speaking to somebody in a role play about the fact that they are allegedly being bullied by someone at work. Let us assume for a moment that the role actor you are talking to is female. Your briefing pack has told you that the role actor has written a letter stating that she is the subject of comments that she feels are inappropriate. In this example, she has not specified exactly what the comments are. Our candidate asks her if she has any idea why the person is making the comments to her. The candidate then says to the role actor, *'Do you think this person is making these comments because you are female, which could mean you are being subject to sexist behaviour?'*

Recognising and acting on blocks

It is entirely possible that asking this question may gain the candidate a mark by virtue of the fact they are probing for further information. However, the actual script may actually state that sexism plays no part whatsoever in the role play. The comments may, for example be about the role actor's political views. In order to stop the candidate following the trail of non-existent sexism, the role actor may use a block along the lines of, *'No, I don't think that's the reason'*. A candidate may ask a further question along the lines of, *'Are you sure?'* The role actor then replies to the effect of, *'Yes, I'm quite certain it is not due to sexism'*. What the role actor is actually doing here is blocking the suggestion that the incident is due to sexism. Whilst the possibility of sexism may have been a good question to raise, it is definitely not the reason behind the comments and the role actor has just confirmed this. Consequently, as a candidate you should recognise this fact, and change on to a different tack. The simplest way of doing this is to ask the role actor directly why they think the comments are being made!

The candidate's role in decision making

Another common example of blocks relates to decision-making. It may well be that you meet somebody who's making a complaint about a member of staff's behaviour. You, the candidate, quite rightly provide them with a range of options of things they could do, in terms of leaving the matter with you to resolve, or making a formal complaint against the member of staff (which is different from just saying they are not happy with the behaviour). Quite rightly, the candidate should offer this range of options to the role actor. This may well gain you a mark for consultation. The role actor, however, will never make a decision for you. If they were to do so, then they would in effect be telling you your answer was correct. They will never, ever do this. Instead, they will reply along the lines of:

> **Role Actor:** *'Well, whatever you think is best' or else 'Well, I will leave the decision up to you.'*

What the role actor is really saying is, *'I will not be making a decision, as that is your job as the candidate. Thanks for consulting me, now get on and make your decision.'*

You would not believe how common it is to hear it candidates haranguing the role actor to try and make them decide which option they want. The role actor will never decide, they are not allowed to. You, the candidate, are the one being assessed, so the examiners want you to make a decision. The reason that the assessors want you to make the decision is because they are marking you on your decision-making ability! No matter how good you are, you will never persuade the role actor to make a decision for you, because they want you to do it for yourself.

Limits on behaviour for the role actor

Another useful piece of inside knowledge lies in understanding the limits of the range of behaviour the role actors can exhibit. Often in a role play the role actor will be briefed to start off very angrily. It will be written into their lines and the script for them to come across as verbally aggressive, confrontational or excitable. However, at the end of the day they are role actors following a script, they work for the police, and are acting in police-controlled buildings. You can be confident, therefore, that while they may come in and be rude and objectionable, they will not start swearing and cursing you. They can't. If they did, someone would likely end up reporting them for inappropriate conduct! So, if you find some role actor starts being very angry, firstly do not let yourself get intimidated or stressed by it, as they are simply acting. They're not really angry with you, because they have never met you before, and you are all working in a fictional environment. They are simply following a script.

Behaviour displayed by the role actor

Next, consider this. Think about the last time you dealt with somebody who was extremely angry over a certain issue. Very angry people are beyond reason. They will not listen to what you are saying, they will not answer questions in a reasonable manner, they will not listen to options, nor will they listen to solutions. Therefore, the role actor's script cannot possibly demand that they remain angry and objectionable for the full five minutes of your role play. It would serve no purpose if the role actor kept shouting at you, or refused to provide information, or indeed refused to listen to you, as quite simply there would be no way to solve the problem. There would be no point in having the role play.

Dealing with an angry role actor

So, what does this mean for you, the candidate? Well, firstly, if the role actor does enter the room very angry, you should feel more relaxed knowing that it is simply part of the script. Even more useful, however, is the fact that you also know that they will be instructed in their script to calm down after a few minutes. As a candidate, your approach should always be to remain calm and polite. Even if the role actor enters the room shouting about some alleged grievance they feel they have, offer to shake hands, and remain polite. They will not immediately become happy people. If you persist and again continually assure them you are there to help but in order to do so you would ask that they themselves sit down and tell you what the problem is, you will find after a minute or two they will comply. They have to. They have a script to get through, which involves giving you further information. They simply cannot remain angry for the five minutes.

Calming the role actor

You should be aware, however, that you only have a certain time period to calm the individual down. If you follow the technique in the previous paragraph, you will get marks for taking control of the situation, being assertive, and for remaining calm and polite (competencies which can be found in the marking guide). If, however, you allow yourself to be intimidated by the role actor, to the extent that you do not say anything or are quite ineffectual in trying to calm the role actor down, after perhaps two minutes you will find they calm down anyway. There is a reason for this. As I have said, they have to calm down after a certain period in order to carry on with the rest of the role play. So it is in their script to do so after having given you the opportunity to show the appropriate skills in controlling the situation. If you do not do so, and the role actor makes the decision to be polite in order to progress the role play, you will have missed out on several marks because the assessors will have wanted you to calm the individual down yourself.

Language used in the role plays

Another limitation on behaviour can be found in the types of language employed. Without doubt, you will find comments which are sexist, racist or homophobic, or behaviours within the exercises which are inappropriate. However, whatever these phrases may be, they will only amount to something, for want of a better phrase, 'mildly insulting'. They will use no excessively offensive words or phrases, because if they did they would end up on the front pages of a national newspaper. If words were used which are generally accepted as swear words, or if examples of sexist, racist or homophobic behaviour were at the more serious end of the scale, no doubt sooner or later candidates would be complaining loudly that they were subjected to such words in the middle of a police assessment centre. As a candidate, you need to be aware of this. My advice is if you find a comment which appears to be slightly odd, and could conceivably be classed as inappropriate, mentally add the F-word to the front of it, and deal with it on that basis. There is a danger that because the scriptwriters water their insulting comments down so much, candidates either miss the significance of them, or do not recognise them at all.

Applying your own standards to inappropriate behaviour

As a candidate, you must understand that the definition of inappropriate behaviour is in effect, 'any type of comment that could conceivably cause offence to anyone'. The common mistake most candidates make is to apply their own standards to inappropriate conduct. My most vivid example of this occurred a few years ago when I was talking about sexist behaviour to a female prospective candidate, who was serving in the Royal Navy. We were talking about application forms, and she remarked to me that she really struggled when asked to give an example of when she'd come across inappropriate behaviour. I was really surprised by this, and told her that I simply could not believe that she had been in the Royal Navy for five years and had never had a sexist comment made about her (with all due respect to members of the Navy, for whom I have the highest regard). She then replied that she couldn't recall any examples. I then stated again that I was amazed that a woman in a male-dominated environment like the Navy had never been the subject of any form of comments about her appearance. Her casual reply without a trace of irony or humour, was that well, naturally, comments were made every day to her by sailors about such things as the size of her breasts, but there was nothing really sexist about it. I make no comment on equal opportunities training in the Royal Navy, but my point is that, in this particular case, this person saw no problem in the kind of language or terms used every day of her working life. If she had she brought these standards, which clearly reflected her own view of acceptable behaviour, to a police assessment centre, she would have failed.

This is why I stress again that the standard you must adopt for the assessment is that of the police, not what you personally may feel is acceptable, or what you're used to in your current working environment.

Focusing on the ability to ask questions

Another key competency for a police officer is the ability to ask the right questions. Therefore, it is logical that the exam writers will wish to write the exercises in such a way that the candidate must ask questions in order to solve them. If the writer designs a scenario which does not require the candidate to ask questions, how would this test questioning ability? It is a certainty therefore that every single scenario, to a greater or lesser extent, will require you to ask questions. These questions will fall into two main types of category.

Ascertaining facts

The first category is to gather basic information in order to evidence whether or not the candidate is thorough when it comes to ascertaining facts. The information given in the answers to this type of question may not necessarily move the scenario on any further, but would be information that in a real-life situation the candidate would be expected to gather. For example, if taking a report of lost property, it would be reasonable to expect the candidate to ask for or check information such as:

- name;
- address;
- description of lost goods;
- contents of items.

These simple questions are basic information gathering. They would result in the candidate gaining marks for gathering basic facts. However, they do not really move the scenario on any further on in terms of the candidate being able to solve the problem.

From an examination writer's point of view, how would the writer want you to solve this lost property scenario? Realistically, in this scenario if somebody is simply reporting lost property to you, how can you, the candidate, actually solve that problem? Within the limits of the examination centre the candidate is clearly not able to go out of the room and start looking for the items. This is because, of course, the item does not exist. The prepared candidate would now be thinking that by this stage there must be more to this role play than simply taking a lost property report. Try to develop the ability to look beyond the obvious. This brings us neatly on to the second category of questions, those which do in fact move the scenario on.

Moving the scenario on

The logic the candidate should be using is as follows. They will have asked the basic questions and obtained basic responses back. The object of the role played will not simply be to fill out a lost property form. There has to be something more to it. If the candidate cannot immediately return the property and as I have just said, they cannot because it physically does not exist, the examination writer must be looking for some other form of action.

At this moment, the candidate does not know what that action is. The key to finding out this out is further questions of the second type that will allow the scenario to move forward.

Asking further questions

So, the prepared candidate should simply continue asking questions. In this scenario, they should be thinking, *'is there anything particularly important or significant about the loss of this person's property?'* The questions they should now be thinking of could consist of:

- What specific items were lost?
- What specific problems will be caused by the loss of the property?
- Is anything in the bag needed urgently?

The answers to these kinds of questions will probably provide further information which will move the scenario on. For example, what if the role actor answers the first of these questions in terms of specific items, by saying there is vital medication inside it?

What if the role actor states that the loss of the property has caused them a specific problem because it contains documentation and the keys to their rental apartment, without which they do not know where they're supposed to stay tonight and have no means of finding out? This will cause great hardship to them and their children.

What if the role actor is a doctor, and inside the bag are urgent case notes that they require for a consultation, without which they will not be able to treat a certain person?

Failing to ask the additional questions

If you do not ask these questions, you will not gain the further information required to move the scenario forward, which in turn means you cannot solve it. The end result of this is likely to be that you fail the role play.

Separate sections of this book deal with solving the problem. However, it is very important that as a candidate you understand that information needs to be obtained and that such information is not just the means in itself to getting a mark. Often that information needs to be utilised in a certain way in order for you to pass the exercise.

Making decisions

The examination writers also need to test the candidate's ability to make decisions, in consultation with others when appropriate. Most scenarios will require you, the candidate, to state how you intend to solve the issue or problem. This amounts to what actions you intend to take. Consider for a moment what would happen in a real-life meeting between a customer service officer and either a member of the public or a member of staff. Once the appropriate questions had been asked, and the situation understood by the customer service officer, it would be logical for them to suggest a number of alternative ways of solving the problem. So far, so good. In real life at this stage, the person with the issue to be solved would usually say which of the options they wanted the customer service officer to take. If the scenario involved a member of the public complaining about a member of staff, the customer service officer may perhaps suggest the options of:

- the customer making a formal complaint;
- the customer leaving the matter with the customer service officer for them to deal with;
- the customer service officer arranging a meeting with the member of staff and the customer to discuss the matter further;
- having explained the situation, the customer service officer taking the matter no further as the customer now understands that company policy had been followed.

In a real meeting the complainant would probably then state which one of these options they wanted.

Your role in decision making within the exercise

In a role-play context, it is clearly good practice to consult with the role actor when making decisions in the same way as the real-life scenario discussed above. However, it must be remembered in a role play that the examination writer will also wish to check the candidate's ability to make a decision. Therefore, in a role play it is highly unlikely that the role actor will actually provide the candidate with a preferred option. So, using the example above, the candidate should indeed outline the four possible options as they see them. This is good, and may well be on the marking guide. However, the role actor will have been briefed in this script not to choose one of these particular options. After all, if they were to do so, they would be giving the candidate the 'right answer'. There would be no purpose in this as far as the assessors were concerned. Instead, the candidate will more likely get an extremely bland answer along the lines of 'I will leave it up to you', or 'whatever you think is appropriate'. To be fair of course, this type of response could also happen in real life.

However, in a role-play environment, if you as the candidate hear this type of response, remember that what the role actor is actually saying is *'Thanks for consulting me, but there is no way I'm going to give you the right answer. Now is the time to make your decision, and tell me what it is.'*

Pushing the role actor for a decision

It is astounding how many candidates continue to try to push the role actor for a response. I have heard candidates ask the role actor five or six times to make a decision regarding what outcome they would like. They would have continued to ask another ten times, except of course the five-minute time limit has been reached and the scenario ends. Candidates must accept that the role actor should be asked for an opinion only once. It is very unlikely they will give it, and once a response is given indicating they cannot, or will not, make a decision, the candidate should make the decision for them and explain it. In this manner, the role actor has been 'consulted' and the candidate has shown they can make a decision.

The need to test different skills

The role play is designed to test a number of different skills. If you study the competency listings carefully, there are only one or two that cannot be tested in role play. These are the ability to create written reports, and engaging in group discussions, as clearly in a role play you will do neither. Every other skill can be tested. A typical role play will be assessing between three and five competencies.

A role play will not therefore confine itself to testing your ability to ask questions. Neither will it concentrate on just your ability to solve problems. It will be wide-ranging in the skills it assesses. It is important to realise this because it will affect the strategy you adopt when dealing with the role play. As discussed elsewhere, time management is vital. If you accept that different skills are being assessed in every role play, it is surely logical to accept that you should only spend a certain proportion of time asking questions. After a certain time limit, you have to move on to something else in the role play because otherwise you will simply fail to display the other skill areas the role play will be looking for. It is possible of course that if you devote, for example, 90 seconds of your five-minute role play to questioning, and then make a conscious decision to move on to do something with the information you have already gained, you will fail to ask a few important questions and so lose a couple of marks. However, you will have the opportunity to display all of the *other* skills that the assessor will be looking for. It is extremely common for candidates to spend the full five minutes asking questions. They get top marks for questioning, but fail completely in all the other skill areas such as generating options and making decisions.

Understanding the purpose of the role play

It is vital therefore that the candidate realises that the role play is not simply a conversation between two people where hopefully the issue will be amicably resolved. It is a showcase designed for the candidate to display the full range of their abilities.

It may be worth while considering the role play and the assessment centre as an assault course. The whole point of an assault course is getting to the end successfully. You're expected to climb over every obstacle and your success is judged on your ability to get to the finishing line within the required time. You're not expected to put your foot into every tyre, to have climbed every rung on a ladder, or to climb up the last inch of the rope on the rope swing. It's great if you can do so, but success is measured by the fact that you reach the required standard in every part of the course, and at least attempt to tackle every part of it.

Role plays work on the same principle. Each competency being tested is an obstacle for you to climb over, but you do not need to complete every one to perfection. Instead, what you need to do is to have tackled it so that you have displayed the ability to deal with it. Being perfect is fantastic, but all attempts to be perfect are likely to result in ruining marks in another competency area.

Finding practical solutions

When discussing role plays with candidates on courses, I find that they often have a common concern that they will not be able to come up with solutions on the day. You know by now that your role play will present you with issues to be dealt with. In order for you to do this, clearly you need to provide solutions. This is a reasonable concern, and clearly those people with customer service experience can be said to have an advantage here.

The key to role plays, however, is to find simple, workable solutions. Firstly, you must treat every issue as the most important issue you have ever come across. Secondly, you must go out of your way to present solutions that would offer the ultimate in customer service and reflect how you would expect to be treated if you were the customer or member of staff involved.

Understanding the principles

There are thousands of potential scenarios, so it is impossible to give standard solutions to them all. The important thing to realise, however, is the principles involved. Imagine that you have just bought a brand new car. You get it home and discover that there is a large dent on one of the panels which must have been there when you picked the vehicle up from the dealer. Clearly, you will want to take the vehicle back to the dealer, but just ask yourself for a moment what response you would ideally expect from the customer service department.

Would you simply expect the dent to be fixed? This would not appear to be an unreasonable request. However, if this was your response, you need to seriously examine your concept of customer care. Such a response indicates a train of thought that will give you real problems if you carry it through to assessment centre.

Personally, I would expect the following. Ideally, I would immediately expect the customer service representative to accept responsibility for the problem. I would expect them to apologise profusely. I would hope that they would offer me a new vehicle, without argument or debate, once they had established beyond reasonable doubt that the car sustained the damage before I picked it up. Ideally they would have a new car available to give me. However, this may not actually be practical. Therefore, it may well be that they would agree to replace the car, but cannot reasonably do so until next week. This may be acceptable to me. However, I would then expect to be offered a courtesy car while the exchange is being arranged. I would expect this car to be of the same specification and type, if not better, than the vehicle I had just bought. I would expect to be recompensed for my time and trouble having to return to the dealer a number of times. I would also expect as a gesture of goodwill that the car would be filled up with petrol when I collected it. I would also expect to be given some kind of discount, or even a free service on my next visit to the dealer.

Upon picking the vehicle up, I would expect to be accompanied by a member of the customer service staff, in order to ensure that the new vehicle was completely perfect.

Providing a Rolls Royce service

This is the kind of approach that you need to bring as a candidate to your assessment centre. If you were the customer service officer and your view was that simply swapping the vehicle or getting the vehicle repaired was acceptable, then trust me when I say it is not. Incidentally, if you find my expectations of customer service unrealistic, I am told that is the process that would happen with something like a Rolls Royce (although I suspect it would never be allowed to leave the showroom less than perfect anyway!)

As an assessment centre candidate, you must be looking to provide a Rolls Royce service to everyone.

Possible solutions

So, whilst it is impossible to provide standard solutions to every possible scenario, below is a list of the kind of simple ideas worth considering. Obviously their application will depend upon the scenario!

- Give the individual a letter of apology.
- If they have been offended by something, get the offender to apologise (in person if possible).
- Put in extra security patrols (usually as a short term measure).
- Ask the complainer to accompany your staff on visits so they can understand your efforts, or so they can see you are doing things correctly.
- Install extra cameras.
- Change opening hours.
- Write a new policy.
- Set aside special places for people to undertake a certain activity.
- Offer free membership.
- Put on extra classes.
- Hold a meeting to publicise the solution.
- Hold a meeting to explain standards.

The solution to any given problem obviously depends upon the actual situation itself. However, as a good candidate you should always ask yourself, 'If I was the customer, what action would I want to solve this problem?'

Being realistic in your solutions

The solutions you present do not have to be earth-shattering but they do need to be realistic. The problems posed to you in exercises tend by their nature to lead to straightforward solutions. Let us say that somebody is complaining to you that there are not enough disabled car park spaces and those that are there are abused by people not displaying disabled badges.

Just think for a moment what solutions you could put in place to solve this. You may consider options such as to:

- utilise your security guards to patrol the area to enforce and educate people about the current regulations;
- start issuing car park tickets for people breaking the rules;
- put up extra signs on the disabled bays so they are clearly marked;
- gain permission from your manager to have more disabled car park bays allocated.

A reasonable solution should not require a master's degree to work out. In fact, the above represents the typical kind of solutions that you might be expected to suggest. A poor candidate will simply have come up with a weak idea such as 'try to get to the centre earlier in the day'.

Practising the process

The key to the solutions issue is getting into the right thought process, not in preparing solutions in advance. The best way to practise is to look at situations in your everyday environment, and listen when people say 'somebody should do something about...'. This is a common moan in any given work environment. Get into the habit of asking yourself what you would do to solve the problem.

Assessors like solutions to be creative, as in the examples given above. They like simple, practical solutions that can be put into place without too much trouble. Even converting a non-disabled parking bay to a disabled parking bay will not require much expenditure, because basically it simply involves painting a symbol on the ground. This type of solution is therefore practical and realistic.

Inventing unrealistic solutions

What a candidate cannot do is to invent some fantastically complex, expensive solution. For example, the candidate would not get any marks for stating that the leisure complex will build a huge multi-storey car park alongside the existing one simply for disabled users. Such a solution is clearly unrealistic.

Despite this, for some strange reason, candidates will often invent solutions that do not exist. If I were using the above as a real scenario, I can guarantee a good percentage of candidates would be saying to the role actor, 'You can use the large disabled car park on the upper car park level'. If this car park did not exist in the documentation at preparation stage, it is complete invention on the part of the candidate. The whole idea of the role play is to at least try to keep things in as realistic a setting is possible. In real life, you cannot just invent things that suit your immediate purpose.

PROBLEMS WHEN DEALING WITH INAPPROPRIATE BEHAVIOUR

With the emphasis on diversity and inappropriate behaviour in the police service, it is beyond doubt that you will be tested a number of times on your ability to deal with these. In the police context, inappropriate behaviour can be classed as a number of things. Clearly the most serious category is that of comments of a racist, sexist or homophobic nature. However, it can also include sub-standard work, or inadvertent offence caused by one person to another. Remember as I explained earlier, in six of the seven skill areas you can get a grade D (the lowest grade), and make your marks up (on that skill area) throughout the rest of the assessment. However, with diversity, a single grade D is an automatic fail of the entire assessment, even if every other mark you achieve on the day across all of the skill areas is an A. It is essential therefore that you understand the importance of dealing with inappropriate conduct. Simply put, fail to deal with inappropriate conduct, using the police service definitions as opposed to your own or anyone else's, and you will fail the assessment centre.

Common problems

Candidates often display a number of weaknesses when it comes to dealing with inappropriate behaviour. These fall into the main categories of:

- failing to recognise the behaviour as being inappropriate;
- recognising that the behaviour is inappropriate, but considering it too minor to deal with;
- recognising the behaviour as worthy of attention, but failing to deal with it (due to time, lack of assertiveness or being unsure what to do);
- recognising the behaviour, attempting to deal with it, but doing so in a weak fashion;
- recognising inappropriate behaviour and then dealing with it in a bullying fashion, so making their *own* behaviour inappropriate;
- recognising and dealing with it, but revealing in doing so issues within their own definition of diversity and inappropriate conduct.

In the following chapters, I will explain how to avoid these traps.

SUMMARY

So far, we have examined the thinking and theory behind role plays, along with the design, aims, objectives and, just as importantly, the limitations of the exercise. Such background is essential in order to understand the techniques required to pass the role plays. In the following sections, we will address each individual segment of a role play, namely the preparation phase, and the interactive phase. The techniques and issues associated with each part will be considered separately for ease of explanation. However, it is vital to remember that the two are inextricably linked. Every element of one section impacts on every element of the other.

6

The role play planning and preparation phase

THE PREPARATION PHASE

An introduction to preparation techniques

Each role play has two stages, the first being the 'preparation phase', which is then followed by the 'interactive phase'. The preparation phase consists of the candidate being given a number of documents to read. The documents will involve an issue for you, the candidate, to deal with in your role as a customer service officer. There is a five-minute time period allowed to read through these documents. You are allowed to make notes if you wish, but you cannot make these notes on the documents themselves. You are allowed to take whatever notes you have made into the interactive phase. Whatever you do in the preparation phase is not marked. Your notes are taken off you at the end of the interactive phase and they are then disposed of. It is up to the candidate therefore what they do with this time. Note that when you are actually doing the role play in the interactive phase, there will be a fresh, unmarked copy of the documents you have just read on the desk in front of you to refer to.

How most people approach role plays

The vast majority of candidates enter the planning phase of a role play with no real idea of what they will do when the clock starts ticking. They simply pick up the papers and begin to read. They have no clear idea of the kind of things they should be looking for in the document. After they have finished reading through the documents, they will pick up the pen and jot down a few thoughts in a random order on a sheet of paper provided. At some point, they realise that a buzzer has sounded and they are then astounded when a role actor enters the room and they realise the role play has begun. This I promise you is the reality of what most people do in role plays. However, the planning phase is vital in helping you achieve the best possible mark, and needs to be approached much more methodically.

How most people plan

Some people, albeit a minority, do attempt to use the preparation time as some form of planning period. However, at best, the plan will consist of a few notable words that the candidate feels may be useful at some point. I can honestly say out of all the thousands of people I have dealt with when it comes to planning role plays, I have never seen one untrained person create a worthwhile plan. In other words, the situation can be summarised as this. The vast majority of people do not plan in a logical way, they just write down a few words they think may be helpful. Those attempting to plan simply write down some words in what they hope is some form of logical list. The key to success in role plays lies completely in the planning. A good plan will probably contain at least half of the marks available in the interactive stage, and will be completed before the role actor has even entered the room. Failing to plan is a lost opportunity, and effectively sets the candidate up to fail. The old military saying has never been truer: 'failing to plan is planning to fail'.

The interactive phase

Once the role actor enters the room in the interactive phase, the candidate is placed under a huge amount of pressure. This is deliberate, of course, as you are also being assessed on your ability to deal with difficult situations. As the interactive phase unfolds, you will have to deal with a number of issues. You will be required to utilise much of the information you have read in the previous five-minute preparation phase. You will have to remember its potential significance, especially in the light of any further information that you are given by the role actor. You will undoubtedly need to ask further questions, and to come up with solutions to resolve the problem. Whilst this is going on it is entirely possible that the role actor will also introduce some further element to do with the situation that will also need to be dealt with.

With so much going on, it is very difficult to keep a clear mental path plotted as to what you intended to do throughout the role play. It is extremely easy to lose track of your objectives. It is easy to forget key points or information that you have read in the previous stage (and remember every word provided is there for a reason!). It is also astoundingly easy to lose track of where you want the role play to go. A good plan will stop these undesirable events from happening.

Remembering the original issue

If in the preparation phase, for example, you are made aware that the person you are about to meet has made inappropriate comments, by the end of the role play be assured you will be expected to deal with them. This is amazingly easy to forget to do under pressure. It is easy to forget that you are meant to come up with solutions to the original issue. This is why it is essential to have a structured plan. Your plan is effectively a blueprint for dealing with the situation you are about to face. It cannot contain all the answers, as until the role actor starts speaking, you do not know what information they are about to deliver. However, a good plan will provide you with a structure to follow no matter what is said. Think of the last time you went for a medical check-up. The chances are the medical staff went through pre-prepared checklists asking you a number of questions concerning the areas they wanted to explore. They clearly cannot know the answers in advance. They use your answers as a cue to ask further questions and depending on your answers to those questions perhaps they wanted to run more tests. This is because they had a plan. They knew the areas they wanted to cover, and probably expected some to be dead ends, but they still asked the questions for the sake of thoroughness. When they got answers that needed no further investigation, they moved on. If they got answers they were unhappy with, they asked more questions then did something about the problem raised. In essence, the doctor had a plan of what he or she wanted to do when you walked into the room. You have five minutes as a candidate to prepare a plan for yourself so that you know what areas to cover when the role actor walks in.

Understanding your role in the role play

Candidates often struggle with the concept of understanding their role. By this, I mean that you must understand that you are required to approach the scenario from the perspective of a customer service officer. If you are tempted to deal with the scenario from any other perspective, then you will create problems for yourself. Typically, candidates approach scenarios from one of three perspectives:

- Firstly, a candidate may try to behave in the way they think a police officer should. The problem with this approach is that the assessors are not looking for you to behave in such a manner. You may well bring perceptions, views and attitudes into the scenario which they positively do not want. For example, many candidates will begin to deal with an issue and from the start take the approach that it is such a minor problem that they almost tend to belittle the feelings of the role actor.
- Secondly, a candidate may bring the philosophy of their own organisation to the role-play. Many companies say they are dedicated to customer care, but at the end of the day they are profit-making organisations and their policies and procedures normally reflect this. Within the assessment centre you are required to act with the utmost integrity and honesty, which involves doing the 'right' thing morally as opposed to looking after the profits of the organisation.
- The third perspective particularly applies to those candidates who have had experience of the police service, either as community support officers, special constables, members of support staff, or those have come into contact with the police. Some candidates bring attitudes which they know exist in the service into the role play. They do this on the basis of the fact they know these attitudes reflect the reality of what goes on. However, the assessment centre is not looking for these 'real life' attitudes, but instead is looking for 'genuine' customer care.

Realising the specific part you are to undertake in the role play

You need to realise the specific part you need to play in the role play you are reading about.

For example, if you realise you're dealing with a complaint from a member of the public, you are there to represent the organisation and act as the person responsible for dealing with that complainant's issue. If you find you're dealing with a member of staff whose performance is unacceptable, then effectively you are taking the role of their supervisor. If you find you're dealing with somebody who has some form of welfare issue, you effectively take on the role of their manager, but also that of the welfare officer. This is important to realise, because the relationship between you and the role actor will impact upon how you tackle the problem.

As a further example, if you're dealing with somebody who is making a justifiable complaint against the organisation, your approach will be one of being apologetic and determined to change whatever is required in order to ensure the same thing does not happen again to someone else. Conversely, if the person who is complaining is incorrect for whatever reason, your approach will need to be that of defending your organisation's actions, whilst still showing respect for the other person's point of view. The relationship between you as the candidate and the person you are seeing will therefore change depending upon the situation. You will remain a customer service officer throughout, but your approach may alter.

This should be uppermost in your mind as you are sitting in your chair looking down at the documents awaiting permission to start reading. When the clock starts, and you're allowed to turn to the first page, it is vitally important that you understand that *YOU* are the customer service officer, and therefore responsible for solving whatever issue walks through the door.

THE CAR SYSTEM: HOW TO PLAN PROPERLY

In order to plan properly, it is essential to have a good structure to work to. This is simply a method of laying the plan out, which will then act as a prompt not just for what goes in the plan itself, but equally importantly for when the plan is being used in the interactive phase.

What is the CAR system?

The system I recommend is based on the CAR system. This involves splitting your as yet unwritten plan for any given scenario into three distinct stages:

- Circumstances;
- Actions;
- Results.

Let's look at the purpose of each section in turn.

Circumstances

In this section of your plan, you should note down the reasons for the meeting, and any other relevant facts that you feel you may need to mention to the role actor in order to clarify with them why you are actually speaking to one another. It is not meant to be a summary of the briefing document. It should simply be a few key words to remind you what the exercise is about. You should use keywords that will remind you what to do, for example:

- introduce yourself;
- explain purpose of meeting;
- refer to complainant letter/report;
- thank role actor for their good work in the past.

You do not have to limit yourself to the facts in the briefing papers though. Use this section of the plan as a reminder of the things you should be doing in the introduction. So, if you have read that the person has an excellent work record, on the basis that everything is there for a reason, note to mention it to them as they walk in.

Actions

In this section of your plan, jot down reminders to yourself what actions may be necessary, and what questions you need to ask. It may be that you are meeting someone who has complained about the way they have been treated and they have also stated that their complaint has been handled poorly in the past. Consider noting in your plan such things as:

- What is the name/date/location of their complaint?
- Which staff member is involved?
- Any other staff involved?
- What happened?
- Did they complain at time? If so, what happened?
- What do they want to be done?
- Why?
- What was the complaint last time? Who dealt with it?
- Why do they feel they got poor service?
- What was the outcome of the complaint?
- Do they want you to reopen that file?

Of course, the actions and questions you jot down here will depend entirely upon the scenario itself. The key is practice, in terms of considering the sort of questions that you may need to ask.

Results

The results section should contain what steps *YOU* feel you must have taken by the end of the exercise. What you write down should be specific to the situation. It may be that a typical 'results' column would look like this:

- Point out unacceptable behaviour.
- Arrange diversity course or refresher if they have already been on one.
- Point out what will happen if behaviour recurs.

- Arrange apology if possible to victim.
- Tell staff of new standards.
- Monitor future behaviour of role actor.
- Inform manager of actions I have taken.

Obviously, all of these decisions depend upon the information contained in the role play brief.

Writing down your plan

You should start each plan on a clean sheet of paper. Before writing anything to do with the scenario, divide the paper into three equal sections from top to bottom, with a line between each section. Label the top section 'Circumstances', the middle section 'Actions' and the bottom section 'Results'. (Of course, in the interests of speed, you could just write in C, A and R!). Insert the role actor's name at the top of the page, along with their status, e.g. guard, customer, councillor, etc. The name of the scenario is always the name of the person you will be meeting. This is so that you will remember who you are talking to, which is very easy to forget under pressure. You should now have a page looking like Figure 4. It does not have to be neat, nor readable to anyone but you. Although it will be taken off you at the end of the assessment, this is not for marking purposes. It is simply to stop a good planner walking out with a blueprint of the exercise they can pass on to someone else. I have laid mine out neatly merely to make explanation simpler.

EXERCISE: ABBOT

Having drawn a blank grid, you are now ready to read the exercise. To give you an example, I will break down the following exercise, which is called 'Abbot'. A prepared candidate will already start to get information from that one sentence. Whoever the scenario is named after will be the person you will be meeting in the interactive phase. So, before you turn a page, you know that you will be meeting Abbot. You should not assume gender, age or background from this, so try to avoid doing so. The first step then is to write in 'Abbot' at the top of your plan, so that you have a constant reminder of whom you are going to be speaking to. The following pages will give you the exercise briefing information in full, just as you would get it on the day.

Then, on pages 116 and 117, I shall reproduce the documents again, but this time underlining key points, and putting in notes as to why certain phrases should be of specific interest to you. To make life a bit simpler, I have numbered each potentially interesting phrase, and provided an explanation underneath.

Role actor's name at top of page

Circumstances

Actions

Results

Fig. 4. An example of a CAR plan template.

Candidate's instructions

Abbot

Contents

- Memo from Customer Service Manager.
- Letter from Abbot.

Memorandum

To: Customer Service Officer
From: Customer Service Manager

Subject: Local minor offender rehabilitation scheme

Dear Colleague,

Please can you deal with this matter in my absence? I have received a letter from a local resident, called Abbot. This individual is complaining about the above scheme. As a new employee, you may not be aware of this. When a young offender is sentenced by the courts, if appropriate they are offered the chance of doing good work in the community rather than going to prison. In essence, the centre offers up to ten young offenders the chance to complete their community service in the centre workshop.

As part of our scheme, offenders make toys for disadvantaged children such as those living in places like Chernobyl, the town in Russia affected by a nuclear accident. In addition, we often take supervised groups of visiting children to meet the offenders in the workshop, so both groups get the chance to understand the other's lives and personal circumstances.

The scheme has proven to be a great success. There is the obvious benefit of the fact that the children are getting toys provided for them. However, research has shown that the offenders are often shocked by the children's stories, to such an extent that many of them become involved in charity work in some way and do not reoffend.

Despite what Abbot appears to think, or the rumours they may have heard, all of the offenders have committed very minor level crimes and have no previous backgrounds of violence or offences against children. Clearly, if they did we would never let them work here.

There is no additional risk to the public as all of the offenders are carefully supervised. Crime, by the way, has fallen at the centre by 5 per cent.

Reoffending rates are 20 per cent lower for this scheme than for other forms of sentence, and the scheme costs far less than prison. All visits are carefully supervised and monitored. A parent's permission is given before any meetings.

In short, this scheme is extremely worth while, and everyone benefits from it. The community especially is safer as there are fewer offences committed by offenders who have completed the scheme.

Please meet Abbot and resolve the issues they raise if possible. I would like to know how the meeting goes.

Regards

S. Bailey
Customer Service Manager

6 The Quarry
Newtown
England

Dear Sir or Madam,

I am writing to express my concern at the new scheme I believe you have introduced allowing dangerous criminals to work in the centre. I believe that you have allowed a large number of hardened criminals to work in your centre, under some alleged rehabilitation scheme. I regularly visit the centre with my young family, and am extremely concerned at this. I have heard rumours about the kinds of crimes that these people have committed, and as a result I and many others are most alarmed at the thought of these animals running amok unsupervised.

I have evidence that the number of crimes committed in the centre has gone up, and it must surely be obvious even to you why this is so. Many of my friends are also concerned, and in fact I have asked for the subject to be brought up at a monthly local community group I attend.

As if this was not alarming enough, I am also told that these animals are working with children as well!

This seems to me just another expensive scheme from well-intentioned social workers. I believe that these people should be in prison, which no doubt would be cheaper and give them a proper lesson to stop them committing crime in the future!

I look forward to meeting you and getting your assurance that this scheme will be stopped in its tracks.

Yours sincerely,

J. Abbot

Memorandum

To: Customer Service Officer
From: Customer Service Manager

Subject: Local minor offender rehabilitation scheme

Dear Colleague,

Please can you deal (1) with this matter in my absence. I have received a letter from a local resident, called Abbot. This individual is complaining about the above scheme. (2) As a new employee, you may not be aware of this. When a young offender is sentenced by the courts, if appropriate (3) they are offered the chance of doing good work in the community rather than going to prison. In essence, the centre offers up to ten young offenders the chance to complete their community service in the centre workshop.

As part of our scheme, offenders make toys for disadvantaged children such as those living in places like Chernobyl, the town in Russia affected by a nuclear accident. In addition, we often take supervised groups of visiting children to meet the offenders in the workshop, so both groups get the chance to understand the other's life (4) and personal circumstances.

The scheme has proven to be a great success. (5) There is the obvious benefit of the fact that the children are getting toys provided for them. However, research has shown that the offenders (6) are often shocked by the children's stories, to such an extent that many of them become involved in charity work in some way and do not reoffend. (7)

Despite what Abbot appears to think, or the rumours they have heard, (8) all of the offenders have committed very minor level crimes, (9) and have no previous backgrounds of violence or of offences against children. Clearly, if they did we would never let them work here. (10)

There is no additional risk to the public as all of the offenders are carefully supervised. Crime, by the way has fallen at the centre by 5 per cent. (11)

Reoffending rates are 20 per cent lower (12) for this scheme than for other forms of sentence, and the scheme costs far less than prison. (13) All visits are carefully supervised (14) and monitored. A parent's permission is given (15) before any meetings.

In short, this scheme is extremely worth while, and everyone benefits (16) from it. The community especially is safer (17) as there are fewer offences committed by offenders who have completed the scheme.

Please meet Abbot and resolve the issues they raise (18) if possible. I would like to know how the meeting goes. (19)

Regards

S. Bailey
Customer Service Manager

6 The Quarry
Newtown
England

Dear Sir or Madam,

I am writing to express my concern at the new scheme I believe you have introduced allowing dangerous criminals (20) to work in the centre. I believe that you have allowed a large number of hardened criminals (21) to work in your centre, under some alleged rehabilitation scheme. I regularly visit the centre with my young family, and am extremely concerned at this. (22) I have heard rumours about the kinds of crimes (23) that these people have committed, and as a result I and many others are most alarmed at the thought of these animals running amok (24) unsupervised.

I have evidence that the number of crimes committed in the centre has gone up, (25) and it must surely be obvious even to you why this is so. Many of my friends are also concerned, and in fact I have asked for the subject to be brought up at a monthly local community group (26) I attend.

As if this was not alarming enough, I am also told that these animals are working with children as well! (27)

This seems to me just another expensive scheme from well-intentioned social workers. I believe that these people should be in prison, which no doubt would be cheaper and give them a proper lesson to stop them committing crime in the future! (28)

I look forward to meeting you and getting your assurance that this scheme will be stopped in its tracks. (29)

Yours sincerely,

J. Abbot

Table 8 lists all of the 29 points highlighted in the underlined documents. This should *not* be written out as part of your planning process, it is simply used here as a means of explaining to you the kind of things that you should be looking out for.

Table 8. Detailed explanation of the Abbot exercise.

Note	*What you should be thinking . . .*
1	This is a big hint that YOU should solve the problem.
2	This is telling you what the person apparently wants to see you about. Read the rest of the brief bearing this in mind.
3	Whatever the report is about, someone somewhere has given a bit of thought to how the scheme is run.
4	Both groups benefit from the scheme, so it has positive effects.
5	The scheme is a success, and you are probably going to have to tell Abbot this if they are complaining about it.
6	The offenders seem to gain as well, as they get upset at hearing about the children's stories.
7	The scheme means that some people at least do not reoffend, which is very good.
8	You should be thinking you need to ask Abbot about these rumours!
9	Why has someone put this in? Are you going to need it to reassure Abbot perhaps?
10	There are clearly circumstances when people would not be allowed to come on the scheme, so it is being risk managed.
11	There is supervision, and crime has fallen. Think why this is in the document. If you are seeing someone who is complaining about the scheme, may this information be helpful?
12	Write this figure down, as it is a big plus for the scheme.
13	Why has someone put this in? Are you going to need it to reassure Abbot perhaps?
14	Why has someone put this in? Are you going to need it to reassure Abbot perhaps?
15	Why has someone put this in? Are you going to need it to reassure Abbot

perhaps?

16 Benefits for all, perhaps you also need to explain this to Abbot.

17 Benefits for all, perhaps you also need to explain this to Abbot.

18 Another hint as at point 1 that ***you*** should solve this problem.

19 Think about this. The only way for you to get a mark here is to tell the role actor that you will be reporting the outcome to the manager.

20 Why does Abbot think they are dangerous?

21 Why is Abbot saying this?

22 What exactly is Abbot concerned about? Ask and you may be able to reassure.

23 What rumours, and from where? Any evidence to back it up?

24 'Animals running amok' – this is unacceptable stereotyping and needs challenging.

25 What evidence? You have been told they have NOT gone up! Does Abbot really have evidence, or is it another 'rumour'?

26 This is a clear opportunity for a good candidate to speak to this group to get the message of reassurance over to everyone. It needs a volunteer: YOU!

27 This is a second prompt, the same as number 24, but also requiring further reassurance about how the scheme works and is monitored.

28 Abbot is wrong here, and this is an opportunity to actually give them the correct facts on the scheme.

29 Prompt for you to fairly but firmly explain that the scheme will continue.

As I have said, the above table is just to get you thinking about what you should be looking for in the preparation phase. You could not possibly write it all down, and even if you could, it would not be workable in the assessment. Upon reading the briefing papers, you should merely be aware of what the points above potentially mean. They will then translate into a plan as shown in Figure 5. Your actual plan will clearly need to be hand written. It should also contain as few words as you can get by with, as that saves you time. I have given my example with full sentences, but that is only for illustration. If I was doing a plan for real, I would just be using single key words. No two plans will be identical. To illustrate this, the Abbot plan is reproduced again on page 284 with the points in a slightly different order.

Circumstances

CSM asked me to deal with your letter.
Scheme for minor offenders.
You have concerns ('extremely concerned') – why?
What are they?
How can I help?

Actions
Question dangerous criminals phrase.
Clarify 'large no. of criminals'.
What rumours? Where from?
What do they mean by 'animals'?
This is unacceptable comment, challenge!
No of crimes gone up? No they haven't, do they have evidence of something I do not know? Why are they saying this? Inform them if they are wrong!
Prison not cheaper, effective alternative!
Why does Abbot want scheme stopped in its tracks?

Results
Make sure I challenge 'animals' comment.
Explain positive side of scheme.
Provide reassurance about scheme in success/monitoring/low risk offenders.
Explain how all involved including community gain from scheme.
Ask if Abbot wants to view scheme with me.
Explains scheme will carry on, and summarise why.
Offer to attend community meeting to explain scheme to others.
Inform manager of outcome!

Fig. 5. A specimen plan for the Abbot exercise.

The relationship between your plan and the marking guide

A good plan can potentially identify up to 50 per cent of the available marks in any given scenario for you. It will prompt you to summarise the situation, which may gain you a mark. It will prompt you to ask a number of questions, some of which will undoubtedly be on the assessor's marking guide. It will remind you of what you need to do by the end of the scenario, which will again keep you focused on what you are doing and so let you spend your time more productively.

A typical marking guide is given in Figure 6 for the Abbot scenario. You can see that even allowing for the fact that obviously I wrote both plan and marking guide, a large number of the issues on the plan are potential scores on the guide. The guide itself is simplified from the real thing, but that does not matter for our purposes.

Abbot Marking Guide

Explains purpose of meeting.	☐
Clarifies concerns from Abbot.	☐
Clarifies what rumours Abbot has heard.	☐
Offers clarification that these rumours are incorrect.	☐
Challenges phrase 'animals running amok' (says why unacceptable).	☐
Explains crime figures.	☐
Explains how crime has not in fact gone up.	☐
Points out no reason for people to be alarmed.	☐
Points out that all participants will be vetted and risk assessed.	☐
Points out crime levels will be monitored.	☐
Points out participants are trusties, who are doing charitable work.	☐
Points out scheme reoffending rates are lower, and is more cost effective than prison.	☐
Offers Abbot chance to visit scheme.	☐
Informs Abbot scheme will be continuing.	☐
Volunteers to take responsibility to attend community meeting and explain scheme.	☐

Fig. 6. A specimen marking guide for the Abbot exercise.

WHAT HAPPENS IF YOU FAIL TO PLAN?

Hopefully by now I have convinced you of the advantages of preparing a plan. If you do not do so, you face massively increased chances of the following things happening to you.

- You will not read through the preparation documentation looking for key points.
- You will not know what initial questions to ask.
- You'll have no clear idea of the way you want the role play to go.
- As the interactive phase comes to an end, you will have no clear guidelines as to what things are left for you to do in order to complete it.
- You will forget the key elements of the preparation document you meant to introduce.
- If, as is likely, the role actor introduces elements that were not actually referred to in the preparation documentation, you may well allow yourself to be diverted by the new information and fail to return to the key issues to be addressed.

Planning is an art and does require practice. How much practice you do is a direct reflection of how strongly you wish to be a police officer.

The difference between reading the scenario and understanding it

This concept is closely linked to that of understanding your role on the day. Any candidate can read through the documentation. However, the trick is to *understand* what you are reading. The preparation phase documents are not just a series of papers relating to the role play you are about to do. The pack will often consist of:

- an indication to the candidate that they are expected to deal with the problem;
- one view of the event or issue (and there may be more);

- some form of contrasting information for you to clarify with the role actor;
- possibly a policy extract for you to use, either to explain the actions of your staff or possibly to be able to see that your organisation has failed to comply with its own standards.

Understanding the scenario

In essence, for you to be able to say you understand the scenario, you need to have the ability to:

- have an awareness of the kinds of things in the documents that are liable to be issues;
- recognise the opportunities the document is providing you with to ask questions;
- recognise any opportunities you are given to note inappropriate behaviour;
- recognise opportunities to highlight issues;
- recognise prompts to offer solutions.

All of the above will in effect provide separate marking chances. If you develop that awareness, it does not matter what the scenario is about, you will be following the right principles. The preparation stage documentation is not there just to be read. It offers you the chance to brief yourself on what needs to be done in the scenario. It must be accorded that respect.

Identifying question areas

I have now repeated several times the fact that every single word presented to you in assessment is provided for a reason. Never is this truer than in the case of role plays. Remember, one of the key competencies is the ability to gather information. There are a number of competencies which measure a candidate's ability to ask questions and gather information. So, your ability to ask questions will gain marks in itself. However, there is a wider implication to this than simply asking questions. In certain role plays, it is likely that the initial information about the issue is designed to prompt you to gather further facts. Therefore, if you fail to ask the appropriate questions, quite apart from losing marks, you will fail the rest of the scenario because you will not have the additional information required to solve the problem. For any given piece of information then, you should be thinking of asking questions to ensure you understand the information properly. A commonly used technique is that of 5WH. When faced with a situation, ask yourself questions based on:

- Who?
- Why?
- Where?
- When?
- What?
- How?

These questions will help you to understand the issue, and give you information without which you will not be able to solve it.

Asking questions properly (5WH)

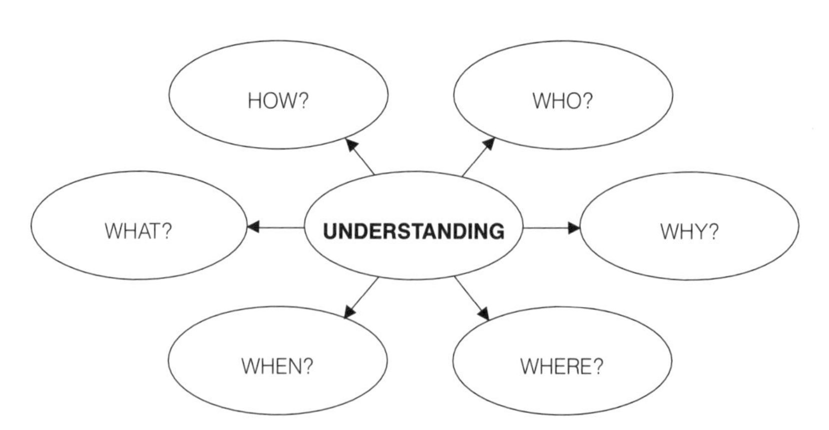

Fig. 7. How questioning leads towards understanding issues.

If you don't ask the questions, not only will you be unable to solve the problem, you will also struggle to demonstrate your ability, for example, to generate options, to be creative in terms of solutions, and to make decisions.

Imagine if you were dealing with a scenario whereby a member of staff appears to have made an inappropriate comment, and you fail to explore the reasons for the comment. You may well fail to spot the possibility that there exists some form of prior relationship between the member of staff making the comments and the person whom the comments were about. This relationship could have a huge impact on the context of the remark, and indeed the solution you come up with.

Understanding prompts in the preparation material

Candidates must therefore understand that prompts on questions to ask are deliberately built into the preparation material. So, while reading through the material, certain questions should spring to mind. Candidates should read the material actively questioning each word, and seeing if each sentence reflects the full story, or needs to be expanded upon. Again, it is impossible to cover all of the permutations that can be used. However, it's worth while providing a number of examples, along with the questions they could in fact generate.

Imagine you are reading through your preparation material and you come across the phrases given in the examples below. A poor candidate will accept these phrases at face value. A good candidate should be reading them, noting that they are in some way vague or need clarification and be thinking of what questions they would wish to ask.

Example One

You are given a report detailing a poor standard of behaviour by a member of staff. The report contains the line, *'The behaviour by the member of staff is surprising given their previous record.'*

This may generate questions such as:

- What previous record? When was this?
- What happened?
- What was the outcome?

- Was the person disciplined?
- If their previous record is excellent, why have they suddenly performed this inappropriate act? Is there some reason for the change in performance?

Example Two

You are given a letter of complaint from a member of the public. The letter is complaining of a certain type of behaviour or incident which they say has happened before. You may wish to consider questions such as:

- What evidence have they got of the incident happening before?
- What did they do about the incident? Were these incidents actually reported to the authorities?
- If not, why not?
- If they were reported to the authorities, what happened?
- Has anybody else suffered this kind of behaviour?
- If so, have they complained about it?
- If they have complained about it, what happened?
- Why do they think the past incidents are connected to this new incident?
- If they believe they are connected, what specific evidence do they have?

Example Three

You are given a report in the preparation phase which states a member of your staff feels they are being bullied. The report contains the line, *'There have been incidents of bullying before, but these were resolved at the time'.*

You may wish to consider asking questions such as:

- What were the details of the incidents?

- Were they happening to the same person?
- Are these new incidents connected to the old incidents?
- What action was taken last time regarding the bullying?
- What do they mean by the term 'resolved'?
- What form did the incidents take last time?

Example Four

You're dealing with a report in the preparation phase about a complaint from a member of the public about an issue within the centre. The documentation contains the line, *'a member of our staff has spoken to the complainant about this issue before'.*

You may wish to consider asking questions such as:

- Who spoke to them?
- Why did they speak to them?
- What action did this member of staff take?
- Was the complainant satisfied with this?
- What measures were put in place to stop it happening again?
- Was the complainant informed of these new measures?
- Is there any connection between the old issues and the new issues?

Hopefully, by now you will get the idea that every line in the exercises is there for a reason, and you are beginning to appreciate how the examination writers will be trying to prompt questions. It is your task to recognise these prompts for what they are.

Testing your questioning ability

The above four examples may all produce information to move the scenario on. However, the exam writers can also insert lines simply in order to make you ask more questions, to test your questioning ability itself. The information you get may not help you to solve the issue, but will get you marks for thorough probing. A typical example may be simply ensuring you get the time and date of the incident that the person is complaining about. If the issue to be solved is the behaviour, perhaps the time of it is irrelevant, but finding it out shows you are being thorough.

Ultimately, the only approach to take to these documents is to study each line carefully, and ask yourself if there is any further information you need to know in order to fully understand that sentence. If so, you must follow the question up. If you have made a mistake, and there is no further information, then you can be certain the role actor will 'block' you. You have lost nothing. On the other hand, failing to ask the question could mean you fail for the reasons already outlined. A good questioning technique will lead you smoothly to understanding the problem, and so allow you to identify the solution. Usually (although not always), you will start off asking questions from your prepared plan, then, depending on the answers from the role actor, you will either ask further questions from your list, or additional ones that arise because of what the role actor has said.

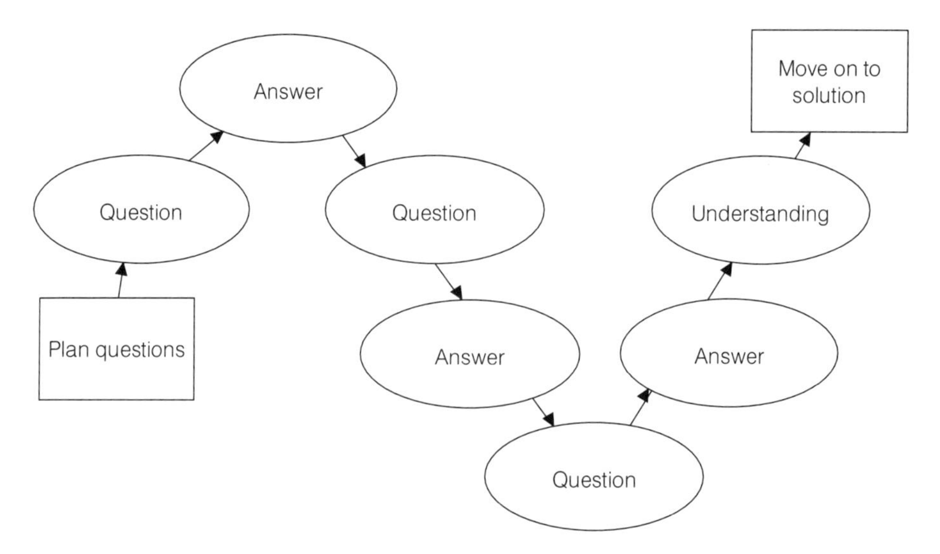

Fig. 8. Questioning.

RECOGNISING, CONFRONTING AND DEALING WITH INAPPROPRIATE BEHAVIOUR

We now approach yet again the subject of inappropriate behaviour. Hopefully now you will have got the message that this issue is particularly important.

You must understand that the use of the term inappropriate behaviour here is as defined by the police service. In the north of England, calling a female 'love' is almost regarded as being normal in many sections of society. However, in the police context it is unacceptable sexism, as it is patronising. Teasing somebody about their looks or the way they dress may be part of normal life. However, in the policing context it may be considered completely unacceptable. In the environment of the assessment centre particularly, if there is some comment or behaviour that makes you think twice, then you will be expected to do something about it. Again, it is impossible to produce a definitive list of inappropriate comments and types of behaviour. Indeed, if I were to do so I would probably be arrested by the police for failing to comply with some politically-correct policy. Suffice it to say, however, that you should familiarise yourself with the concept of inappropriate conduct and behaviour, and this can easily be done by reading forces' diversity strategies and codes of conduct. I personally work on the basis that if you would feel uncomfortable using that phrase or exhibiting the particular type of behaviour in front of the individual concerned, or the group it is meant to depict, then it is probably inappropriate. Do not use it.

Introducing inappropriate behaviour in the preparation phase

Remember the limitations imposed on the assessment centre exam writer. In terms of inserting inappropriate behaviour into the preparation phase, there are really only two main ways of going about it. These limitations exist because whatever the behaviour actually is, the candidate will have to refer to it in some way in the role play. So, the first and most obvious way is that the documentation will contain an element of inappropriate behaviour concerning the role actor you are about to meet – either as victim or offender.

The second way of introducing it is to somehow suggest that the inappropriate behaviour has impacted on the role actor, either as a victim or observer of the behaviour. In order for you, the candidate, to show that you're dealing with this behaviour, you will have to discuss it with the role actor, and explain what you intend to do about it. Remember, the role actor may be either victim or offender.

We will deal with how to challenge inappropriate behaviour when discussing the interactive stage itself. For the purposes of this section, it is sufficient merely to recognise it and understand that you should note it somewhere on your plan as a reminder to deal with it in the role play. Just as important as dealing with it, however, is showing that you intend to take steps to ensure it does not happen again. Obviously, this will depend upon the context of the role play itself.

COMMON MISTAKES IN THE PLANNING PHASE

The following sections discuss the common mistakes that people make when preparing a plan. The biggest mistake of course is not actually doing one to begin with!

Not reading quickly enough

Remember that the exercises will been piloted on several hundred people by the time you take them as a candidate. Therefore the exam writers will have determined that the average candidate of the standard required will be able to read through the material and prepare adequately within the five-minute period. As far as the assessment is concerned, the excuse that candidates did not have enough time to read the material is unacceptable. The moral of the story is that if you cannot read through the documentation within the time allowed, and make the necessary notes, it is not that the time period is too short, nor that the documentation is too long, it is quite simply the fact that you are not reading it quickly enough, or are spending too long thinking about certain elements. You therefore need to develop your reading or decision-making skills.

Time management

As a candidate, you have to be extremely disciplined about how you utilise your time. In the preparation phase, you have five minutes, or 300 seconds, to read through the sheets of paper provided and prepare some sort of plan. Logically therefore, as a minimum you must read through to the end of all the documentation. If you fail to do so, it is almost inevitable that the last paragraph on the last page (which you did not get the chance to read) will contain the one vital piece of information without which you will never solve the role play. Failing to read all the material and translate it into a written plan is likely to lead to the consequences I have already pointed out. You, the candidate, are therefore required to plan your time efficiently. As you open the documents, before you begin to read, just have a glance through to see how many pages there are and how much information is contained upon them. If at first glance you realise that the first page has a lot of writing, that the second page has only three lines, and the third page is a small newspaper cutting, you can allocate your reading time accordingly. You will clearly spend more time reading the first page than the remaining two pages, as there is more information there. You also need to be aware throughout that you will need to make notes.

Not working quickly enough

I suggest you do not read the entire document before you start to make notes. If you do, the chances are you will run out of time and end up with very little on paper. The technique to spend your time wisely is to read through at a brisk pace, jotting keywords into the correct part of your plan. Do not copy whole sentences, just write down enough words to stimulate your memory when speaking to the role actor. Do not spend too much time on one page. Go through the documents quickly, noting what issues you feel you need to pick up on.

Not understanding what you are reading

The preparation documentation should not simply be viewed as a briefing. It should be viewed as a blueprint offering opportunities for candidates to score marks in a number of core competencies. The briefing documents therefore will contain prompts that, if you know your stuff, will shout out to you what the assessors are looking for. It needs to be read in this context.

Poor understanding of the planning process

If you have not fully understood the planning process, you will waste a lot of your precious five minutes writing down things that are not relevant, or miss out things that are. The plan is not simply a way of recording information: it is meant to be a blueprint for you to follow when you are speaking to the role actor. If you follow the guidelines that I've given, you will produce a good plan which can be followed in a logical and rational manner. If you try to write everything down from the information provided on to your plan, in effect attempting to summarise the documentation, it will probably not work. A good plan is not simply about remembering the information you have been given. It is a prompt for you to ask appropriate questions, to be able to check information, to act as a reminder for you to put forward options, and also as a checklist of things you must do by the end of the role play. Things such as options and checklists will not be found in the preparation documentation. However, they still form part of the plan because they are part of the blueprint you require to complete the scenario successfully. The preparation document itself should act as a prompt for you to include these things on the plan.

Putting too much thought into what information goes where

Another common failing with candidates is the amount of stress they put themselves under when formulating a plan. Using my system, I split the plan up into three distinct segments: Circumstances, Actions and Results. Many candidates will correctly identify the piece of information or issue which needs to be brought into the interactive phase. They then waste a good 15–20 seconds attempting to decide which category of the CAR system it should go into. Whilst in broad terms it is helpful if you can put information under the 'right' heading, it is by no means essential. The whole purpose of the plan is to prompt you into saying or doing the right things at some stage in the five minute role play. If you include a piece of information in a different section of the plan from the one it *should* go into, it really makes no difference whatsoever. The important thing is to ensure that you mention it. There are no set rules as to what type of information should go under what heading. Indeed, as your preparation material is not marked, it does not matter. Provided you have identified correctly the information that needs to go on the plan, that is good enough.

Failing to use your plan

Planning is a difficult concept to grasp. What I find astounding though is the mass of people who do not actually *use* their plans. Many candidates prepare a really great plan. They take this plan into the interactive phase with them. However, under pressure, they simply forget to use it as a checklist. In the heat of the moment, they forget they have created a blueprint for themselves to follow and consequently do not use it. Bearing in mind the pressure you will be under, it is almost inevitable that you will miss certain parts out of the interactive phase that you covered on your plan if you do not remember to read it. This will probably cost you marks. Your plan is your checklist and your blueprint. Make sure you use it.

Failing to be flexible in the face of changing circumstances

This is linked in with being able to follow your plan even if additional or unanticipated factors appear. You can be confident that in some exercises the exam writers will have built in a surprise for you, whether in the form of some further information or inappropriate comments or behaviour. Flexibility is another competency being assessed. As a candidate, you cannot simply ignore an issue presented to you by the role actor. Neither can you really afford to leave it until the end of the role play to deal with, as inevitably you will run out of time. You need to be flexible enough to deal with that incident or behaviour there and then in a definite manner. Once you have done so, return to your plan. I promise you that the changing circumstances, while they may impact upon your final decision or course of action, will not make your plan redundant, due to the limitations placed upon the exam writer. The logic behind this is as follows. Every word in the preparation phase has been put there deliberately. If an issue is set up for a candidate to examine, the structure of the assessment itself is too well defined to allow the role actor simply to do away with the issues contained within the preparation phase in favour of something else. It simply cannot happen. Any new information will either impact on the original issue, or require solving in addition to the original issue.

What happens if (when!) something happens that your plan has not anticipated?

No matter how good your plan, it is extremely likely that in a number of the role plays, some new factor will be introduced. Remember, the plan is exactly that: a blueprint based on the circumstances as you knew them at the time you devised the plan. In real life, circumstances always arise which will impact on any plans you may have. As a police officer, you may be assigned to go and arrest somebody at their place of work. Your plan may be to take some of your colleagues and cover the front and rear entrances and walk up to the front door. This may be a good plan. However, if on arrival you discover that the person you plan to arrest is working with a large hammer, you may have to alter this basic idea. This does not mean your plan was bad, it simply means that a factor you did not know about has come into play. In this situation, you have to quickly make a decision as to what you're going to do, and then do it. Having done so, you can return to your basic plan for arresting the individual. The same concept applies to plans for role plays. Expect the unexpected to happen, and then, rather than panic, deal with it using the same principles we have discussed throughout this book, then you can return your plan. The principles for dealing with any given situation remain the same. If a new factor is introduced in a role play by the role actor, it simply means you have less time to think about the situation and must deal with it there and then.

SUMMARY

- Remember the purpose of the preparation material.
- Make sure you have planned properly.
- Consider what issues are likely to come up.

- Write down what actions you need to have completed by the end of the interactive phase.
- Stick to your plan, but be flexible.

How to practise

In Chapters 13 and 14 of this book you will find practice role plays, along with suitable plans. One of these is the full Abbot exercise, used as an illustration in the main chapter. Use these to help you practise planning. Your completed examples do not have to be identical to mine. If I were to replan them I can assure you that the second plan would not be identical to the first, but it does not matter. Provided that the main points are covered in some form or other, that is sufficient.

Planning is a difficult concept to master. However, being able to plan effectively will give you a huge confidence boost. Just as importantly, a good plan will channel your thinking and performance towards dealing with the key issues in the scenario.

7

The role-play interactive phase

WHAT IS THE INTERACTIVE PHASE?

So far, we have covered in some detail the first part of the role-play exercise: the planning phase. I will now explain the second part, the interactive phase. It is here that you will meet one of the characters referred to in your preparation phase documentation. In this case, having read the previous sections of this book you know who this will be: 'Abbot', as in the name of the scenario. Abbot is the name of the person you will actually meet.

Meeting the role actor

Once the five minutes of your preparation phase has finished, some form of buzzer will sound and you will either enter the room where the role play is about to take place, or if you are already in a room, the role actor will enter. As soon as that buzzer sounds, the five-minute period allocated for the exercise begins. Once the five minutes have passed, another buzzer will sound to signify the end of the exercise.

The person you deal with in the room will have been involved in some way in the scenario covered the preparation documents. They could be the person who has written a letter of complaint, or a member of staff whose behaviour you are required to discuss with them. They could be a member of the public concerned about some issue to do with the leisure complex, or a senior manager who is querying some policy. In any event, the role actor will remain in character from the moment they enter the room until the moment they leave.

Within this five-minute period you are required to deal with the problem and issues and reach a successful conclusion using, of course, your plan.

THE PRINCIPLES OF ROLE-PLAYING: WHAT ARE ASSESSORS LOOKING FOR?

Role plays allow the examination writers to assess almost all of the competency areas. Broadly speaking, they will be looking for candidates to display the skills of information gathering, questioning and creativity in terms of creating options and decision-making. In addition to this, assessors will wish to see candidates consulting with the role actor where appropriate, and summarising information for the role actor where needed. Role plays are the best opportunity assessors have to put the candidate into real life situations. Theoretically, the assessors therefore wish candidates to behave in as natural a fashion as possible, in order that they gain a true insight into a candidate's ability and potential.

The artificial environment of role plays

In reality, role plays are conducted in a completely artificial environment. As a police officer, I have dealt with thousands of situations which reflect the ones the assessors use. In none of them have I been able to guarantee that I will be able to reach a solution within five minutes. In none of them have the other parties been almost evasive and reluctant to give me information until I ask specific questions. When I have asked the other party what solution they ideally would prefer, they have almost invariably told me. These factors alone make role plays unrealistic.

Improving your role-playing performance

Candidates need to understand that the role play is not simply a conversation between two people. Neither is it a proper customer service environment. The role play is an artificial mechanism designed to test your abilities in certain competencies. If you, as a candidate, can understand that the role play is designed to test your skills levels, as opposed to your ability to present yourself as a nice person, you're already well on the way to improving your performance. Despite what the examination writers would have people believe, role plays are not free-flowing and natural in their layout. In the national sergeant and inspector examinations, both of which make extensive use of role plays, candidates are aware that they have to do certain things within a certain time period, and perform accordingly. Very few people can simply get by with charm and a sparkling personality!

Treating the role play correctly

The role play therefore must be treated as what it is: an examination. For example, many candidates upon meeting the role actor will engage in what amounts to small talk. They ask the role actor if they had a good journey to the leisure complex, if they are seated comfortably, or make references to the fact that they too have experienced similar sorts of problems to those the person is complaining about. They try to empathise with the role actor, basically in a very human attempt to get the role actor to like them. The reality of course is that the role actor will never like them, as they are simply playing a part. If the candidate's small talk is not on the marking guide, and it invariably will not be, then no marks will be awarded for it. All small-talk provides in a role play is a very effective method of wasting precious time!

INSIDE KNOWLEDGE ABOUT ROLE PLAYS

In a similar way to the rest of the assessment centre exercises, with role plays certain constraints are placed upon the examination writers. To begin with, it is essential that the exercises are as fair as possible to candidates. In terms of role play, the police try to achieve this by having very strictly defined scripts for role actors to use. Theoretically, the response given by the role actor in Cumbria should be the same response as one in Cornwall. The script therefore has to be kept fairly simple. This is for two reasons. Firstly, the role actors are usually ex-police officers or civilian staff. They have no formal acting experience or training. Therefore, to put it bluntly, they have no real acting ability. Secondly, the preparation time allowed for role actors before the assessment centre amounts to about a week. Therefore, for any given script, there is only a short period of time for the role actors to learn it.

Of course, the purpose of the role play is to allow a good candidate to solve the problem. The script has to take into account the information provided in the preparation phase, and use that as a springboard for the candidate to start the conversation with the role actor. The role actor's script therefore has to correlate with the information provided in the preparation phase.

The practicalities of the scripts

The role actor must tell the truth when asked questions by the candidate. This is not because they are inherently honest, however. It is because of the design limitation of the role play process. Consider a scenario in which the candidate has to speak to a role actor about an apparently racist comment they have made. If the role actor completely denies making the comment, there is no way within the five-minute time period for the candidate to deal with it effectively. In order to do so, they would have to stop the conversation and go and make enquiries into such things as witnesses, closed-circuit TV footage and any other means of ascertaining whether the role actor is telling the truth or not. This is clearly impractical. The role actor therefore will have to agree if a specific allegation is put to them – in this case, that they did make the comments.

This is not to say that they cannot disagree with the context of the remark, or say that the remark has been misunderstood or misheard. So, in the example given in the previous paragraph, if asked directly if they have made a racist comment, the role actor may well say no. This is because in their perception the comment they made was not racist. However, if the candidate then quotes back the words used, and asks if they did make this specific comment, then the role actor has no option other than to agree that they did. The issue for the candidate then is to point out why it was felt that the comment was racist. This is completely different from the role actor denying that the comment was actually made.

Exaggeration within the role play

The role actor can of course exaggerate. Imagine you're speaking to a member of the public who's complaining about the number of crimes in the area. The role actor may come out with a line stating that there have been 'hundreds of crimes' on their estate in the last few months, and state their (possibly incorrect!) belief that crime is going up dramatically.

Upon hearing this, a strong candidate should recognise it as a statement of opinion and not a fact. The candidate may well have information from the preparation phase which clearly states that in actual fact crime has not risen in that particular area. While it would be good practice for the candidate to ask the role actor why they feel crime has increased, and in particular do they possess any evidence of such an increase, this is a classic assessment centre method of setting up the candidate to go down the wrong track.

Avoiding the trapdoors

Although the exercise writers would deny any such thing, what they have actually done in this case is to place a 'trapdoor' in front of the candidate. The role actor's script contained the line about crime apparently going up as temptation to the candidate. If the candidate then takes this at face value, they will deal with the rest of the role play as if there has in fact been a large increase in crime. The strong candidate will politely inquire as to the nature of the evidence and reasons why the person believes the crime rate has gone up. The chances are no such evidence will be forthcoming from the role actor, and what the role play was looking for was for the candidate to explain to the role actor that their fears about crime were in fact unfounded. This should be backed up by the actual crime figures being explained to the role actor.

This technique of attempting to offer the candidate a trapdoor to fall through is extremely common in role plays. Candidates need to be conscious of looking beyond the obvious. If you're dealing with a member of staff who states that they have only had a few days off sick which is no big deal in their opinion, specifically ask them how many sick days they have taken off. It may well be that the actual number, which the role actor will have to provide you with if they know it, far exceeds the policy you may have been handed in the preparation phase outlining unacceptable sickness leave. If you simply accept the role actor's assurance that the sick leave is not too bad, you will not find out they have contravened the policy.

Listening to every word

The key point to remember here is that you need to listen to every single word that the role actor says. Each word has been carefully scripted. You should be constantly on the lookout for words or phrases that are vague, or perhaps a little bit elusive. You must develop the instinct to be able to recognise these answers immediately, and challenge or question them. One of my favourite questions to deal with such vague or ambiguous phrases is to ask, 'What do you mean by that?' It is especially effective if you repeat back what they have just said. So, if I was in conversation with the role actor, and I was concerned about the fact they were continually late for work, I may well ask them was everything all right at home. If they were to answer, 'Everything's pretty much OK,' I would immediately be suspicious. This comment is completely different from saying, 'Everything's fine'. I would therefore immediately say to the role actor, 'Everything's pretty much OK, what do you mean by that?'

Feeling intrusive with your questions

Some candidates struggle with this concept as they feel that they may be perceived to be intrusive, or that they are somehow asking personal questions of the role actor, which they think will lose marks. If the script includes such lines, then the marking guide will *expect* you to ask such questions. Indeed, asking difficult questions is a key characteristic of a police officer!

If there is no relevance in the question then the response of the role actor will simply be to 'block' the candidate as discussed earlier.

Having said all this, there is another thing to remember. Role actors cannot lie, although as I have discussed they may have a different perception of the 'situation'. What they can do is make you extract information from them instead of volunteering it all on one go. For example, imagine you're speaking to somebody whose work performance has dropped since last July. Hopefully, by this stage you have recognised that if a specific date has been included, there is a reason for it. So, your starting point for this conversation should be to ask what happened in July that may have affected this person's performance.

If dealing with this scenario, my first question would be, *'your performance has dropped significantly since July. Did anything happen in July that caused this?'*

Because the role actors are instructed not to give candidates information too easily, they would probably come back with an answer on the lines of, 'Nothing much really'. My next question would be, *'You have said nothing much really, can I ask you what you mean by that?'* The role actor may well then say something like, *'Well, I just had one or two issues at work, not worth speaking about really'.* At this stage, as a candidate I would know I was on to something. My next question therefore would be, *'What do you mean specifically by one or two issues?'* At this, the role actor may open up a little bit and say, *'I had a minor disagreement with somebody back then, but it's sorted now'.* As a candidate, I would then ask questions specifically about the incident: who was the person concerned? What led to it? How did it impact on their current behaviour? Logically, there will have to be some link with the performance issue because otherwise it wouldn't be in the script!

You can be certain that what the role actor will not do when you first question them about July is give you an answer revealing everything that has happened. If they did so, the assessor would be unable to mark your ability to ask questions and extract information.

The importance of time management

You should remember all the way through this that you have only five minutes to show the assessors you have all the skills they are assessing in the role play. Broadly speaking, as we have already said, this is your opportunity to ask questions, generate options, make decisions and explain how you will put them into effect. If you spend three minutes asking questions, you will probably score extremely well in the area of gathering information; however, you will have only left yourself two minutes to display all the other skill areas. Therefore, in the assessment centre, while you may well have got a grade A for gathering information, you will probably have failed the other six competency areas. You have to pass each competency in order to be successful: fail one area and you will fail the assessment centre overall.

Being time conscious

It is necessary therefore to be extremely time conscious. In effect, you need to split up your five-minute period into three distinct stages. These stages are those utilised in the planning phase, using the CAR system discussed earlier:

- clarifying the *circumstances*;
- outlining the *actions* you intend to take;
- explaining the *results* you intend to achieve and how.

The amount of time given to each of the three sections will obviously vary depending upon the role play. Whilst all role plays will require you to clarify some information or ask some questions, some are designed specifically to make you ask a lot of questions. In others, less emphasis is placed on the questioning, but you may be required to explain policy or decisions you have made. It is therefore impossible to provide a definitive guide as to how long out of your five minutes you should spend on each section. Broadly speaking however, you should aim to complete your introduction and opening within 30 to 45 seconds. It would be sensible to ensure you do not spend more than two to three minutes clarifying information or asking questions. The final minute to minute and a half or so should be spent outlining options, making decisions, and telling the role actor what you, the candidate, intend to do to solve the problem or issue.

The rough timing is shown in figure 9, but the exact amount of time you spend on each stage will obviously depend upon the demands of each individual scenario.

Flexibility within the scenarios

It cannot be stressed enough that these times are extremely flexible. It will all depend upon the make-up of the scenario itself. What will remain constant, however, is the fact that the first minute will probably be taken up with clarifying information, and the last minute with explaining how you intend to solve the problem. How the three minutes in between are spent is scenario dependent.

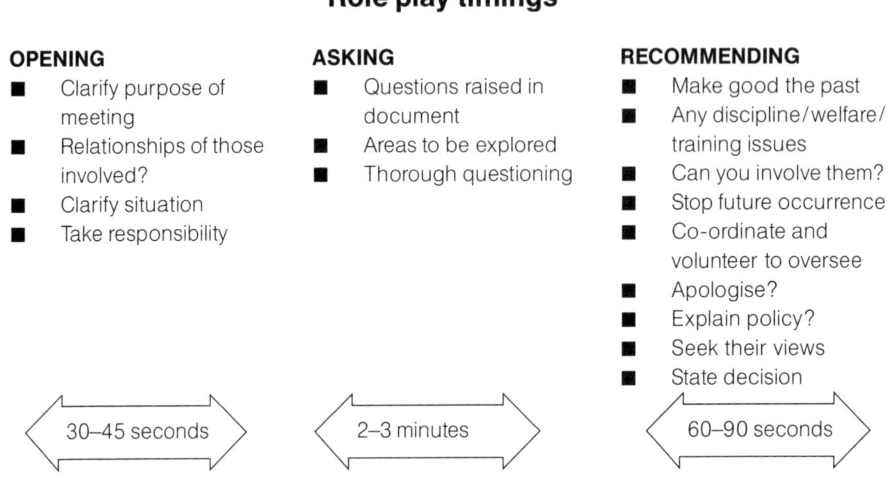

Fig. 9. Timing of a role play.

The main implication for time management is this: if you find yourself reaching the end of the first two minutes of the role play, and you are still asking questions, you must be disciplined enough to attempt to move on. Hopefully, by this time you will have established the information needed to move on to the next stage using your 'signposts'. If you haven't, then your questioning technique is probably wrong. As you approach the last 60 seconds, if you are still explaining the options to your role actor, it is time for you to start making recommendations and justify them.

Time management is crucial. Under pressure, many of us become long-winded and start to explain things in the longest possible way. You simply cannot afford to do this in a role play. It is also vital that you gain the skill of forcing yourself to move on even when it may not feel natural to do so. Ultimately, the bottom line is that if you spend five minutes asking questions, you'll pass the questioning section, but will fail everything else.

THE TECHNIQUES OF THE INTERACTIVE PHASE

Following your plan

I have spent a great deal of time explaining the importance of the plan. It is vitally important that, even under the pressure of the interactive phase, you follow it. By all means briefly introduce yourself to the role actor. Depending on the way the role play is written, it could be that you effectively begin the conversation. For example, if you have been instructed by your 'manager' to speak to the role actor about an issue, they may well be expecting you to begin speaking first. If on the other hand, the role actor has 'asked' to see a representative of the organisation, it is possible they will begin speaking first. It does not matter for the purposes of the plan which takes place. If the role actor begins speaking first, it will probably be to impart information. For example, the role actor may be reinforcing the contents of a letter they have written. Alternatively, they may be stating a viewpoint that you already know they hold because you received this information during a preparation phase. This viewpoint will probably not be a surprise to you and a strategy to deal with it should have been built into your plan.

Using your blueprint

You must always remember the three CAR stages: the *circumstances*, the *action* you're going to take, and a *result* you intend to achieve. Your plan is your blueprint for dealing with the role play. If you have planned properly, you will find that the demands the role actor is making of you will already be covered on your plan. The good candidate will follow their plan through, asking the questions required, listening to what the role actor has to say, and then linking this information with the rest of the plan in terms of the results required.

If you fail to follow your plan, you will rapidly lose track of what you are trying to do. You will almost certainly miss questions you meant to ask and, by the time the last few seconds of your five-minute period arrives, will probably have forgotten to outline some of the results you intended to achieve. The plan is your lifeline. As I have said before, it is ignored at your peril!

Being flexible (while following your plan)

The most valuable item of your preparation is obviously your plan. It is extremely unlikely, however, that your plan will be sufficient to cover every eventuality within any given scenario. Your plan is there to provide a blueprint to the main part of the role play. It provides a series of logical steps for you to follow. What it cannot do is anticipate additional factors that the role actor may be instructed to bring into the interactive phase. For example, you may well have prepared an excellent plan to deal with a particular given scenario; however, you do not know what the role actor will say to you. Let us imagine that with no warning whatsoever in the interactive phase, the role actor suddenly makes an inappropriate remark. Clearly, your plan will make no provision for this. As a candidate therefore you must be flexible enough to recognise what has been said, and then be able to deal with it. There is a golden rule when it comes to flexibility of this type: ensure that you deal with whatever issue arises straight away. If you do not, for example because you decide to leave it until the end of the scenario to address, then there is a very high probability you will forget or run out of time. Either would result in a devastating impact upon your mark. When such issues arise, deal with them immediately. Take whatever action is required and return to your plan.

This is not such a difficult thing to do as may at first appear. For example, because of the limitations of the role play, everything that was given to you in the preparation stage will still be relevant. Therefore, any new information or direction that the role actor is scripted to introduce into the interactive phase can only move the scenario so far. Remember, the whole scenario will have been quality assured to ensure that a competent candidate is able to complete it within five minutes. If the role actor were to introduce something that would have a massive impact on the direction of the role play, then it would have made the five-minute planning time irrelevant. So, it is fair to say that while certainly you may find that the role actor brings in new issues that you are required to deal with, by and large they will either fit in neatly with what you already have planned, or else be something that can be easily and quickly dealt with.

Following up comments by the role actor

In this context we are moving the concept of gathering information one step further. When preparing the plan, you will be aware by now that you have to look for 'missing' information. A good candidate will be looking for generalities or vagueness and making a note to ask questions about those areas. In the interactive phase itself you will find that the role actor will not simply pour their heart out to you the first time you ask them a question. Candidates are expected to display the ability to 'probe' the role actor in an appropriate manner.

Dealing with issues

The core competencies of being a police officer require candidates to deal with issues directly. This means you have to be open and frank with people, without being confrontational or overly aggressive. So, if the role actor has made an inappropriate comment, then you must clearly point out that comment, explain why it is inappropriate, make sure that by your wording you have explained or shown that you are against that kind of comment and then come up with a firm tactic to deal with that particular remark. If you are vague you will lose marks. In the real world, if a motorist is parked illegally on double yellow lines for no good reason, the police officer would be expected to clearly explain that he has committed an offence, explain what the offence is, and then tell the individual what they intend to do about it. The assessors will be looking for evidence of your ability to do this.

The same principle applies to other issues, whether these involve solving a problem from a member of the public, dealing with welfare or discipline matters, or justifying and explaining to a complainant why a specific course of action has been taken.

Consulting

Part of the skill of being a police officer is the ability not just to impose your own solutions on the community, but also to be able to ask the community for their solutions, or their opinions on the action proposed, when it is appropriate to do so. To illustrate this, it would be perfectly reasonable to expect a police officer to consult a member of the public who's complaining about children playing football outside their house as to what solutions they would suggest or what action they would like the police to take. Conversely, it would be completely unrealistic to ask a sexist for their views as to whether or not they should be reported.

Consulting requires two stages. Firstly, it requires the candidate to decide whether or not the situation is appropriate for such consultation. In the context of role plays, the vast majority of the time you will be able to consult the role actor in some way. This is not because you as the candidate have no proposals of your own, but instead to allow the person complaining to have their say. It does not mean of course that you will agree to carry out their suggestion, as it may be unreasonable or unfair. Alternatively, if the facts were so grave as to almost obligate you to take a certain course of action with the role actor (such as in the case of racist behaviour), there may be no opportunity for you to consult in this matter. However, what you are always able to do is to ask the other person how they feel about the proposed course of action. To illustrate this, imagine you're dealing with a member of staff whose performance is unacceptable. As a good candidate, you are aware that you must deal with this firmly but fairly. Having ascertained the facts, you have decided to give the individual a formal written warning. Clearly, it would be foolish to ask the individual if they are happy about being given this. However, it would be reasonable to ask if they understand why they've been given the warning and asked for their feelings on the situation. (For more information on possible sanctions against people who have done something wrong see 'Dealing with inappropriate comments or actions' on page 157.)

Getting feedback during the role play

Remember that within the assessment centre environment, despite the fact that you are assessed on the skill area, and therefore must effectively consult, you will never get a proper answer in response. The role actor will never say to a candidate that they are happy with the course of action taken. If they were to do so, they would be telling that you have got the answer right to that scenario. Conversely, they will never tell you that they are extremely unhappy, because they are telling you that you have got the answer wrong.

Instead, you'll get an answer which is totally non-committal. The usual response if you ask a role actor for their solution to a problem will be something along the lines of, *'That's your job. I was hoping you would be able to help me.'* If you discipline somebody about their behaviour, and then ask them how they feel or if they understand why you have taken the action, they will probably answer along the lines of, *'It's not really down to me'* or the old favourite, *'Whatever you feel is appropriate'*. These are the best answers that you will get.

Persuading the role actor

Remember, this is a totally artificial scenario. You are expected to ask the question in order that the assessor can tick the box marked 'consulted with community'. Do not expect a proper answer, and do not commit the very common mistake of attempting to persuade the role actor of your point of view. It is amazing how many candidates actually try and influence the thinking of the role actor. Remember, the role actor is working to a script. The script will give the candidate the opportunity to 'consult'. The same script will *not* give the role actor the opportunity to be persuaded. As a candidate, you need to ensure you have consulted, acknowledge whatever response you get, and then move on. You have your mark for consulting, there are no marks for you being able to persuade the role actor to your point of view, and therefore any further debate on a subject is simply a waste of your five minutes.

Outlining options

Once you have fully understood the situation, you should come up with a number of alternatives in terms of courses of action available. Obviously, the nature of these options will depend upon the scenario. At its most basic level, there always things you can do. You can either do nothing, or you can do something. To do nothing is clearly unacceptable, as after all you are being assessed on what you *can* do.

Many candidates get hung up on these options. It is not necessary to present in-depth, fully workable ideas that would be completely practical in the real world. After all, you only have five minutes to solve the scenario. So, imagine you're dealing with a shopkeeper who is complaining about nuisance youths coming into her shop all time. The shopkeeper (not unnaturally!) wants you to do something positive to stop this happening. You should be able to generate a number of possible solutions to such a simple scenario. For example, maybe the store could install closed-circuit television, employ a security guard, or move the cash desk to the door to discourage the youths from coming in.

Being creative with your solutions

However, remember the assessors are also looking for your ability to be creative. In terms of options, therefore, always be mindful that it may not entirely be the candidate's responsibility to solve all aspects of the problem. In this scenario where youths are causing problems inside a shop, a good candidate would consider the reasons for the youths being there. Is the shop selling goods which makes such behaviour likely or inevitable, in which case the storekeeper can perhaps do something about it themselves? Are there very simple security issues that can be introduced by the store? The police service is particularly keen on partnership working, so in some ways it is ideal if the storekeeper will agree to some acceptance of this, and therefore go some way to help provide the solution. Note, however, that this is not you ducking responsibility. Instead, you are taking responsibility for finding a joint answer to the issue.

Imagine that the store is a sporting goods shop. Consider whether or not there are any facilities available to provide youth activities. It may well be that a practical solution to stop youths gathering outside the sport shop could be for the storekeeper to arrange a young persons' football tournament.

It is not the practicality or viability of these options you will be marked on. The assessors are merely looking for candidates to show that they can think beyond the immediately obvious.

Avoiding flights of fantasy

One word of caution. While your proposed options do not need to be thought out exactly, they should not be wild flights of fantasy either. Imagine in a role play you find yourself dealing with some important local dignitary complaining about being unable to find a car park space when they visit the centre. It may be reasonable to suggest options such as asking the role actor to pre-book a car park space, saying you will put cones out to ensure they have a bay. It may be feasible to allow them to use a staff parking bay. Both of these will be considered reasonable options. However, if as a candidate you were to suddenly invent a ten storey car-park with one thousand extra spaces, which did not exist anywhere except in your own imagination, this would be regarded as being simply foolish and be marked accordingly. Options need to be reasonable and realistic.

Final words about options

Your suggestion must never be seen to show favouritism to a certain group. For example, if you were to allow the local dignitary to use a disabled parking space, your own ethical standards would be open to question. Being a local dignitary in itself cannot be enough to justify favourable treatment in any way. There would need to be legitimate requirements for them to park in a certain place in order for you to justify making such provision. If the action were to disadvantage other people, such as in this case the disabled, this would in itself be unacceptable.

Having generated your options, you now need to consider what your recommended solution, i.e. which option you will pick, needs to cover.

WHAT MAKES A GOOD SOLUTION?

Solutions should take into account three elements. These are:

- find and deal with any factors that may have led to the incident;
- repair any damage (as in, making good what has happened);
- ensure it will not happen again.

If all three are not considered, then there is no way that your solution will serve any real purpose. Imagine you are the customer service manager at a garage. A customer has come to complain to you about the fact that the receptionist was rude to them. They complain that your receptionist was uninterested to such an extent that several pieces of work on the customer's car were not carried out because the receptionist did not write them down. Furthermore, the customer is so disillusioned with your company that they have no intention of using you again. In order to solve this problem effectively, you would need to consider the three elements above. If you're not very good at your job, you would simply arrange for the work that has been missed on the customer's car to be fixed. That would certainly solve the immediate problem. However, it takes no account of the reason why the receptionist dealt with the customer in the way they did in the first place. Such a simple approach also totally fails to put anything in place to stop the receptionist doing the same thing again in the future. Therefore, it would be a very weak solution.

Finding stronger solutions

A good manager would undertake to find out exactly why the receptionist acted in the way they did. Perhaps there are personal issues that the receptionist needs to be given help with. Maybe they need more training. Conversely, maybe they just could not be bothered, and therefore need some form of disciplinary action. Certainly a good manager would arrange for the incomplete work to be done, probably at no extra charge. In order that they could reassure the customer that there would be no repeat of this behaviour, they would also put some form of quality assurance in place to ensure that the member of staff concerned did not act in the same way again. This may consist of telling the customer that the receptionist will complete some form of action plan for three months in order to ensure that they come up to the high standards that the company expects.

By doing this, the good manager has shown the customer that they are fully aware of the problem and are prepared to take steps to make sure that it never happens again. Simply fixing the damage caused is a weak approach from a marking perspective.

Finding out why problems have occurred

This scenario relates directly to the assessment centre environment. If a problem exists, you must find out if there are reasons why it has occurred in the first place. You should then do something about those reasons. Having done that, you should then take the appropriate action with regard to the person or group who has caused the problems. Finally, you should put something in place as a form of monitoring to ensure that those problems never happen again.

So, if a member of staff is underperforming, do not limit yourself simply to dealing with their underperformance. Find out if there are any background reasons for this, whether these be welfare, training or discipline issues. Having done this, then deal with the issue of the behaviour itself, but also put some form of monitoring in place to ensure that their performance remains up to the required standard.

Making decisions

By this stage in the role play, you will have outlined your options to the role actor, and consulted them. As I have just explained, they are very unlikely to tell you the option they actually prefer. A common failing at this stage is for candidates to almost try to 'force' the decision out of the role actor. Quite simply, if it is not in the role actor's script to give you a decision as to what they want (and it will be very rare indeed if it is!) you will now need to make a decision as to what course of action to take. Do this clearly and decisively. You are being assessed here not so much on the decision you make, but on the fact that you *do* make a decision. Many candidates give themselves huge problems in this area. They will offer the role actor a number of options, and get a non-committal response back from them. Instead of then immediately making their decision and moving on, weak candidates will at this stage start debating the relative advantages and disadvantages of each and every option with the role actor. This is pointless, as the role actor will have been told not to indicate which, if any, option they themselves prefer.

Needing to be decisive within the role-play

At this stage, the range of options you have provided should now become a single solution, recommended by you. The correct technique here is that once you have consulted, and the role actor has given their non-committal answer, immediately tell them which option you think is best, why and how you intend to implement it. Use a form of phrasing along the lines of, *'In that case, what I intend to do is to utilise option... What I intend to do is to speak to the member of staff concerned, challenge them on their behaviour, and take any appropriate disciplinary action I feel is necessary.'* By using this form of words, you are clearly explaining to the role actor (and the assessor) the decision you have made and the actions you will take to support that decision.

You need to be decisive in the role play. It never fails to amaze me how hard this is for people. On courses, I often tell people that I want a 'yes' or 'no' answer to a specific question. Frequently, students will still answer 'Well, I think if this were the case...'. Clearly, this shows a total lack of decisiveness.

Decisions and reasoning

Having made your decision, and explained this to the role actor, a good candidate also needs to explain why they have made that particular decision. Very briefly, tell the role actor why you have picked that particular option over the other options. The only tricky bit here should be summarising your thought process. Hopefully, there was a reason why you chose one particular option over another. If there wasn't, you really need to go back to the start of your thought process! The explanation should only take a few seconds. If you are going to discipline somebody, tell them why. If you suggest a meeting with somebody, tell the role actor why and what purpose you want such a meeting to serve.

Final consultation

Having done all this, you will now be approaching the last few seconds of the role play. It is good practice, if you have the time, to say to the role actor something along the lines of, *'I have explained what I intend to do, how do you feel about this?'* Again, do not expect to get a proper answer. That is not the point of the question. The point of the question is simply to make sure you get any potential marks for consulting the role actor on the proposed action you are going to take.

THE ROLE PLAY AND INAPPROPRIATE BEHAVIOUR

Dealing with inappropriate behaviour in the interactive phase involves the same set of principles as in the preparation phase. Inappropriate behaviour can be introduced into the role play in one of two ways.

Firstly, it can be described in writing within the preparation phase. In this case, it would need to be noted in your plan, and within the 'actions' section of that plan you would need to ensure that it was introduced into the conversation and dealt with accordingly. When introduced in the written phase, you have the advantage of it being in black-and-white and therefore are able to build it into your plan.

The second way to introduce inappropriate behaviour is to build a line into the role actor's script. Using this method, typically you will be in the middle of a conversation with the role actor, and they will drop in a scripted line which needs to be dealt with. This can be the more difficult one to pick up, because as you are reading and following your plan and at the same time trying to listen to what the role actor is saying, you have the additional pressures of the assessor being in the room with you.

Being 'overly' politically correct

In either case, the principles involved in dealing with the inappropriate behaviour remain the same. As stated numerous times in this book, many prospective candidates will no doubt feel that I have been overly politically correct. I would be the last to disagree with such a comment; however, this is the environment in which the police service operates and your own personal perception of what is politically correct or incorrect is irrelevant. It is the police perception that you have to abide by. Within policing circles, there was widespread disbelief several years ago when a police training centre took the decision not to sell Rowntree's Yorkie bars in their canteen. The reason for this was the launch of a Yorkie advertising campaign with the slogan 'they're not for girls'. I make no comment on this, other than to say it serves as a useful example of the extent to which political correctness has overtaken the police service. The moral of the story is that as a candidate you are required to abide by the standards the police have set, irrespective of whether a reasonable person would consider them sensible. If you fail to do so, then you will fail in your application.

Recognising inappropriate behaviour

Inappropriate behaviour is not just about racist, sexist or homophobic comments or actions. While this group is clearly vital in terms of such behaviour, inappropriate behaviour can be applied in a much wider context. It could be considered inappropriate behaviour to be lazy, to smoke in public view, to tell jokes while in a serious meeting, to be asleep on duty, to make fun of someone's disability and a million or more other things. The key test in deciding whether behaviour is appropriate or not is to consider whether somebody may, and I stress the word *may*, be offended. It is not about your own personal standards. It is not about what may or may not happen in the real world.

Many years ago, along with a colleague, I was first on the scene at an incident where someone had tied a rope around their neck and thrown themselves off a high wall. When we arrived, there was nobody else about. The body was suspended from a pipe so that it was about four feet off the ground. My colleague without a flicker of a smile remarked 'We are going to be hanging around here for ages'. It was the first (although not the last) time I'd heard this remark made in this type of situation and both of us immediately burst out laughing. The reality is that our laughter was simply a coping mechanism for dealing with a tragic situation. However, it would be considered to be completely inappropriate (and we certainly would not have laughed had any of the family been there). If you're dealing with such behaviour in a scenario, it will need to be treated as being highly inappropriate – regardless of the fact it was simply a coping mechanism that did not cause any harm because it was not witnessed by anyone else.

Being aware of and recognising inappropriate behaviour

The biggest problem people have with inappropriate behaviour is recognising it as such. I have already referred to the fact that in some places it is common for people to refer to females as 'love'. Many females will regard this as patronising, and to be honest, quite rightly so. Many northerners may potentially trip themselves up at assessment by using these phrases in role plays and so creating issues for themselves regarding diversity.

I would urge you from the moment you apply for the police service to consider what you say to people and read as much as is possible about the phrases that are considered inappropriate. Train yourself not to use such phrases. Do not think you can simply avoid saying them on the day, as under pressure you will forget and use them. When I first joined the police service, patrols were routinely described as 'single manned' or 'doubly manned'. As I progressed in the organisation, I realised that this particular phrase was frowned upon. Indeed, at one meeting I used it myself, upon which my (female) Superintendent actually challenged me. Since then, I've taught myself never to use the phrase 'manned', and instead use the word 'crewed' instead. This constant monitoring of your own phrases will enable you to eradicate any potential troublesome phrases before the assessment day. If in doubt, don't say it.

Dealing with inappropriate comments or actions

Having identified an inappropriate comment or behaviour, you now have to deal with it. The next step in this process is to challenge such behaviour. Again, for the majority of us who do not routinely 'challenge' people in our working lives, this can be quite difficult. In this context, candidates are required to clearly show the assessor that they recognise the inappropriate behaviour and have the moral courage to point it out clearly to the offender. A good challenge may use a form of wording similar to, *'Can I just stop you there? You have used the phrase... about people from a certain group. I personally find that phrase quite offensive.'* Ensure that you are firm, but polite. Do not cross the line of being arrogant or bullying, as that will also get you a poor mark – it will be felt that you were acting oppressively towards the person yourself. In Figure 10 I have shown how you should tackle inappropriate behaviour.

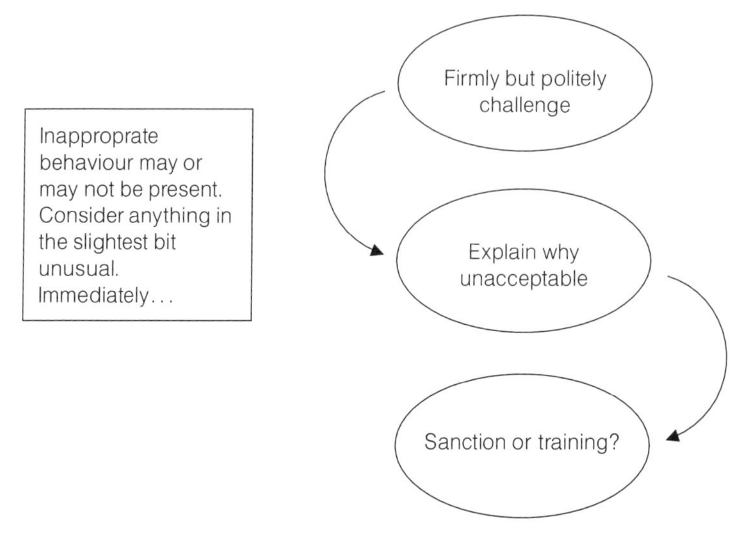

Fig. 10. Dealing with inappropriate behaviour.

Looking at someone directly when challenging them

This approach leaves the assessor in no doubt about your feelings towards a particular phrase or behaviour – you have shown as a candidate you have the ability to tell somebody that what they were doing was wrong. It is a skill, however, that is particularly hard to do when face-to-face with somebody. Ask yourself how long it has been since you looked someone else directly in the face and said what they were doing was wrong and unacceptable. For the vast majority of us, such occasions are few and far between. It is a skill to be practised.

Explaining why certain words or behaviours are inappropriate

Having challenged the behaviour, a good candidate will now explain briefly why that behaviour is wrong. After all, it is possible that the person behaving unacceptably does not realise that their actions or words are wrong. Using the example given above, many northern males would be surprised at being told that calling a female 'love' was patronising. It is important to explain why something is unacceptable for two reasons.

Firstly, the reaction of the offender to the explanation will affect the manner in which you, the candidate, deal with the individual. If the person was genuinely unaware and could not reasonably have been expected to know that their behaviour was wrong, then you may deal with it more leniently than if the person does not care if they have caused offence or in fact did so knowingly. Secondly, by explaining why you find the behaviour unacceptable, you are giving the role actor the opportunity to understand your reasoning and perhaps to supply an alternative explanation that may put their actions in a different light.

Deciding an appropriate penalty for unacceptable conduct

It needs to be remembered that the kind of behaviour you will come across will probably be at the lower end of the scale. For example, you will never encounter a role actor who is a member of the Ku Klux Klan, as the action you would take against a clearly racist organisation should hopefully be obvious. Instead, the behaviour is likely to be at a moderately low level. The temptation for candidates here is therefore to deal with it as if it is not particularly serious. The danger with this approach is that the assessor may view your response as being weak and inappropriate in itself.

My own view is as follows. The behaviour will never be enough to justify dismissal in the case of an employee. This is because of the practicalities of the role play environment. If the behaviour was that serious and you simply dismissed the role actor from the company, the role play would immediately come to an end and the assessor would be unable to mark you any further. So, in terms of options, it is safe to discount that of dismissal with regard to employees. This does not prevent you of course from using the possibility of dismissal as an option, although it will not be your final solution.

Showing the assessor that you will take positive action

Conversely, simply giving people advice is likely to be seen as weak. How many times have you been told off by your boss, then walked away and laughed about it with your friends? In any event, it will have had no long lasting impression on you. So, with regard to employees who display inappropriate behaviour, what is left? I would always recommend giving a member of staff a written warning about behaviour. This shows the assessor that you're prepared to take positive action and have a strong enough character to be able to put something down in writing which will go into a colleague's personal file. It is an effective compromise between a weak bit of advice and dismissal.

Giving written warnings

Personally speaking, there would need to be a very compelling reason for me not to give somebody a written warning for inappropriate behaviour. Such reasons could include, for example, that they were being influenced by somebody else, perhaps by bullying and that was why they were displaying inappropriate behaviour. Interestingly enough, I myself am constantly challenged on this piece of advice by prospective candidates. They often feel that they would be judged as being too harsh for giving out written warnings for what may be considered trivial issues. The beauty about written warnings though is this: to begin with, in the role play, the person you are giving a warning to doesn't exist! So, if they feel you dealt with them harshly, or that you are a bit of a 'square', it doesn't matter. Remember, you are not there to be liked. The role actor is present to give the candidate the opportunity to score marks – it is up to you whether you take that opportunity.

Monitoring future behaviour

Once you have dealt with someone for inappropriate behaviour, then it is important to show the assessor that you will ensure there is no repeat. The best way of achieving this is to explain to the role actor that you will be monitoring their behaviour for a set period. It does not matter what period you say, as you aren't really going to do it! Pick anything from a month to six months. As a final touch, if it is a member of staff, you could add that at the end of the period if they have not 'reoffended', you will put a note praising them for their change of attitude into their personal file.

What if the inappropriate behaviour does not come from an employee?

If the person you wish to challenge does not work for you, clearly you cannot give them an action plan, or even monitor their future behaviour in all probability. What you can do, however, is inform them that if they continue their behaviour, then you will consider asking them to leave the centre, and seek their exclusion from it. Do not make this into an ultimatum though, for the same reason that you would not dismiss an employee. It is too confrontational, and could be construed as bullying on your part. Simply explain politely that such an action would be one of your possible options.

SCALARS: IT'S NOT WHAT YOU DO, IT'S THE WAY THAT YOU DO IT

It is important at this stage to give a brief explanation of 'scalars'. These are quite a difficult concept to grasp in some ways, but can be explained broadly as follows. The assessor wants to see not only what you do, but the way in which you do it. So, each skill area effectively has two interlinking marks attached to it. The first mark is given for hitting the *behavioural statement* concerned. In the case of inappropriate behaviour, the mark may be for challenging the inappropriate comment. The second is a mark given for the *manner* in which you hit it, i.e. whether you did so in a confident manner, or were weak or uncomfortable in dealing with such behaviour. It is best explained by example. Imagine in the role play you are dealing with a staff member who has been performing below standard. There will be a mark for challenging the role actor on their behaviour, let us say their unacceptable sickness record. In addition, however, there will be a grade for how you actually did it, on a sliding scale from say, 'assertive' to 'unassertive'.

The two scores are merged together by computer. So, two candidates can say exactly the same thing, but get different grades for the exercise as they will have been graded differently in terms of, in this example, assertiveness.

You cannot know what scalars are in existence for any given exercise: however, there is one big learning point. Whatever you say, whether it is a decision, asking a question or whatever, you may as well say it confidently. If it was the wrong thing to say, it does not matter because you appeared assertive. If it was the right thing, however, then you will gain marks by being confident, as opposed to losing one for an apparent lack of confidence.

COMMON MISTAKES IN THE INTERACTIVE PHASE

There are a number of common problems candidates have with the interactive phase. If you find you are having difficulties, it will normally be to do with one of these factors.

Not asking questions

It is a key skill of a police officer to be able to ask questions. The assessment centre is specifically designed to test a candidate's ability to do just this. It is a simple fact that you will be unable to complete the role-play exercises based on the information you are given in the preparation phase alone. In order to resolve the issues you will encounter, you will need further information. The only source of this further information is the role actor. The role actor will not volunteer this information unless you ask the right questions. It therefore follows logically that you must be able to recognise issues or responses that require further questioning. As part of your preparation you should train yourself to a clarify ambiguities or unanswered issues that appear in your everyday conversations. For example, if a friend tells you they have just bought a new television, don't settle for just finding out what make it is: ask what the specification is, what size it is, which channels it gets, where did they buy from, how much did they pay, was there a warranty included in the price and so on. If you're told someone is going on holiday, do not simply accept the fact that they're going to Spain: ask them what part of Spain, where that is in relation to the nearest main city, how far it is from the airport, how long it will take them to get there, how much it will cost, whether they are they going by coach or taxi or other means and so on. Certainly, you will become a bit of an irritation to your friends; however, the whole point is to train yourself to ask questions in order that you look beyond the immediately obvious.

Failure to look out for key statements

Be on the lookout also for key statements that really need further investigation. If you ask a colleague how they are, and the response is basically that they are 'fed up', don't leave it at that. Ask them why they are fed up, is it to do with work, is it something at home, is it perhaps their work colleagues, in what specific way are they fed up and what can you do to help. This does seem slightly silly in some ways, but it is a key skill of a police officer. As a police officer, whether you are speaking to the victim or a perpetrator of a crime, most people give you the version of the truth they want you to have. You need to be able to establish the actual facts of the matter.

Not being assertive enough

In a role play you will be expected to deal with a number of situations. It is quite possible that you will be called upon to challenge behaviour, or to defend the organisation from unfair criticism (assuming of course that your organisation was in the right!). Many candidates are not used to looking people straight in the face and explaining that something is unacceptable. In an attempt to compensate for this, candidates will often use such phrases as *'It's not that I object so much, but some people would find your behaviour unacceptable,'* or, *'Look, I am not trying to be funny, but, well, you know, some people may find it a little bit naughty of you to say what you did'*. Using this kind of language or phrasing clearly shows that the candidate is uncomfortable when dealing directly with issues and that can be suggestive of a lack of assertiveness. Practise saying to your friends and family what you would intend to use as your challenge.

Being too assertive or aggressive

Some candidates confuse the fact that they are acting in a customer service environment within the assessment centre with their perception of how they think police officers would be or should be out on the streets. These candidates, when met with a role actor who is angry and shouting at them, will stand up and start ordering the role actor to sit down and be quiet. The candidate then tries to force the other party into submission by constantly talking over them, or telling them to be quiet and pointing at them. This is definitely unacceptable. Assessors are not looking for candidates to intimidate the role actor into compliance. They are looking for a candidate to establish communication at a reasonable level, understand why the role actor is upset or angry and deal with it in a rational and fair manner.

Failing to confront issues

There are two ways in which people can fail in terms of not confronting issues. One way is by simply not realising that there is an issue there to confront in the first place. For example, you may be speaking to a member of the public complaining about a group of travellers who have set up camp in a field adjoining their property. The member of the public is extremely irate at the fact that the travellers are there and (wrongly) thinks that the crime rate has gone up as a result. It would be a common failing for candidates to spend so much time sympathising with the dilemma of the member of the public, possibly not realising that there is no actual problem, that they ignore a racist remark that the role actor makes.

The second way of failing is committed by those candidates who recognise the issues, but cannot effectively deal with them. This is very similar to the issue of failing to challenge. Weak candidates end up using phrases like, '*yes, that kind of comment is not very nice,*' and then attempt to go on to some other part of the scenario. Again, this will impact very heavily on their marks.

Once you have recognised an issue, whether in the planning or interactive stage, make sure you deal with it in a positive manner. Trying to avoid it, or going around the houses in terms of condemning the behaviour, will simply cause you problems.

Failing to generate solutions

Another key skill area is that of being able to generate solutions to problems. Prospective candidates become really hung up on this particular issue. The problems presented are not huge – in fact, being fair to the system, many of them are in fact extremely straightforward. By way of preparation, make sure you visit your local force's website frequently and read as many of their publicity bulletins as you possibly can. You will see all kinds of initiatives and solutions that forces have suggested at some point. For example, you may read in one newspaper that a local shopping centre has started playing classical music in order to deter groups of youths gathering. Quietly file this away somewhere as a potential solution should you ever encounter a similar scenario at the assessment centre. If you come across a minor problem in your own work environment, consider what you could possibly do to solve it. While you are at work, listen out for any day-to-day problems that arise. You may work somewhere where two departments share a common resource, perhaps access to a typist or the use of a van or lift at certain times, thus putting them into conflict. Think what you would do to solve this problem if you were the manager. Note what solutions are put in place by your manager. Try and follow this mental philosophy:

> *'To begin with, I have to do something, because doing nothing is simply unacceptable and I will fail. On the other hand, I cannot simply give one party whatever it is they want, at the expense of the other party, as that would be completely unfair. Therefore any solution has to be a compromise, where everyone gets what they need, as opposed to what they want.'*

Failure to explain solutions

In a role play, giving your solution will only get you a certain proportion of the marks. You really need to explain, very briefly, why you have chosen that particular solution. Imagine if you were at a crossroads with a friend. You do not know which way to go. You are not sure that your friend knows the way to go either. Then they suddenly announce they are going to the left. That would be good, in terms of the fact that they have clearly made a decision; however, wouldn't you feel better if they explained why they wanted to go left? Hopefully, they would provide you with a rational explanation as to their decision.

Failure to address all of the problems

Remember, role-play scenarios are designed to be completed by a competent candidate within five minutes. It is expected therefore that you will solve all of the issues within that time period. It is going to cause you a huge problem if you do not cover them all. You need to ensure that your planning stage has been effective and you have identified what issues need to be addressed prior to entering the interactive phase. In addition, you also need to be flexible enough to deal with whatever the role actor comes up with. It is far better to deal with every known issue quickly, rather than go into great depth over one or two issues and miss another one out completely. The problems tend to be fairly obvious. The trick is to manage your time effectively in order to be able to deal with them all.

Failure to follow the plan

It takes a lot of practice to create a good plan. It takes a lot of self discipline on your assessment day to put that practice into effect and create a plan suitable for the interactive phase. It is extremely easy for candidates to take that plan into the interactive phase and because they are under pressure, or because the answer to one question is not quite what they expected, to forget all about that valuable piece of paper they are holding – and go into freewheel mode! If this happens, you run the risk of losing track of exactly what you wish to achieve in the role play. Remember, the plan is your blueprint. It provides a logical checklist of the things that you should be aiming to achieve within the five minutes. As I have said, it is unlikely to hold all of the marks you will require in order to pass that individual role play; however, it will hold an extremely high proportion of them and in any event a good plan will be a prompt for you to complete certain key tasks by the end of the time period. If you do not use your plan, you stand a huge risk of losing track of what you're trying to achieve. The consequence of this will be that you will start to panic, which will make the situation go from bad to worse. You will then probably forget that you even had a plan in the first place. That is a very difficult situation to retrieve. Use your plan.

Failure to manage time correctly in the planning stage

This point applies to both the planning and interactive stage. With regard to the planning stage, you have five minutes (or 300 seconds) to complete the three sections as in the CAR model, on top of which you need to read through the documentation to begin with. This time limit is non-negotiable. If you find in your practice that you cannot read quickly enough ahead, then practise reading faster. If you find your plan is too long to write, find a way to write more quickly. Perhaps you need to use fewer words, just using key ones to jog your memory. Do not use complete sentences as they take too long to write on to your plan. Remember, the exercises are designed so that a competent person can complete them within five minutes. If you cannot do that, you're not doing it correctly.

Failure to manage time correctly in the interactive stage

The same philosophy applies to the interactive stage. It is impossible to give a definitive proportion of the five minutes to spend, for example, on questioning, or how long you should spend generating solutions. This is because it obviously depends upon the nature of the individual scenario. What can be stated, however, is that you have only five minutes to complete the task, so if you're spending two minutes dealing with your opening circumstances and another two minutes asking questions, you will clearly run out of time. The role plays can only really be practised by doing mock exercises with a friend.

Failing to time yourself during the assessment

As stated already, I would strongly advise you to take some form of timer with you into the assessment and use that to monitor your progress within the role play. If most of your questions are answered in the preparation phase, then there may not be many questions you need to ask – and if you're watching the clock, you'll react accordingly. Certainly, by the time four minutes appears you should be starting to wind the scenario up, in terms of telling the role actor what your solutions are and how you intend to implement them.

Wanting to be liked

Most people like to be liked. It is a trait of human nature. Many candidates will start making small talk with the role actor. In the real world, this may be all well and good and may win over an angry customer. In a role play, the role actor is precisely that, an actor. They will not be convinced – they don't care. They are there to deliver a script. Don't waste your time. Say what you need to say to gain your mark. Then move on.

Believing that you need to convince people of your sincerity

This is similar in a way to trying too hard to make small talk. Candidates will often spend a great deal of unnecessary time trying to convince the role actor of something. As I have said, it is good practice when making a decision to tell the role actor clearly what decision you have made, and then explain why. You do not have to explain it in great detail, nor do you have to convince the role actor that this will be in their best interests. Once you have explained something to them and asked them for their opinion, then you will get your tick in the box and your mark. Any further repetition of these comments on your part is simply a waste of time and means you will be unable to say other things which may have got you additional marks. Remember, the key point about a role play is that it is a play which is scripted for the role actor and you have your own part to play. Admittedly, you do not know what your lines are as such, but you should be aware that whatever those lines are, it is a waste of time to repeat them.

WHAT IF IT ALL GOES WRONG?

With the best will in the world it is possible that something will happen and you will lose track of where you should be going with the role play. Although it feels unnatural, by far the best strategy to deal with this is to come to a full and complete stop. Do not fall into the trap of rambling on in the hope that some divine inspiration will save you. Obviously it is always better not to lose track of the role play, but if you do, the assessor will be interested in how you recover. If you recover smoothly and in a logical manner, you will not be heavily penalised. In fact, you may even gain some marks because you were able to cope with the pressure of realising you have made a mistake. The main thing that will kill your role play is if you say to the role actor something like, *'I'm sorry, I've lost track of where I am, I don't really know what to do'*. You cannot do that on the streets as a police officer, so therefore it is unfair and unrealistic to expect to be able to do it in a role play.

Losing track of where you are

So, if you do lose track of where you are in the role play immediately stop. Take a moment to read back on your plan and identify where the role play appeared to go wrong. Invariably, one of two things will have happened. The first is that you failed to identify a key issue or to ask an important question. Sometimes, under pressure you can think you have asked a question that in actual fact you haven't. If you think this may be the case, simply ask the question again, starting off from the last point you thought you still understood the scenario. The other thing that may have happened is that you have failed to listen to the role actor, or misunderstood them. In this case, do what you do in real life, and simply ask them to repeat the last thing they said. Try and think your way out of the problem. If you have to go back to the beginning of your plan, then so be it. You will not be allowed to restart your five-minute period and as you will be working under a lot of time pressure, you'll need to skip through the sections very quickly. However, you will still be making progress in gaining marks.

Listening to the role actor's lines

The other key factor in recovering the role play is to do with the lines spoken by the role actor. Consider carefully what the role actor said. Were they really trying to prompt you ask a further question? Were they somehow giving you a hint of the direction they want you to take? Examples may be along the lines of the role actor saying, *'I enjoy my job most of the time'*. This is really screaming out for you to question them further as to what they mean by the inclusion of the words *'most of the time'*. If they are complaining to you about a particular issue, and use a phrase like *'I will take the matter into my own hands,'* this is really demanding that you explore further what they mean by this. Remember also that any line that is repeated is begging for you to follow it up. If in doubt, the tactic of desperation is simply to repeat the line back to the role actor, and put on to the end of it the words, *'Can I ask you what you mean by that?'* If nothing else you are clarifying what has been said and may even get a mark for it.

Can a poor performance be saved by a good one elsewhere?

This is a frequently asked question. The answer is yes and no. The way the marking guide is made up is covered elsewhere in this book. However, for the purposes of this answer consider the following. Each role play will be testing on average between three and five competencies. Those areas will also be tested in other exercises a number of times throughout the day. Candidates do not pass or fail individual role plays. Instead, when the marks are added up at the end of the assessment day, each of the seven competencies is marked individually. Candidates pass or fail each individual competency. So, assume for a moment that a candidate performed badly in one particular role play. The first question is, has that candidate actually performed as badly as they think? The scenario may be testing their ability to show resilience, utilise communication skills and their ability to respect diversity. So, it is difficult for the candidate to know exactly which skill is being assessed in any given situation. If they did badly with regard to communication, there are a number of other opportunities to bring up their marks for that area throughout the whole assessment.

Overall, it is indeed possible to make a mess of one role play and make up the marks on another exercise. On the other hand, it is better not to need to make anything up! Suffice to say that if you feel you have made a mistake in one role play, carry on regardless. It is still possible to pass, and fretting about what has just happened will only ensure that you do fail. In actual fact, many candidates feel they have done far worse than they have anyway! This is the reason why I never give course students feedback until after they have their exam results. Frequently, I am contacted by a candidate the day after they have done their assessment, fretting about their perception that their performance was awful. I will not discuss it at that point, as almost invariably a week later they will have been told they have passed. Being aware of your mistakes shows such a high level of awareness of the process, that there is an excellent chance that while you may have slipped up somewhere, your overall performance should get you through anyway.

SOME HOME TRUTHS ABOUT ROLE ACTORS

Their training and abilities

It is a common belief that the role actors and assessors are highly trained. The reality is that the course these people undertake consists of ten working days. Within these ten working days, they have to be taught each of the formats for all of the exercises. There will be a lengthy input on diversity. There will be all kinds of theories for them to take on board. The amount of time devoted to telling them how to carry out any particular exercise is extremely limited. In acting terms, the assessors and role actors are only marginally below the position of karaoke singers in the hierarchy of the music profession! They're not therefore experts. They do not know a huge amount about how to be objective, how people perform under pressure or occupational assessment in general. By way of comparison, the average course duration for you to be able to drive a standard police car is three weeks. So do not overestimate the actor's abilities. In many cases, they will be as new to the process as you are. While forces may try to suggest that despite the short training, these people are experts, the logistics of the recruitment process would suggest otherwise. Most forces will recruit once a year. Therefore with the best will in the world assessors do not get the chance to gain a great deal of experience to add to their somewhat brief training. Remember that if you start to feel nervous!

Resisting stereotyping the role actors

One more thing about the role actors – do *not* stereotype in the preparation phase. If you do, it is very easy to be thrown when someone walks in who is the total opposite of what you expect. For example, imagine you are reading in the preparation phase about a security guard who has 20 years' service in the role, but has a very sarcastic attitude and a reputation for being the first to use some form of physical force to eject people from the centre. Most people will already be expecting to meet some bolshie bruiser of a male guard. They will then be put off balance if a petite, extremely attractive female walks in. Do not assume anything about the role actor.

Personal bias

People like people like themselves. Being human, assessors also like people who seem to be quite nice, are polite, appear to be trying their best and generally appear to be good eggs. This is why I would always advise that as the role actor comes into the room, you give them a smile and introduce yourself. As the buzzer goes for the role actor and assessor to leave the room, say thank you and give them a parting and respectful smile. If they make a mistake, which is quite frequent, avoid grimacing or doing anything which will make them feel stupid. If you do so, they can take it out on you in terms of marking. This advice may seem to be against what I have said about efforts to make the role actor like you. However, politeness does not cost you anything. Don't bother shaking hands though, everyone's too nervous.

The whole system is theoretically meant to be objective. However, as with everything involving the judgement of human beings, it is anything but. For example, the current system is based upon the police promotion examinations. A number of years ago it was suggested that attractive female candidates were dealt with differently by male assessors. It became apparent that in role plays designed for the role actor to be aggressive, male role actors tended to be less 'angry' and give information a lot more easily to good looking females than to unattractive females or males. Allegedly, the service got around this by giving instructions highlighting the practice. I mention it here only to illustrate the fact that the assessors are human and you need to take that into account.

Actor backgrounds

It is also worth noting that your role actors and assessors will not always be police officers. In any assessment centre you will find a mixture of police and support staff, mixed with retired officers and retired staff. These individuals will simply be brought in on the day, having completed the basic two-week course. It is entirely possible that some of them will have little more experience than you at assessments, especially if you are applying to a small force that only recruits at long intervals.

Is the system fair?

I am often asked whether or not I believe the system is fair. Having been involved with police recruitment for so long, I answer as follows. Within the conceptual framework it is designed around, the system is probably as fair as it can be. However, it still allows far too much weight to be given to the opinions of individual markers and that also means that individual assessors' abilities impact too heavily on candidates. For example, I know apparently excellent candidates who have failed at interview. When I have debriefed these candidates, it will often emerge that some particular trait of the assessor or interviewer has impacted on their performance. For example, one student who was a superb candidate came back to me having failed his assessment. Upon debriefing him, it became apparent that the assessor had seized on the fact that he was ex-military. The female assessor hadn't questioned him at any length on his examples and in my opinion simply had a bias against people in the military.

The variation between assessment centres

On the other hand, there is the problem of what one assessor considers to be overly aggressive behaviour being considered as a good example of assertiveness by another. The service attempts to explain away such arguments by saying that it compares the performance of each assessment centre with the others. It therefore argues that statistically by comparing each individual geographical centre with other centres, it can ensure that no particular place fails or passes more candidates than any other one. I believe that while this may be true, and that there is no systematic bias between assessment centres, there are, however, frequent cases of individuals being judged differently, depending upon the individual assessor they find themselves facing. I would argue that you could take a candidate through identical assessment centres with different assessors and find they are marked differently – which would inevitably affect whether they passed or failed. I would further argue that this is the real reason why the police service will not allow videotaping of assessment centre performances. With the cost of recording and storage facilities being so low, there is no reason why each candidate could not be given a DVD of their performance in order that, should they fail, they will be able to view this in order to develop their skills further. I would again argue that the real reason the service will not do this is because it would give the candidate the opportunity to compare their performance with another candidate's. This would give definitive proof of discrepancies existing in relation to marking. If totally committed to an equal level of marking, why not give everyone a copy of their performance? I would be interested to understand the reason why the police feel they cannot do this.

However, the reality is they do not feel this way, and there is no effective appeals process. Candidates can only work within the confines of the system as it currently stands. If you can't beat them, all you can do is ensure you understand the rules of the game and play it to the best of your ability.

FINAL INSIDER TIPS

Below are a final few things for you to consider in the final few seconds before your exercise commences.

Listen to the lines

Make sure that you pay attention to what the role actor is saying. They know what the scenario is about, and you don't (well, not entirely!), so work on the basis they have further information to give you, and listen to what they are saying. Bear in mind that you will probably need to ask them further questions.

Say 'Hello'

Politeness costs nothing, so say hello as they enter the room, and introduce yourself. Introduce yourself, and gesture for the role actor to sit down. As I have said, don't bother shaking hands; both you and the role actor will have sweaty palms anyway. Smile and thank the assessor and role actor with a single nod or word as they leave the room.

Help the role actor

Do not talk over the role actor. Give them time to say what they want to say. If they make a mistake, pretend you have not noticed and let them recover graciously.

Watch out for the hooks and blocks

This is linked in with what they are saying to you. Make sure you understand the concept of hooks and blocks.

Time yourself

Keep an eye on your timer. Although the instructions say that you cannot take a timer in, no one will object to a digital watch. Just activate the timer as the door opens and the buzzer sounds. Stick to the time limits, and be constantly aware that you have to get through all of your plan within the five minute period.

Remember that it is a totally unrealistic situation

Remember, it is all artificial. You now know the time limits and what the role actors and exam writers can and cannot do. As the role actor is just that, do not be overly concerned about 'persuading' them, just use them as an opportunity to score marks. If there may be a mark for empathising, say one thing to show you empathise, get the mark, and move on!

HOW TO PRACTISE ROLE PLAYS

In Chapter 13 you will find four practice role plays, headed 'Candidate instructions'. These pages contain the full candidate instructions for each of the role plays and are in effect what the candidate would be given on the day.

Chapter 14 contains the marking guides for each scenario, along with instructions for anyone who may be role acting for you. In addition, to help with your practice, I have included a specimen plan using the CAR system.

Note that the first exercise is the 'Abbot' scenario used to explain the basics at the start of this chapter. Here, it is reproduced in full, but this time with the role actor instructions and marking guide.

SUMMARY

Unless you happen to be in certain professions, the chances are that you will not have done role plays before. Many candidates find them daunting and understandably so. However, the knowledge you now have about them will give you a huge advantage.

The best way to prepare is practice. Get a friend to read through the scenarios, and role act for you. Vary them as much as you can. By doing this you will be vastly increasing your chances of passing.

8

Interviews

THE TWO TYPES OF INTERVIEW: NATIONAL AND LOCAL

The original concept of the national recruitment system was to introduce a standardised method of assessing potential recruits across England and Wales. However, there are a minority of forces that still use their own internal interview process as well as the national system. It should be stressed that any such interview is *additional* to the one undertaken on the assessment day. As only a minority of forces use it, for my purposes I shall refer to this as the 'local interview'. I will deal with it in a separate section, as many candidates will simply not have one. The following pages relate to the standard initial interview that most candidates will undertake.

THE NATIONAL RECRUITMENT MODEL INTERVIEW

Explanation of format

The interview is defined as a 'structured interview'. In days gone by, the assessors would have effectively made up their own questions. Basically, if the assessors liked what they heard by way of an answer, then the candidate would pass. If the assessors didn't like what was being said by the candidate, they would fail. Using this technique, many good potential officers were rejected and certain undesirable ones accepted. There was no way of evaluating, never mind evidencing, the decisions made as to who passed and who failed. The national system was devised to rectify that situation.

The competencies discussed at the beginning of this book form the basis of any structured interview. In the interview, you are encouraged to be yourself and are not expected to consider yourself still in a customer service environment.

Gaining marks

Each question is designed to give the candidate the chance to evidence certain specific skill areas. I have already explained that within the seven competency areas, each has a number of 'sub-competencies' or 'sub-behaviours' within it. For every sub-heading within any given competence and for each piece of 'evidence' you supply, you gain a mark. At the conclusion of the interview, your marks for the competencies are added up with those of earlier exercises and your total mark for the assessment worked out.

You, the candidate, must therefore understand two key elements about what you are aiming for when you give an answer:

- You must aim to provide example evidence of the specific competency being assessed in that question.
- Your evidence itself must be specific, in terms of describing a defined example.

So, telling the interviewer what a good sense of humour you have will not get any marks, as contrary to popular opinion having a good sense of humour does not appear anywhere in the competency list whatsoever (check if you don't believe me!).

Types of question

From a candidate's perspective, there are advantages to structured interviews. In a traditional type of interview, you can be asked anything, from who you think should be the next prime minister to where you see yourself in five years' time. Traditional questions may ask you how you would deal with any given situation or how you feel about certain things. Typical examples could be:

- What would you do if you were on patrol as a police officer or police community support officer and saw a fight outside a pub?
- What does your family think of you wanting to be a police community support officer or police officer?
- What kind of things do you think you will deal with in your first few days as an officer?

Each of these three questions asks you to anticipate what you would do in the future. None of them actually asks you for any evidence of what you have done in the past.

Seeking competency evidence from your past experiences

Competency-based questions effectively disregard what you think you *may* do. Instead, they seek specific examples from your past when you have displayed certain skills or found yourself in certain types of situations. The theory is that if you displayed certain skills in your past, and can evidence (i.e. explain) these at the interview, then this is a good predictor for skills you will be able to use and develop in the future.

So, the types of question you will get at the national assessments will be along the lines of:

- When have you shown an appreciation of diversity?
- When have you had to show resilience?
- When have you worked as part of a team?
- When have you had to consider the needs of a customer?

This is good from the candidate's perspective as you can start to think of evidence months before your assessment date. But it gets even better!

Under the police assessment system, candidates are actually given the competency areas that the interview will focus on. So, you are told (more or less) what questions are going to be asked. How good is that?

Actually, the service is not giving away all that much. After all, there are only seven competencies, so there are only seven areas that you can be questioned on. These are the main competencies, which I defined at the beginning of the book as:

1. the ability to respect other people's cultures and values and beliefs;
2. the ability to work as a team;
3. being aware of the needs of the customer and the community;
4. the ability to communicate;
5. the ability to overcome problem issues;
6. the ability to take responsibility;
7. the ability to react well to pressure.

Competencies not being assessed

So, there is a maximum of seven question areas that could possibly be examined. However, careful study of the welcome pack will normally reveal that certain competencies will not be tested in the interview. Usually, only four will be assessed. So, typically the 'frequently asked question' answers in the welcome pack may well inform you that, for example, problem solving and community focus will not be assessed. That means you will only have to revise or prepare for five questions. Even better though is that communication is not normally the focus of a separate question. This is because your communication skills can be assessed by your behaviour at the centre – for example in the way you speak, your confidence, report writing skills and so on. All being well you should only need to prepare for four questions. However, for the sake of completeness, all seven questions will be covered over the following pages.

A word of caution though: the competencies examined at interview do change from time to time, one will drop out for a year while another comes in, so make sure you understand what the welcome pack actually says!

Being familiar with the competencies

The wording of the question can of course vary greatly, and this is another reason why it is important that you are familiar with the competencies. For example, consider the competency of being able to react well to pressure. The questions exploring this competency area could be asked in several different ways, such as:

- Tell us about when you have worked under pressure.
- Tell us about when you have had to keep going under difficult circumstances.
- Tell us about when you found yourself under stress in your work or home life.

The moral of the story is to be completely familiar with your competencies.

How long do answers need to be in interview?

The assessment centre format is usually to have four main questions asked within a 20-minute time span. These four main questions will be the same nationally for everybody. Whether you do the assessment centre in London or Lancashire the same questions will be asked. Logically, therefore, a candidate has five minutes to answer each question. Incidentally, this should apply to both police and PCSO recruitment.

Making the most of the five minutes

Candidates often query whether or not they have to speak for the full five minutes in order to pass. The simple answer is no. You are marked on the quality of your answer, not the quantity. One candidate described to me how she misheard one particular question, and started to answer the question she thought had been asked. Three minutes into her time the interviewer told her this and asked her to answer the question. Of course, the assessor was under no obligation to mention this error, and could easily have let her carry on and fail. (Having said that, she was a very attractive girl, and bearing in mind my comments about the assessors and human nature...) When the candidate listened to the question again, and realised her error, she started again and got a grade B for that particular competency. This is pretty good considering the fact that she only had two minutes of her time left.

Fortuitously for this particular candidate, when she heard the question properly, she noted that it was one that she was well prepared for and she was able to give a good evidenced answer. Overall, giving an answer in two minutes is not to be recommended. If you have five minutes allocated to give an answer, it is foolish and wasteful to speak only for three. You can only be given marks based on what you say, and if you only speak for three minutes out of the five-minute period, you're wasting 40 per cent of the time allocated for the question. This is simply not good practice. It doesn't mean you will fail, but it does mean you're missing out on chances to pass.

Styles of interview

Everyone therefore will get the same main four questions. The way these are asked will also be the same. However, although this is a national system, the interviewer will probably have the discretion to run your interview in a variety of styles.

Basic question style

The first style involves the interviewer asking you a question (they may also allow you to read it on a card), then remaining silent for the next five minutes. If you, the candidate, stop talking, the assessor will say nothing. Using this style of interview, the assessor will not interrupt you, or say anything at all until the end of the time allocated for that question. They will then move on to the next question. If this happens, do not necessarily read anything into it. Perhaps you have done so well that the interviewer does not feel the need to ask more questions of you. Alternatively, perhaps the interviewer's technique means they would not ask anything further irrespective of how good or bad your answer was. In this type of interview therefore, you will only be asked the four competency questions as previously discussed.

Additional questions style

An alternative interviewing style is to ask further questions of the candidate based on the answers to the question they have just been asked. This is a process known as 'probing'. These additional questions are intended primarily to test the candidate's understanding of what they're saying or to clarify ambiguities. They may also be used if the interviewer is not convinced that what the candidate is saying is entirely true. Some interviewers like to bombard candidates with probes, almost trying to turn the interview into a confrontation. This is actually bad practice, but regrettably does go on. Therefore, you need to be prepared to deal with it. In any event, probes always link to the answer that the candidate gave to the preceding question. Probe questions are therefore unique to each individual candidate; the main questions (i.e. the competency ones) stay the same.

Probes are best explained by example. If the main question is 'tell us about when you have experienced working as a team', depending on what the candidate says, the following could well be probes:

- Who else was on your team?
- What were you trying to achieve as a team?
- You said there was somebody not pulling their weight on the team, what did you do about it?
- How did they feel about that?
- What did you learn from the way you approached the problem?

These probing questions depend totally upon how you answered the main question. The effect of this is that your interview may be completely different from that of the person who went before you. The four main questions will remain the same, but the probes will be completely different.

Alerting the interviewer or causing concerns

Be aware that if you say something that potentially highlights an area causing concern to the interviewer, that area will be probed. For example, the candidate may use the phrase 'local undesirables' in some context in an answer. A probe may well query what they actually mean by this. It would then be easy for candidates under pressure to start using inappropriate or judgemental phrases about groups such as drug addicts or 'yobs'. These could well be interpreted as suggestions that the candidate is likely to be judgemental and biased in their dealings with certain groups, which is clearly an undesirable quality for a police officer.

Probes, if indeed you get them, are not something to be concerned about – in fact they are to be welcomed. They are an opportunity to show off what a good example you have of the competency being assessed.

If you have prepared a good five-minute answer, the chances are that any issue the interviewer wishes to probe will probably have already been considered, and you were therefore going to mention anyway. As ever, the moral of the story is thorough preparation.

PREPARING YOUR ANSWERS

As has been said, the interviewer may or may not decide to interrupt your answer with probing questions. However, it is good practice to assume they will not and prepare therefore to give an answer for the full five minutes allocated to the question. This is a long time to talk for, but remember, if you can do so, almost irrespective of what you're saying, you will be scoring highly on communication and confidence if nothing else. Being able to speak for this time period does require careful and thorough preparation though.

Using CAR for your answers

My recommendation for completing your preparation may seem a little complex, but becomes easier to understand when illustrated by example. Basically it revolves around breaking your answer down into the same three distinct stages which were used in role-play preparation, i.e. the CAR (circumstances, actions, results) system. When asked a question, and just as importantly when preparing your answers in advance, you should use these three component parts. The use of CAR does differ slightly in interview however. I will now explain how the system fits with the interview and the competency listings.

Circumstances

The first part of any answer should be to describe the situation you found yourself in at the time of your example. You need to provide some form of verbal picture for the assessor, which will allow them to understand how you came to be in the place you were when the example happened. It should be a brief description of:

- why you were there;
- what your job was;
- what was your role;
- how long you had knew the people concerned.

Obviously, the factors you mention here will depend upon the question itself. Ideally, just aim to set the scene for the interviewer. By way of comparison, imagine you have just met someone at a party for the first time, and are telling a story about work or college. As they do not know you, or anything about you, you need to give them the basic background before telling them the story. This introduction will only last between 30 and 45 seconds. It is literally an introduction to the circumstances you found yourself in, nothing more.

Actions

This is the most complex part of the CAR system, and in essence requires you to carefully examine each of the competencies for any given specific competency area.

Consider the competency area of diversity. The main heading of diversity is followed by a number of sub-headings (the sub-behaviours). The strong candidate should be aware of these from the competency listings. The more of these sub-behaviours you evidence in your answer, the higher you will score. Logically therefore, you need to mention or 'hit' as many of these sub-behavioural statements as possible. You will probably never hit all of them, but should aim for as many as you can. As a rough guide, if your answer hits three-quarters of the sub-behaviours, it should be fine. If you only hit half of them, you need a stronger answer. If your example only hits a third, change the example. Again, this concept is much easier to explain by example which I will come to shortly.

Results

In this third part of your answer, you will effectively tell your interviewer what you achieved in the incident you have just described. Ideally, you will be able to describe in this section what outcomes your actions had, what you learnt from them, and what effect they had on the people around you. Ideally, you will also provide a definite outcome, such as the fact you received a thank-you letter, or that as a result of you resolving the situation, the individual concerned still sends you a Christmas card every year.

WHAT IS EVIDENCE?

Often candidates can get very confused by the concept of 'evidence'. For assessment purposes, my own definition of evidence as:

> *An explanation of what actions the candidate specifically took, in terms of words, behaviour or responsibilities, along with a definite outcome for the situation being explained.*

This definition sounds more daunting than it really is. Put simply, it means that for every answer you give, you must keep in mind the principles introduced at the beginning of this chapter:

- You must aim to provide example evidence of the specific competency being assessed in that question.
- Your evidence itself must be specific, in terms of describing a defined example.

The difference between making a statement and providing evidence

There is also a distinct difference between making a 'statement', and providing 'evidence'. Imagine you are answering a question about team working. Many candidates will give an answer along the lines of:

> *I am very good at team working, I work in a factory with many others and you have to work as a team.*

This is not evidence. Instead it is a simple statement about teamwork in general. There is no specific information contained within it about the candidate, or specifics showing that they are in fact a good team worker.

Example 1

A far better, *evidenced* answer would be:

> *I work in a team of six people on a production line at a car factory. My section assembles car seats. Each of us has a certain job to do – for example, I put the cloth on the seat, whilst others fit the adjustment mechanisms. None of us can do our job properly unless the others do theirs. We have a target to reach each shift, and as we all work together, we have achieved ours consistently for the last three months.*

This candidate clearly provides evidence of exactly what sort of team they work in, along with the fact that they have a specific role and recognise other people have specific roles as well. The candidate also acknowledges the fact that it is necessary for all team members to work together in order to achieve targets, and goes on to prove that they are a key part of this team because the team meets its targets each month.

Compare this answer with the first one given and you will hopefully see the first answer is the candidate simply making an unsubstantiated claim about him or herself.

Example 2

Consider a further example of the difference between making statements and providing evidence. The question this time is to provide an example of having shown respect for diversity. Think about this answer:

> *I am very aware of diversity, and have a lot of friends who are from different backgrounds to myself. Many people of different beliefs and backgrounds to mine went to my local school.*

There is no evidence whatsoever contained within this answer. It is simply a series of statements. It gives no indication as to what way the candidate has interacted with somebody with different beliefs to themselves. Therefore, it would score poorly. A far better answer would go along the lines of the following:

> *In my current job, I work in a post-room with a colleague who has a different religious background to mine. I am a Christian, whereas he is Muslim. We share desks, and after having worked with him for a few weeks, I realised that I knew nothing about his faith. This was particularly obvious when it came to things like his eating habits, and the fact that he used to pray several times a day. I simply had no idea why he was doing certain things, and realised I knew nothing about his religion. I decided to ask my colleague to tell me about his religious beliefs, as I was interested. He explained to me for example that he did not drink alcohol, nor eat certain foods. Because of this I adapted my own work routine. For example when I discovered that certain kinds of food were distasteful to him, I stopped bringing them in for my lunch.*

This second example clearly shows that the candidate has worked with someone of a different background to their own, and has evidenced interest and respect for that person's lifestyle. This type of answer would therefore score much more highly.

Being truthful in your answers

Evidence does not mean you need documented proof of what you're talking about. The word 'evidence' is simply a term used to refer to a specific example. The interviewer will not follow up on what you say; no one will contact your current employer to see if you really did work with somebody of a different background, or that you really did hit the target for three months running. You should clearly be truthful in your answers. If you lie and are detected in that lie, that itself will throw doubt upon your level of integrity and you would doubtless be failed.

The importance of preparation

If you look at the competencies again, each one is broken down into an average of 12–14 sub-behaviours. It is probably fair to say that the vast majority of candidates do not bother to think about these at all. The next section aims to explain to you how vital these sub-behaviours actually are, as in effect they can be considered to be part of the marking guide.

USING THE CAR SYSTEM AND THE COMPETENCIES TO DEVELOP ANSWERS

The best way to illustrate using the CAR system to develop competency-based answers is by example. In order to do this, I have illustrated below an example answer to a question on the competency of diversity. For the purposes of explanation only, I have broken it down into the three CAR sections – circumstances, actions and results. At the beginning of each section, I have provided an explanation of what the answer is trying to achieve. The words in *italics* are the actual spoken words that would make up the answer. Words in normal print are explanations. When you read this section, have a marker in the page that details the competency behaviours for diversity (page 30). The numbers in brackets after each point in the answer refer to the specific sub-behaviour that this piece of evidence hits.

'Can you tell us about when you have experienced diversity?'

Circumstances

In this competency, the assessors are looking at evidence that shows you can respect the beliefs of people who are different from you in some significant way, whether that be in terms of ethnic origin, religion, sexual orientation, disability or other similar factors.

In the opening part of the question answer I will outline the situation in which I found myself. I intend to provide sufficient detail for the assessor to understand the context of the example. This should take no longer than between 30–45 seconds.

> *At the moment, I work in a busy office with a team of about 20 people. About six months ago, a new member of staff joined the company, and sat at the desk opposite to mine. This individual was clearly disabled, as he used a wheelchair. After I introduced myself, I realised that I had little experience of working with disabled people, and had no idea of how my new colleague would view his new situation, or indeed me. As he appeared a bit nervous on their first day, I decided to see if I could help him settle in more quickly to the organisation.*

By telling the interviewer this, within the first few seconds of your five-minute time period you have neatly set up an interesting example. They now know that you have a grasp on what the question is actually asking, can summarise a set of circumstances and are able to begin a conversation in the interview confidently. All these things will have already started to get you marks.

Actions

In my full explanation of this phase of the model, I made reference to building the answer around the particular competencies for that specific question area. With this answer, ideally you should be referring back to the pages with the sub-behaviours lists on (pages 30–36). As you go through this answer, look at the headings for diversity. Each of the sub-behaviours for each competency has been allocated a number. I have used the reference for each competency hit (i.e. 1.2, 1.3 etc) after each sentence to show how I have referred it back to the answer. For each sub-behaviour you can fit into an answer and evidence of course, you will get a mark. I have split the answer into paragraphs only to make it easier to see how I have hit each sub-behaviour.

I realised that being the new member of staff is quite difficult sometimes; I wanted to ensure that my new colleague felt that I understood his perspective. I spoke to him and introduced myself, explaining that I remembered my own first day, and asked if he had any questions I could answer for him, or anything I could do to help him (diversity sub-behaviour 1.1).

He explained to me that he preferred to be as independent of help as much as possible, and so for example did not want a fuss made, nor unnecessary patronising concessions made because he was in a wheelchair. I explained that I was unsure of any help I could or should offer, and he simply smiled and said he was a normal person and just wanted to be treated as such (diversity sub-behaviour 1.2).

Over the weeks, I got on with my new colleague extremely well. Occasionally, something would happen which would cause frustration, such as for example, the other day, my colleague experienced discomfort in his back. This made him a little bit short on patience, which is perfectly understandable. I ensured I remembered his position and took account of it (diversity sub-behaviour 1.3). *Occasionally, there would be some disagreement between people in the office, for example recently there was a debate over the layout of office furniture. I acted as the arbitrator for all parties in the office, and pointed out to them all that everyone works in the same office, and that we all had responsibility to ensure everyone, whether in a wheelchair on not, could manage with the workspace allocated* (diversity behaviour 1.4). *Once I pointed this out to everybody they calmed down and agreed to the new layout* (diversity sub-behaviour 1.5).

One time, an office night out from work was planned. My new colleague, who was usually very sociable in terms of going out with us, was very quiet, and appeared reluctant to actually come. Having noticed this, I asked him why he wasn't going, and he explained that in the bar we intended going to he could not get up the stairs without being carried, and therefore did not want to go. I realised we were effectively excluding him, switched the night out to a venue my friend would be comfortable at, and he then happily attended the night out (diversity sub-behaviour 1.6).

Another way I have shown respect for his disability was in use of language. I have had to challenge several people who made inappropriate comments or remarks, explaining that remarks they had made could potentially be offensive. On each occasion, the person who made the comments apologised to the group as a whole, and there were no repeat comments from that person (diversity sub-behaviour 1.7).

I found that my friend was extremely independent in his views, and that I had to respect these. For example, he did not like me to help him out of his car into a wheelchair when we were sharing lifts. I quickly found that in his opinion this was considered patronising behaviour (diversity sub-behaviour 1.8).

As we spent more time together, I began to recognise things that he considered annoying. I noticed, for example, that with some work colleagues, if a conversation between them, my disabled colleague and I started up, they tended to speak to me rather than him. Because I knew he found this annoying, I was able to avoid doing it myself, and quietly tell others not to do so either (diversity sub-behaviour 1.9).

As our friendship grew, we were able to speak more of difficult issues. For example, if we went out to a location where there was not a disabled toilet, I would on occasion help my friend into a toilet cubicle. When we discussed this, I realised that if I showed any shyness or awkwardness about it, he felt even more embarrassment. We now openly laugh about such issues as we are so comfortable about it (diversity sub-behaviour 1.11).

In terms of honesty, my friend told me after a few months that he was quite awkward with me when he first came into the office. But he appreciated the manner in which I had tried to understand his position. Because of our friendship, we are now extremely open with one other, and talk in depth about his condition. In return, I often share personal issues with him myself (diversity sub-behaviour 1.12).

Gaining marks by linking behaviours to evidence

You should be able to see that by breaking my answers down aiming for each sub-behaviour I have provided a clear evidenced example for each. Each one effectively represents a mark.

Note also that in the answer above, there is no illustration of sub-behaviour 1.10. This is because in the context of the story, I was unable to evidence it. That is not a problem, as long as your example hits three quarters of the behaviours, you should be fine. Having said that, of course the more the better!

Results

This phase is simply a chance to round the story off. A positive ending is desirable. In this case I would be saying something along the lines of:

> *We are now great friends, and still work together in the same office. We often socialise together. Through my experiences with my colleague, I now feel I have a much greater understanding of disabled issues and this is where my understanding of diversity came from.*

Length of answers

Summarising the circumstances as already stated should take up no more than a minute. The next four minutes should be devoted to your evidenced examples of the competencies. This may seem a strange way of answering a question or developing your answer. However, if you practise you will be able to create a logical narrative within the five-minute time period, which will score well. In terms of timings, my answer above is meant as an example. The actual length of what you prepare will depend upon your style of speaking. Don't try to learn your example word for word for two reasons. Firstly, it will be very difficult to do and make you sound like a robot. Secondly, if the question is slightly different from what you expect, then you may not able to be flexible and adapt your answer. If you have learnt it word for word, you will have more difficulty changing parts that may not be relevant.

Preparing answers for all competency questions

In order to fully illustrate the CAR system to you, I have provided example answers to the remaining six competencies. Remember that while it is always worthwhile preparing example answers for all seven competencies, in your actual interview you will usually only be asked for four, which you should aim to find out before the assessment. In the 'actions' section of each answer, after each piece of evidence I have included (in brackets) the competency behaviour reference number related to that skill area. So, for example, where my answer states something like, *'I challenged him on his comments, and pointed out they were sexist and so unacceptable'*, I have also put a reference such as 'Ability to communicate sub-behaviour 4.10'. If you look at the competencies for communication (on page 33), you will see that the answer given hits that behaviour. As you work through the exercises, compare them with the competencies listed at the beginning of the book. When you are giving your examples, you can list the behaviours in any order you wish that best suits the example. As I have moved through the examples, I have deliberately missed some out due to the fact that they did not fit into the example (and to show that not all of them need to be in), and changed the order.

Remember, these are only for illustration. Your answers may be longer or shorter depending on your personal style.

Over the following pages I have provided illustration answers for the remaining six competency areas. As you read each one, try and follow how each piece of evidence has been linked to a specific sub-behaviour. I have again provided the reference number for each piece of evidence so you can compare it with the competency being tested.

Can you tell us about a time when you have had to work as part of a team?

In this competency, assessors are looking for evidence of your ability to realise that in the police you are a small but important piece of a larger machine. They want evidence that you have worked with a group of other people towards a common goal, and have developed mutual respect within that group.

Circumstances

I work in a busy supermarket. It is quite a big store, employing about 100 people who work in shift patterns. There are a number of jobs in the store, ranging from manager to driver through to cashier. Each one of us has our main tasks, for example I am a shelf stacker, but we are expected on occasion to rotate around and do different jobs as the need arises.

Actions

As so many of us work in the store, each of us has our own specific job. However, depending on what is happening in the store, on occasion you can become part of other teams. For example, every now and then we have a store cleanliness day. When that happens, I will work with 10 or 12 other people, to tidy the store from top to bottom. Conversely, when the tills are extremely busy, a similar number of us will be put on to a particular sector of checkouts, so we become part of that team (team working sub-behaviour 2.1).

Working within such an environment, it's really important that we all work together. For someone who is quite ambitious, it has to be said there is no great incentive to work on the checkouts, as there is no particular status associated with it, but at the end of the day somebody has to do that task and I ensure I volunteer to do my turn (team working sub-behaviour 2.2).

Clearly, some jobs inside the supermarket are better than others. For example, one of the most unpopular jobs is clearing up spillages. I ensure that I volunteer for this at least once or twice a week. I feel by doing this I improve my credibility with my colleagues, and am contributing to the team by doing tasks that are unpopular (team working sub-behaviour 2.3).

Working in a fast-moving environment with cash means you have to have confidence and trust between colleagues. For example, when I hand my takings over to another member of the supervisory team to check, I have to trust them that they will do so honestly. On the other hand, when a lorry full of frozen food arrives, it is essential that I can trust my colleagues on the freezer department to have cleared the right space for us to put out the new stock. If we did not have this trust, we would be unable to complete our respective tasks, and the job would not get done (team working sub-behaviour 2.4).

As part of a busy team, I am used to giving and receiving help. For example, last week I was restocking a particular product. I only had half an hour to restock the shelves before the store opened, and would have been unable to complete the task by myself. My colleagues offered to help me, and between us we were able to get the job done. It works both ways of course, and only yesterday one of my colleagues asked me to help them move some boxes from one part of the store to another (team working sub-behaviour 2.5).

I believe that part of being a team player is the ability to assist other people in their work. As I have just said, we all help one another to achieve team objectives. Last month, I was asked to help a new starter to the organisation. My new colleague was just out of school, and did not really know shop procedures such as stock rotation. I noticed this, and explained the system fully to him so that he was able to do his job properly (team working sub-behaviour 2.6).

Clearly part of being in a team is about working with colleagues and assisting them. The best example of this recently occurred when we had several delivery lorries arriving at the same time. Sometimes this can happen shortly before the store is about to open. I took charge, and assigned each of us individual and specific tasks, one section of the team bringing the stock in to the store, and another getting the store ready for opening (team working sub-behaviour 2.7).

Each of us is assigned to a department within the store, with responsibilities for certain areas. Being a supermarket, there is a great emphasis on cleanliness. Usually our manager gives team leaders certain tasks to do with cleaning. I was appointed a team leader as I enjoyed the challenge of being able to work in a well-organised team, and work towards a common goal (team working sub-behaviour 2.9).

When I started with the company, I made an effort to get to know my team members by sitting with them on tea breaks, and chatting to them as we worked. By showing an interest in them, and also proving that I wished to learn from them, I soon became an accepted part of the team. I also ensured that I went on social events, and actively participated in any team events that were taking place, such as a recent charity netball game. This team working helps to generate new ideas, both from me and my colleagues. For example, recently we had to move a lot of stock from one location to another. I suggested one method of moving it, which was accepted, but another member of staff pointed out that by loading the trolley in a slightly different way, the process could be simplified even further. So that was what we did (team working sub-behaviour 2.8).

My own particular role within the store team is working on the checkout. I am frequently required, however, to help out other departments. Although we have our own targets, the store as a whole has others to hit, and we all recognise that to do so we have to pull together. For example, if the administration department do not order the correct stocks, then we do not have the right product to sell to customers. Nobody would be able to do their own job in that case. We therefore all have to work as a team. Everyone is interdependent on everybody else (team working sub-behaviour 2.10).

Results

This is why I believe I am experienced in the area of teamwork. Working in such an environment, which is constantly moving, and working different hours to other members, we get along amazingly well. Between the small teams inside the store there is a friendly atmosphere, and in-store competitions are often the subject of good-natured rivalry. We all realise that we're there to achieve a common purpose, and that the only way we can achieve that common purpose is by working as individuals in support of our teams.

Can you tell us about when you have dealt with the needs of a customer?

In this competency, assessors are looking for evidence of your ability to look at issues from the customer's point of view and do everything in your power to help solve a genuine problem or misunderstanding.

Circumstances

I work as a shop assistant in a dry-cleaning store. It is based on a high street, and is extremely busy. We are part of a high street chain and have targets along with policies and procedures to comply with. Having said that, the company is proud of its attitude to customer service, and staff are allowed a certain amount of latitude to solve customer problems depending upon the circumstances.

Actions

Obviously the aim of the organisation is to make a profit. Having said that, the company philosophy is that it is better to make a fair profit by looking after the customer. Our customer service policy is based on this principle. Last week, I was working in the shop by myself when a customer came in complaining about a very expensive dress that had been given to us for cleaning. The customer stated that when she got the dress home it was marked in such a way as to make it unwearable. The customer was extremely upset, and initially demanded that the dress be replaced. The cost of cleaning it was actually quite small and the replacement value would have been well in excess of the amount that the company would have made by cleaning it (customer focus sub-behaviour 3.1).

Having said that, I was very conscious of customer satisfaction. I explained to the customer that because it was such an expensive dress, I could not immediately authorise the cost of buying a new one. I explained to her instead that I would refer the matter to a manager upon their return. The manager would normally send the dress to head office, and they would decide on what action would be taken. I told the customer that this would take an average of 10 days to actually do. The customer understood this, but was concerned because they actually wanted the dress for a party that weekend (customer focus sub-behaviour 3.2 and 3.3). *Once she had gone home, I thought about any other solutions I could come up with to try and sort out the customer with a dress for the party. I knew that the company would not allow me to authorise the purchase of a new dress, because as I have said it was a very expensive one. I looked at the damage closely, and noticed that the damage was actually on a rear seam. Although I am not an expert in dress repair, I wondered if it would be possible to get the dress repaired, rather than replaced. I consulted the customer, and asked her how she would feel if we actually repaired the dress. She stated she would be quite happy with this* (customer focus sub-behaviour 3.4).

Effectively the customer wanted the dress for the weekend, so as soon as my colleagues returned to the shop from their lunch break, I decided to take responsibility for taking the dress across the street to a seamstress (customer focus sub-behaviour 3.5).

As it transpires, the dressmaker estimated it would not cost much to repair the garment. As the estimates were so reasonable, I decided to take responsibility and arranged for the work to be done. I also asked the dressmaker what she thought might have caused the problem. She thought that at some stage of the dry-cleaning process, something had caught on the hem, so the fault was probably indeed with the company. I took the repaired dress back to the shop, spoke on the phone to the customer, and apologised for the incident (customer focus sub-behaviour 3.6).

I explained that the damage to the dress was in fact our fault, and the actions I had taken to get the dress repaired. I was able to tell her the dress was already repaired, and arrange for her to come into the shop to pick it up (customer focus sub-behaviour 3.7).

When the customer arrived to pick up the dress on the following afternoon, it was in an as new condition, repaired completely, and presented to her in a free dress cover I prepared. I also explained that as it was our mistake, not only would we clean it free of charge on this occasion, but I gave her a number of gift vouchers. She felt by the end of the conversation that I had treated her with respect and dignity (customer focus sub-behaviour 3.8).

Working in the shop has taught me to consider carefully my attitudes and behaviours. For example, I personally may not find someone's taste in clothing suits mine, but I have realised that commenting on this can easily cause offence. At the same time, I have learnt to treat other people's property with respect, as it may have sentimental or other value attached to it (customer focus sub-behaviour 3.9)

Working in the store has disciplined me to always appear professional. Doing so, in my case by being smartly dressed, knowledgeable and polite, clearly impacts on our business. In fact, last year I was awarded the employee of the week award on two separate occasions (customer focus sub-behaviour 3.12).

Results

Because of my approach on this occasion, the customer wrote in a letter of thanks to the shop, which my manager commented on. The company did not make any money on that particular transaction, and in fact may have lost a little by the time the cost of the repair was factored in, but in the long run, that lady will tell her friends about the customer service she received. I am sure we will get a great deal of business because of it. I personally feel I did the right thing by showing the customer how much they were valued.

Can you tell us about when you have shown good communication skills?'

In this competency, assessors are looking for evidence of your ability to communicate with other people. This area will probably be assessed by the way in which you speak and write as opposed to being a separate question, but at least by preparing it you are covering potential angles just in case. Remember here that communication involves being able to listen to other people as well as being able to tell others what you want.

Circumstances

I work in a call centre for a large well-known telecommunications company. I am a supervisor on a unit of 10 staff, and am responsible for meeting unit targets, as well as managing the staff. In addition to this, however, I am sometimes called upon to train new staff members. The way the training system works is that new entrants to the organisation will attend a full-time training course. Because my specialism is customer service, I am often asked to give them a presentation on the customer services side of the operation.

Actions

I go about this a number of ways. Firstly, once I know I am with a certain group, I will check which particular part of the customer service operation they will be working on. I have prepared a number of simple-to-use guides which I have stored as Word documents on my computer, in order that I can give them to staff attending the course as a means of reference (communication sub-behaviour 4.1).

I am conscious that I need to ensure that people understand what I say, as they often come from different backgrounds and with differing levels of educational attainment. For example, some are graduates who have not been in the workplace before, others are people approaching retirement age. In order to check that they have taken on board what I have said, I will often ask them to repeat information back to me in their own words. For example, if I explain a certain policy to do with returned goods, I will ask member of staff to explain it back to the rest of the group. In this way, I know that the information has been properly understood by the student (communication sub-behaviour 4.3).

As part of this training, I will often start up discussions between individual groups in order to examine such concepts as customer service. With such a wide range of people, their ideas of customer service vary widely. Therefore, I have to ensure that each group is always prepared to listen to the other one, and treat their opinions with respect. This can be quite difficult sometimes. For example, often the younger members of the team can be extremely profit orientated, whilst the older members of the team are more customer focused. As a trainer, I have to ensure both groups have their say, but also fully understand the ethos of the company (communication sub-behaviour 4.4).

Obviously, when I am working in this environment it is sometimes necessary to use different ways of speaking to people, depending upon the audience. For example, sometimes we show groups of teenagers around the call centre, with a view to letting them see what the working environment can be like. When speaking to groups like these, I ensure that I do not use any technical phrases, and I try to come across quite informally, in a manner to which they can relate. Conversely, if a senior manager from a different call-centre is speaking to me, I know that I am able to use much more technical terms, and indeed would be expected to do so as a mark of professionalism (communication sub-behaviour 4.5).

Because of my work in the call centre, working on telephones, speaking to scores of different people everyday, along with my training work, I feel I'm a confident speaker. In particular, with respect to the training side of my job, I often have to adopt an authoritative tone. For example, sometimes a new member of staff will disagree with company philosophy on one particular issue, such as last week when one member of staff felt our refund policy was too generous. After debating the points with her for a few minutes, I then had to give a further definitive answer in terms of that policy, and instruct her clearly on what she needed to do in order to comply with this (communication sub-behaviour 4.7).

When working with my team, I believe that on many occasions, although not all, it is necessary to explain some of my decisions. For example, recently I refused to support a team member's application for promotion. They were clearly very unhappy at this, and initially they had considered putting in a grievance against me. I explained to them that I needed to be sure that they fulfilled the requirements of the job, and that I felt they did not have the experience, qualifications and background for the post. When I explained to them clearly the reasons for my not supporting their application, and evidenced it, they realised themselves that they were not suitable. They accepted the decision as they realised that even had they gone forward to the next selection stage, they would have been unsuccessful (communication sub-behaviour 4.8).

I have found that by explaining to the team exactly what is required of them, they respond much more effectively. Each Monday, I hold a team briefing, where I explain our goals for the week, and what tactics we will be using to achieve them. I then invite staff comments and ask for any suggestions or improvements. At the conclusion of this meeting, everyone involved knows exactly what is expected of them, and how they will meet those requirements (communication sub-behaviour 4.9).

In addition, I have found it far easier in the long run to deal with issues as they arise. For example, I recently had cause to speak to a member of staff who was being persistently late. As this staff member was quite a good friend, I realised that it would be slightly awkward to speak to them about this breach of work ethic. However, I felt it would be unprofessional of me not to deal with it. On the next occasion they were late, I immediately asked them to come to the office to see me. I made it quite clear that their behaviour was unacceptable and outlined the consequences that would follow if they were late again. The result of this was that they have not been late since, and I gained the respect of the department by dealing with the issue immediately (communication sub-behaviour 4.10).

Results

Because of my experience, therefore, I feel I am a good communicator. On the feedback sheets that students are asked to complete after my training courses, I always achieve a very high rating for my communication style and presentation. Students also often comment on my approachability. I have been complimented by senior managers on my communication style, and recently a member of my staff told me that they respect me more because I deal with things there and then, rather than avoiding the subject.

Can you tell us about when you have had to work to overcome a problem?

In this competency, assessors are looking for evidence of your ability to identify a problem or issue, and then do something positive to deal with it.

This question is really about customer service. Note that in this example, the competencies have been placed in an order to suit the flow of the answer, which is perfectly acceptable.

Circumstances

I work in a bank usually on the front counter, meeting customers, taking in money, paying into accounts and generally dealing with customer issues and problems. It is a routine part of my job to deliver customer service, part of which involves dealing with people's problems as they arrive at the bank. I have worked there for about five years, and pride myself on my ability to do my very best for customers. Last month, I was working on my normal place on the front counter when a member of the public came in. He had an account with us and had his monthly wages paid in direct to that account. His household expenses were then paid out of that particular account. The customer was very angry, as he had tried to use his bank card to buy something that day and discovered that it had been refused. When he had checked his balance with us, it indicated that his wages had not been paid into the bank. He had phoned his company, who had told him it was the bank's fault. He was therefore very angry, and wanted to make a complaint as well as get some money out.

Actions

Initially the customer was demanding that we pay several direct debits due on that particular day, and also allow him to take money out of the account. On the face of it, this seemed to be an entirely reasonable demand. However, upon checking his account there appeared to be no money in it. I therefore had to make a decision about what to do in terms of paying his direct debits and giving him his money, which did not appear to be in the account. I decided to investigate the matter further before making a decision (team working sub-behaviour 5.4).

I gathered as much information about his account as was possible – his account number, how much money should come in each month, the source from which it should have arrived and so on. I also checked that no payments had been made on his behalf by ourselves, and asked him what was the effect of these not taking place. In short, I found that his mortgage had not been paid either, which meant he would be liable for a large additional fee for missing that payment (team working sub-behaviour 5.10).

I went through the various computer systems that the bank possesses, searching for the customer's previous credit history, and seeing if there were any further explanations on the system as to why this error had occurred. For example, I checked various databases to ensure there were no problems with past payments, nor past credits. I then phoned the customer's employer and confirmed that the payments had in fact been made. It quickly became clear that the payment had been made by the employer, but it had not arrived at the bank (team working sub-behaviour 5.11).

I had to collect all this information as quickly as possible. I double checked the account numbers, dates and amounts, as well as customer details, to ensure that the information I was gathering was in fact correct (team working sub-behaviour 5.8).

*By this point, I had quite a lot for information, some of which was relevant and some which was not. For example, looking back in his file there were quite a few entries regarding how his address had been mixed up from when he moved house several years before. This was clearly not important in this particular case (*team working sub-behaviour 5.9).

The gentleman was quite upset at this stage, and was almost on the point of being rude. I reminded myself, however, that he was under stress, and decided that I would not take sides until I knew the full facts of the matter. As he was being rude to an extent, another of my colleagues had decided to be as unhelpful as possible. I had to take her to one side, and remind her that this was completely unfair, and that she should actually keep an open mind about the situation until the full facts of the matter were established. I pointed out that if this had happened to her, she too would be unhappy (team working sub-behaviour 5.3).

Having gathered all this information, there was no doubt that the bank had made a mistake. Because of this, we had clearly caused the customer some upset and distress. I therefore came to the conclusion that I was morally obliged to sort out this problem fairly, and there and then. The situation was causing him unnecessary stress, and I needed to take action immediately to relieve this (team working sub-behaviour 5.7).

I realised that there were certain factors in this situation that could not be changed. Because of the direct debit problem, the gentleman had incurred fees from other lenders. This was a simple fact and could not be changed. However, the gentleman would therefore be out of pocket, and this certainly could be changed. In addition, he had no access to money for the weekend, a situation that could also be remedied. I decided that the best way to deal with this would be to arrange access in some way to his account for money for the weekend (team working sub-behaviour 5.5).

I realised that the main problem here was the fact that the payment of his wages had been made by his employer, but had failed to arrive. The knock-on effects of this were symptoms of the main problem. This was the fact that for some reason our computer system did not record the payment. I realised that any solution would have to include not just paying the gentlemen his money back, but ensuring that such a problem did not happen again (team working sub-behaviour 5.6).

Having got to this stage, I checked company policy as to what could be done in this particular matter. Normally, in these circumstances, the customer would have to wait for the funds to be cleared or traced before any money could be released to them. I felt, however, that this was unfair and not very flexible. Upon reading further into the policy, however, it did say that under certain exceptional circumstances, for long-standing customers with a good banking record, if a member of staff believed that a genuine oversight had been the reason for the problem, they could credit the account with uncleared funds and cancel any additional charges (team working sub-behaviour 5.2).

Taking these factors into account therefore, I told the customer I would be crediting his account with the facility to go overdrawn to the amount of the missing money. This would effectively mean that payments would be made on his behalf and he could take money out until his wages had in fact arrived. I also told him that as the whole thing was our fault, there would clearly be no bank charges involved. I also informed him that the bank would pay any other charges incurred as a result of our mistake. I then phoned the computer department, and asked them to double check the computer path that should have been used by his firm's money arriving with us. Almost immediately, they phoned me back to say they had spotted an inputting mistake on the system, and as a result of that, they were able to repair the fault and guarantee it would not happen again (team working sub-behaviour 5.1).

Results

Initially, the customer was extremely angry with the bank, and wanted to close his account and take it elsewhere. Because I took a genuine interest in his problems and was so professional about dealing with the short- and long-term implications of the issue, the gentleman was extremely pleased with our customer service. A few days later, a letter arrived from the customer to my manager. In the letter, the customer thanked me for my efforts, and was clearly satisfied that the problem that caused the issues in the first place had been resolved. This was because I believe he had received extremely good levels of customer service from me in terms of recognising and rectifying the problem.

Can you tell us about when you have had to take responsibility for an issue?

In this competency, assessors are looking for evidence of your ability to deal with an issue, ideally by doing more than would be reasonably expected of you. Good examples will often involve you going beyond what the average employee in your place of work would be expected to do.

Circumstances

I work as a delivery driver for a large furniture company. My job is to deliver the furniture from the warehouse to the customer's address, to position it in the room of their choice, and occasionally to collect payment. In addition, if the customer has any complaints or issues with the furniture I have delivered, I'm responsible for notifying the salesperson back at the office and ensuring that any returns or collections are also arranged. A few weeks ago, I delivered a particularly expensive leather suite to a customer who lived quite a way out of town. Upon arriving at the lady's house, she looked at the furniture and immediately noted that a small footstool was missing. She was quite disappointed, as she was having guests round a few days later and wanted the furniture in position for them.

Actions

I immediately took responsibility for dealing with the problem. I assured her I would look into the matter as soon as I returned to the office, and see why the stool had not been included with the delivery (personal responsibility sub-behaviour 6.9).

On returning to the office, I checked the delivery note and saw that there was no mention of the stool on it. Having checked the original order however, I saw that the lady was indeed correct, and that she had ordered and paid for the additional item. In other words, it should have been part of the order, but had been missed off for some reason. The manager queried why I was looking at the invoice, then as she herself was reading through it, one of the warehouse staff took me to one side, and stated that he had in fact made a mistake and missed the item off my delivery for the day. He wanted me to say that there must have been a mistake on the woman's part, and to play down the impact the missed item had on the customer. However, I felt that this would be ethically and morally incorrect. I therefore told the supervisor that a genuine mistake had been made by the warehouse staff, and that I would do my best to rectify it. She fully accepted this, although I believe she did later speak to my colleague over the omission (personal responsibility sub-behaviour 6.1).

I told the warehouse manager I was happy to sort out the problem for the customer, as I felt that we as a company had let her down. I volunteered to take the additional item back to her house. This would mean I would be late finishing work, but again I felt I had to do it to be fair to the customer (personal responsibility sub-behaviour 6.11).

I therefore phoned the customer, told her what had happened and apologised. I also explained what I proposed to do, in terms of bringing the item to her house that evening if she was agreeable (personal responsibility sub-behaviour 6.10).

She stated that that evening would not be convenient, as she had to go out. However, we agreed a mutually convenient time the following day for me to drop the item off. I checked my work for the following day, and ensured I would be able to meet the agreed time (personal responsibility sub-behaviour 6.6).

At the appointed time the following day, I arrived at the customer's house and took in the stool. She was extremely pleased that I had kept my word and turned up at the appropriate time. She was also pleased at the attitude of the company in admitting its mistake, and doing its best to rectify it. She especially appreciated the fact that I was willing to deliver it effectively on my own time the night before. I actually think she was a little bit surprised I offered to do this. However, I am extremely proud of my attitude towards my job, and explained to her that, simply put, I did not want to let her down (personal responsibility sub-behaviour 6.7 and 6.8).

Although my job could be considered mundane by quite a lot of people, I like to do it to the best of my ability. That is why I was committed to getting the customer's delivery right, and delivered to her on time. Because of my commitment to the role, I have received a number of comments in my personal file from my manager commending my enthusiasm. I have delivered hundreds of pieces of furniture to addresses all over my local town, and not received a single complaint. Because of my attitude towards customer service, I have received well over a dozen thank you letters from various people. Because of this, my manager was happier to give me increased responsibility recently and recommended me for a small promotion (personal responsibility sub-behaviour 6.3, 6.4 and 6.5).

Results

A few days after this incident, the manager called me into the office and told me that the lady concerned with the furniture had phoned up. She was delighted with her furniture, and called specifically to tell the manager about my attitude towards customer service. They were particularly pleased that I had taken responsibility for dealing with the customer's issue. Had I not done so, and waited until the manager in either the showroom or warehouse was available to deal with it, then the customer's furniture would have been delivered late and she would have been disappointed.

Can you tell us about a time when you were put under pressure?

In this competency, assessors are looking for evidence of your ability to find a positive way forward under moderately difficult circumstances. It does not need to be a matter of life or death, simply a time when you were under time or other pressure to complete something, or else there were other factors involved which made an easy solution difficult.

Circumstances

I work as a supervisor in a fast food restaurant. It is an extremely pressurised environment, particularly at busy periods such as main meal times. It is very easy, if you are not careful, to let the pressure get to you a little bit. Recently, a customer came into the shop and placed an order for a large quantity of food. One of our most popular members of staff served the individual, and was tied up for some 15 minutes filling the order. This is a long time in a fast food restaurant. The order was difficult in terms of sorting out the correct items from a staff point of view. After about five minutes, the customer began to get irritated at what they perceived to be an unnecessary delay. In actual fact, some of the items they had ordered needed special cooking, and therefore would inevitably take longer to prepare. The customer started to make sarcastic remarks to our staff member. I was busy with another customer at the time, and only heard half of what was being said. I intended to go and speak to the customer to explain the delay, but could not get away from the customer I was with. All of a sudden, my member of staff suddenly lost their temper due to the sarcastic remarks from the customer and actually swore at them. This is completely against company policy.

Actions

I was now presented as a supervisor with a difficult situation. There was no doubt that the customer was being awkward and sarcastic, and in fact I had heard some of the comments myself. However, the staff member was also quite excited at this stage, and the two protagonists were set to begin arguing. At the same time other customers were beginning to show discontent at the increasing length of the queues, whilst other staff members were either watching what was going on and therefore not serving, or also making unhelpful comments in support of their colleagues (working under pressure sub-behaviour 7.3).

I realised that there was a potential flashpoint in the restaurant at this stage. I told the member of staff to go into my office to get him away from the scene, and got another member of staff who had not witnessed the events or had any dealings with the customer, to complete the food order. I apologised for the incident to the rest of the customers in the restaurant and considered what other actions I now needed to take (working under pressure sub-behaviour 7.12).

There were clearly two opposing viewpoints here. The member of staff felt that they'd been doing their best to help the customer and been the subject of unnecessary remarks. The customer on the other hand clearly felt that they'd been getting an unacceptable level of service, and had got so frustrated that they had continued making the comments. I realised that I had to deal with these two conflicting viewpoints (working under pressure sub-behaviour 7.8).

The customer was by this time this quite irate, and I asked to speak to him in a quiet corner of the room. I explained to him the reason for the actual delay, and the fact it was simply because of the size of the food order he had placed. I also apologised for the fact that my member of staff had used inappropriate language. He accepted this apology, and also conceded that perhaps he'd been overly sarcastic. By speaking to him in this manner, I defused any further confrontation. He left the restaurant quite happily, having declined my offer of making a formal complaint against the member of staff (working under pressure sub-behaviour 7.10 and 7.11).

I then went to speak to the member of staff in my office. As I did so, I was met by a small delegation of other staff members. They stated that in their view the staff member had been provoked, and that there should be no further action against him. As I have said, he was a popular member of staff, and they knew that because of the circumstances combined with this I could take disciplinary action against him. The staff were very unhappy about this prospect. However, I felt it was my responsibility to the company and its standards as a manager to take appropriate action (working under pressure sub-behaviour 7.7).

When I was speaking to the member of staff, I described what I had witnessed, and that I had a certain amount of sympathy for him. However, I also explained that the language he used had been completely unacceptable in the cold light of day. I was exceptionally careful not to side with him, or the customer. It would have been easy for example, to sympathise with him to such an extent that I did not manage my responsibilities effectively (working under pressure sub-behaviour 7.10).

After speaking with my colleague, he declared that he could not see that he had done anything wrong. He was adamant that the customer was wrong to make the remarks that they did, which I agreed with, but also that he was justified in swearing back at the customer. Clearly this was unacceptable to me and the company, no matter how much I liked the individual (working under pressure sub-behaviour 7.9).

I gave the matter some thought for several minutes, whilst asking the member of staff to remain in my office. Having thought the matter through fully, I came to the conclusion that even though he was a popular member of staff and had been provoked to a large extent, his actions, and more especially his attitude afterwards, were completely unacceptable. Although it was a very difficult decision therefore, I decided that the only course of action open to me was to dismiss him for misconduct. As I say, this was a difficult decision to make because of his popularity and the fact he was a good worker. I felt, however, that such a decision was necessary because of the poor example that had been set to other members of staff. The decision was deeply unpopular with his friends in the restaurant, but I felt it needed to be made (working under pressure sub-behaviour 7.4 and 7.1).

Results

Because I dismissed this individual, there was clearly a great deal of upset at the restaurant. At the end of the evening, I called everyone to a meeting in the training room. I explained what I had done and why. I outlined the fact that whilst I appreciated that there were certain pressures on the member of staff at the time, such a loss of temper was completely unacceptable and against the whole ethos of the company. This was especially true bearing in mind that we were in a location where there were lots of children. Although two members of staff still felt my decision to be wrong, the rest of them discussed it over a period of about half an hour and came to understand why I had taken the action I had. The next day, some of them apologised to me for their initially hostile attitudes the previous night. We now have an excellent working relationship once again. This was an undoubtedly difficult decision to make, but I felt that I did the right thing in terms of upholding standards.

GENERAL ADVICE

What to do if it all goes wrong

Anyone can have a bad interview. It happens to the best of us. Anybody can have an off-day, a mental block, or little sleep the night before and produce a performance which does not do them justice. Clearly, in an ideal world this will not happen to you on your interview day. Sometimes though, fate takes a hand. If it does, you can only be philosophical about it.

Reducing the chances of a poor performance

Most poor performances, though, are the fault of the candidate. The best way to start, or at least reduce, the chances of a disaster taking place is preparation. The more prepared you are, the more confident you will be and you'll lessen the likelihood that you will stumble and fall.

Using thinking time

If the worst does happen, and you lose the thread of your answer, then you're far better off simply stopping talking for a moment. Take a sip of water if there is one available in the room. Use these few seconds as thinking time. Try and collect your thoughts. Do you remember the question you were asked? If so, can you identify the point at which your answer started to veer away from the subject?

If you can recall this point, apologise to the interviewer, and start again from that point. If you have simply lost track of the question completely, and that is extremely common in interviews, swallow your pride, explain to the assessor that you have lost your train of thought, and ask them to repeat the question. It is better to do this than carry on spouting a load of rubbish. You will get more credit for this than trying to bluff.

Dealing with the artificial pressure

Clearly it is better not to be in this position, but if you recover, the panel will have respect and sympathy for you. It is those who simply give up in the interview who commit assessment suicide. As I have said elsewhere, if you cave under the artificial pressure of an assessment centre, how on earth can you expect the assessor not to be concerned that you would behave in the same manner on the street as a police officer or a PCSO?

SUMMARY

Formatting your answers using the method shown here is undoubtedly a difficult concept to grasp. However, if you can manage to do so, formulating a focused, five-minute answer that will score well is far easier. I promise you that you will immediately feel the benefit in the interview.

A final thought

One final thing to consider – if you do struggle trying to apply the principles I have spoken about here, how do you think you would have fared if the first time you gave any real thought to your answer was the moment when you were asked the question in your interview? Prepare thoroughly, and start now!

THE LOCAL INTERVIEW

Before paying too much attention to this section, you should first understand exactly what the local interview is. So far in this chapter, I have been referring to the interview that you will undertake on the national assessment day. This is the competency-based interview and will apply to all police officer and police community support officer candidates. Within the PCSO system, however, it is possible that the interview will be a combination of a competency-based session together with some traditional type questions. You should be able to find this out by asking the recruitment department directly. If it transpires that yours is simply a competency-based interview, all of the rules and questions as given in the previous chapter still apply. However, it is possible you will also need to prepare for some local interview questions.

Establishing if a local interview will be held

As a police officer candidate you should be aware that a minority of forces have introduced their own interview, normally (but not always) after the national assessment day has been passed by the candidate. I will refer to this interview as the 'local interview'. This interview is likely to be a mixture of traditional and competency-based questions. In the case of PCSO candidates, I would recommend that you also prepare for these questions, whilst police officer candidates only need to undertake the issues in this section if your research indicates you will have to do another interview.

Again, ask the recruitment department directly if a local interview will be part of the assessment process in the force to which you are applying.

What are the differences between the 'local' interview and the national one?

Although it varies from force to force, the local interview is normally a mix of old and new style of questions. So, everything that has been said so far about national interviews must also be considered and prepared for. However, the local interview is also likely, although by no means guaranteed, to cover other areas. Because of this, you do need to prepare for these additional questions. It is far better to spend time preparing and not need the work, rather than not to do the work and need it.

The local interview format

The local interview will probably last anywhere between 20 and 45 minutes. There will be up to 12 main questions, but as ever there are likely to be probing questions from the panel in addition to these. There is no time limit per question. The interviewer will instead allow you to speak in your own time, although if you seem to be taking too long, they will find some way to move you on to the next question. The competency questions that will come up in the interview will be of the same type as the ones already discussed. I will now explain the 'soft' questions, which cover different aspects of your motivation as an individual. Remember, though, that your answers are still being assessed against the core competencies.

What follows is a general examination of the types of question that come up regularly at interview. The way they are phrased can be altered in a thousand ways; however, if you prepare answers for them, you will find that at least some will come up in one form or another and you will be much better placed to tackle them.

THE MOST COMMON THEMES

I have included a list of potential questions at the end of this chapter, from page 222. Remember the questions cover common themes, and they can be worded in countless ways. When dealing with these questions, you need take this into account.

I will now cover the most common themes, and the kind of points you should be thinking about when preparing your answers. All of these questions are in addition to the competency questions previously covered.

The most typical question areas revolve around the following areas:

- Tell us about yourself.
- What skills and experience do you bring to the role?
- How do you plan your day?
- What would you do on your first day (week or month)?
- How do you deal with conflict?
- How do you relax at the end of the day?
- How would you deal with inappropriate conduct?
- What sort of things do you think you will be doing in your new role?
- What preparation have you have undertaken for the role?

I will now examine each of these questions in more detail.

'Tell us about yourself'

This is a very common local interview question, and is partially intended to get you to relax at the start of the interview. You should prepare a brief summary of your life and career. Include a brief background, your employment history and main qualifications. The panel will already be looking for skills to mark, so your answer should portray you as a keen individual who is comfortable with speaking. If you dry up within 30 seconds, the interviewer will have reservations about your communication skills. There will also be a question mark over whether you have anything relevant to say. Plan something along the following lines:

I am Sarah Smith, 34 years of age. I currently work as a section supervisor for a high street bank. I have been there for about three years, and supervise four staff. Before that I worked for a housing department for two years, advising tenants about various customer service issues. I have an active social life, and enjoy going to the gym and socialising. I also enjoy spending time with my five-year-old son. I've applied for this post for various reasons, but mainly because I want to give something back to the community.

Giving an answer along these lines tells your interviewer:

- you have good communication skills;
- you have the ability to summarise information;
- what work experience you have that may be relevant;
- that you recognise the need to have good communication skills;
- that you have a social life away from work and are therefore probably a balanced individual;
- that you want to join the service for the right (community-based) reasons.

You also need to ensure you practise this answer numerous times, in order that you are able to deliver it comfortably and logically to the assessor.

'What skills and experience do you bring to the role?'

Knowing what skills you should aim to bring is easy. Simply use the core competencies. Pick out the four you feel most confident with. Refer to each with a very brief example. If you are a lorry driver, don't limit your thinking to believing that the only skill you have is driving. Instead, build on the fact that your job means you have to be motivated and self-disciplined, realise the need to obey rules and regulations, and be methodical about even mundane tasks. Humour incidentally, as I've said before, is not a core competency. Therefore, you will not gain any marks by saying that you have a good sense of humour.

A typical example may be along the lines of:

> *I am aware of the core competencies for this role and believe I can evidence them. For example, I work as a cashier at a local supermarket. I have to be good therefore at communicating with people and sorting out their problems. I deal with both complaints and exchanges, so have to be good at problem solving. Being in retail, I work with people from many different backgrounds and so I believe I have a good understanding of people's diversity.*

Your answers may need to be a bit longer – remember, mine are there simply to give you some ideas. The rules of 'evidence' can be relaxed a little bit for this question, as interviewers are unlikely to probe further for specific evidence.

'How do you plan or prioritise your day?'

All this question is looking for is an explanation of how you go about your normal working day. Ideally, your answer will show effectively that you would normally sit down at the start of each shift and consider the following:

- Prioritise your workload to complete the most urgent tasks first.
- Plan your day through recording meetings and events in a diary.
- Use your professional knowledge and experience of the role to ensure if, for example, you are patrolling, then you are in the best place to deal with issues. If there is a problem with parking at a local school as children are being dropped off, then you would ensure you were there at that particular time, not two hours later when the problem has sorted itself.
- Perhaps you speak to the previous shift or use some form of intelligence briefing to find out what has happened in the previous few days on your patch.

Never suggest that you will be unable to plan your day as it will depend upon what kinds of incidents are given out by the control room over the radio!

'What would you do in your first day (week or month)?'

This question can be phrased a number of ways, and is seeking evidence of what kind of self-motivation you have in terms of integrating yourself into the role. Consider the following kinds of actions:

- Visit every office in the building and introduce yourself to the occupants, asking what they do and how your job fits in with theirs.
- Visit and learn all the local landmarks, such as main roads, churches, pubs and so on.
- Introduce yourself to key local people, such as residents' groups, community leaders, head teachers, councillors and shopkeepers.
- Get to know your colleagues by speaking to them at every opportunity.
- Read previous briefings so you know what is going on in your area.
- Ask more experienced colleagues what they think the problems in the area are.

'How do you deal (or when have you dealt) with conflict?'

This question is looking at your communication skills, and your ability to cope with pressure. The completely wrong approach when answering this question is to start off along the lines of, 'I used to be Royal Marine, so can handle myself'. This will be considered confrontational, arrogant and aggressive. The service wants people who can recognise that:

- conflict is usually due to breakdown in communication;
- good communication skills can be used to defuse tension;
- listening to people will help them understand what the other person's

issues are, enabling them to negotiate with people in order to get them to calm down;

- only as a very last resort, should the minimum level of force required be used.

Conflict of course can be extremely minor in nature – for example, disagreeing where to go for lunch is a conflict. There is no need for it to be overly dramatic. Do not pick the time when someone wanted to have a scuffle with you outside a pub, as you should have had the common sense to avoid such a situation in the first place!

'How do you relax and deal with stress at the end of the day?'

No matter which way you look at it, policing is at times stressful. The foolish answer to this kind of question is to say that you do not get stressed. Everyone gets stressed to a certain extent. Think of some methods that you use to relax, perhaps such as:

- going to the gym;
- reading;
- talking things through with friends or family;
- taking the dog for a walk;
- sport.

Be very careful about mentioning going to pub after work. You most certainly do not want to give the impression you are a potential alcoholic!

'How would you deal with inappropriate conduct?'

This again should be an easy question. Here you must take exactly the same stance as that already spoken about with regard to role play and proposals, as well as at the competency interview stage. This basically consists of actions such as:

- challenge the behaviour immediately;
- explain why the behaviour is unacceptable to the offender;
- consider reporting the matter to management;
- support the victim;
- monitor the future behaviour of the offender.

Think of a few examples when you have done so.

'What sort of things do you think do you will be doing in your new role?'

Consider what you put in your application form in answer to this question. Leave out the dramatic and exciting parts of the role. I know you really want to join the job to get involved in high-speed pursuits and chase bad guys! That is certainly what I joined for, and I had my fair share of excitement. However, a far better approach is concerned with community and reassurance activities, as discussed in the application form section (Chapter 3).

'What preparation have you undertaken for the role?'

Again, consider your application form answer to this question and what was discussed in Chapter 3. Ensure you provide definite examples of how you did something positive to prepare. Remember that fitness training has been mentioned by everyone! Make sure you're able to answer questions such as the name of the Chief Constable, the number of divisions, the number of officers in the force and the force's objectives. You should find the answers to all of these questions on the force's website.

TYPICAL QUESTIONS ASKED AT LOCAL INTERVIEWS

1. What kind of tasks do you think you will carry out as a PC/PCSO?
2. Tell us what skills and abilities you feel you bring to the role.

3. Why do you want to join the service?
4. Tell us about the Policing Plan for our Force.
5. If one of your team mates is not doing their fair share, what would you do?
6. If one of your team mates was acting inappropriately, what would you do?
7. What have you done to prepare for the role?
8. Describe what you see as 'neighbourhood policing'.
9. Who do you see as the 'community' and how would you familiarise yourself with the community in your new area?
10. What do you see as the role of a police officer or PCSO?
11. Police officers/PCSOs must always be looking to develop themselves. How would you do that?
12. When have you had a disagreement with another person?
13. When have you had to make a difficult decision?
14. When have you had to show determination?
15. What do you think the force's goals and objectives are?
16. What would you do if on duty you encountered someone threatening you with a broken bottle?
17. What would you do if you saw a pensioner being bullied by local youths?
18. Tell us how you plan your day.
19. Has anyone ever challenged your personal style?
20. How do you deal with mundane jobs?
21. You are on patrol one night, and a drunken member of the opposite sex tries to kiss you. What would you do?

22. On patrol one night, a female approaches you and says that she has been kissed against her will, and is crying. What would you do?
23. When have you had a difference of opinion with someone?
24. How do you decide the order of importance of tasks?
25. Why do you want to do this role?
26. How do you cope with stress?
27. Tell us what you know about our force.
28. Why do you want to join this force?
29. How should we recruit more from minority groups?
30. When have you influenced someone to your point of view?
31. What in your life are you most proud of?
32. How would you deal with a difference of opinion with someone?
33. How have you prepared for this interview?
34. Tell us about yourself.
35. What do you think makes a good team?
36. What skills and abilities do you bring to the role?
37. When have you dealt with diversity?
38. Tell us about when you took a course of action that did not work.
39. What are your strengths/weaknesses?

Remember, these can be reworded a thousand ways!

SUMMARY

If you do have to do a local interview, you are only one step away from being offered a post. The interview must be treated with the same respect as the rest of the assessment process. As with everything, the secret is preparation and practice. Consider the questions here, and how they could be amended or rephrased. Get a family member to test you by asking you questions, and get them to put them to you in a different order. Practise speaking the answers out loud.

Remember, pass the interview and you are in. Don't get so near to being offered a place, and fail for the sake of a few hours' preparation.

9

The written exercises: reports and proposals

WHAT ARE WRITTEN REPORTS?

As a police officer, you will clearly need to put pen to paper (or finger to keyboard) every single day. There are few activities that you will carry out which will not require some form of writing. It is inevitable then that the assessment centre will use some method to test your ability in this area. When the system started out in 2004, this was tested by means of two types of exercise. Firstly, the candidate was given some form of information and asked to write a report on an issue that this information covered. The second exercise consisted of the candidate being given information and then being required to write a letter to somebody.

The proposal exercises

After a few years, this format dropped in popularity. It was replaced by two 'proposal' exercises. In these exercises, candidates are again given briefing papers. They must then write a proposal based on what they have read, providing a solution to a problem posed in the pack.

In essence, these two types of exercise are very similar. The guidance given therefore is equally applicable to both. The formats may change from time to time, but the basic premise behind them all is the same.

Ultimately, you will be required to complete two written exercises, each one lasting 20 minutes in total.

The format

Whether you are required to prepare a letter or a proposal (which is just another name for a report), the basic format will remain the same. In your role as a customer service officer, you will be given a set of papers to read through. These could consist of, for example:

- a letter of complaint;
- a report from a manager;
- a report from another member of staff;
- a newspaper clipping.

These documents will describe some form of problem or issue. You will then be asked to write a report for a nominated person, often your manager, perhaps a colleague or conceivably a member of the public. You will be given a specific period of time for this, usually around 20 minutes. You are free to split your time between reading and writing as you see fit.

As with all of the exercises at assessment, the writing exercises will have been piloted to ensure that a typical competent candidate can undertake them inside the time limit. So, if you run out of time, you are not doing it right!

The report template

Note that sometimes you will be told to write your answer on a 'report template'. This is a fancy phrase which simply means you will write your reply on to a form the assessors have designed. At the top may be a space to fill in with your name, the name of the person you are addressing the report to, and perhaps the date and title of the report. Obviously, you should complete these sections if they are there. In recent years, this has been sent to the candidate as part of the welcome pack.

Understanding the written exercise

The first mistake many people make about the written excerises is to fail to understand exactly what the exercise is searching for. It is not simply about being able to write neatly, using correct spelling, punctuation and grammar. Clearly, these qualities are certainly assessed, but the exercise is about far more than that. It goes almost without saying that your handwriting needs to be legible in order for the exercise to be marked. You'll be allowed a small number of grammatical and spelling errors, the number of which seems to vary depending upon the individual marking it. For our purposes, it is sufficient to say that you should write as neatly as you can and if you have doubts about spelling a certain word, use a different one instead.

What the written exercise is examining

The purpose of the written exercises, however, goes far beyond your ability to simply put words down logically and accurately on paper. As has been described, the format of the exercise is to give the candidate what amounts to a briefing sheet. This briefing sheet will outline the issue or problem, and the candidate is required to produce a written response to that problem. What the exercise is examining is your ability to:

- assess information given to you a written format;
- understand and summarise that information;
- see both sides of the problem;
- generate creative solutions;
- evaluate solutions;
- make a decision;
- convey that decision and the rationale behind it in writing.

Many candidates fail this exercise because they fail to appreciate these qualities. In many ways, the written exercises can be regarded as a role play, the only difference being that instead of having a role actor to speak with, the candidate's thought processes and decisions must be justified on paper.

Your answer may be grammatically perfect, written in an exquisitely delicate hand, with no spelling mistakes whatsoever. However, if you have failed to understand the problem as outlined to you in the briefing sheet, you will fail.

Time management

As with all of the assessment centre exercises, you must be constantly aware of the time. The length of the exercise is normally about 20 minutes. This includes reading time, but there are no set limits on the proportion you take to read through the material provided to you, or how long you spend preparing your written response. In short, you can if you wish spend 15 minutes out of your 20 reading through the given material. If so, you will need to prepare a pretty good response in the remaining five minutes in order to pass.

Writing speeds

Everyone writes at different speeds. It is therefore difficult to say for any given exercise exactly how long you should spend reading as opposed to writing your response. On average, however, as the amount of written material is roughly the same as that provided in the role plays, you should aim to complete your reading of the material in just over five minutes. This will leave you 15 minutes to write your answer. Remember, you can be marked only on the written response you have provided.

Candidates therefore must be extremely disciplined when it comes to time. As ever, you should take some form of digital watch into the assessment room with you. Start it when the assessor says go, and be conscious of how long it is taking you to read the document. Train yourself to be disciplined enough so that when you arrive at the five minute phase, or thereabouts, you are able to start writing your answer. If you do not become this disciplined, it is extremely easy to find yourself starting your written answer with only eight or nine minutes left.

Length of written work

People often ask how much they should write in these exercises. Again there is no straightforward answer to this. Three pages of indecipherable rubbish will score far lower marks than one page of relatively neat writing, with a well thought out, logical response. On the other hand, some people can write three pages easily. You have to be the judge of your ability. On average, however, most people will write between one page and a page and a half of A4 paper. I once had a student who was criticised on his feedback for writing too much, which is typical of poorly trained markers.

One final word of warning with regard to timekeeping. Several students have told me that during this exercise, the invigilator has marked the time off by using a clock on the wall. Whilst this has the advantage of everybody presumably being able to see the clock, it is clearly very difficult with an analogue clock with hands to judge the time exactly. There have been various accounts therefore of assessors misjudging the timing of the exercise, in one case calling time after just 18 minutes. Be conscious of the time yourself, and be ruthless with yourself if you are taking too long to read one section.

The limitations of the exercise from a writer's perspective

This exercise is basically a role play, but instead of having a role actor to speak to, you have a sheet of paper on which to put your ideas. As such, all of the same restrictions considered in the role play section apply. There are, however, some additional ones.

The exercise writer has to give you all of the information you need to complete the bulk of the exercise, as there is no role actor from whom to get further information. So, the old rule, 'every word is there for a reason', is even truer in this case. If a phrase in the briefing literature sounds a faint alarm bell, then act on it.

The only thing that the assessor need not give you is information that may relate to solutions to the problem posed. This is because they want to assess your creativity when it comes to solving issues, again just as in role plays.

Many candidates have a problem being creative, but you have to remember that the police are only testing you at a very low level.

How the exercises are developed

The exam writers will always be on the look out, as in the case of the role plays, for items they can borrow to write scenarios. So, read the news yourself and think whether what you are reading about would be a good scenario or not. If you see an article in the paper about two neighbours arguing over a shared driveway, consider how you would go about solving it. Police officers become very good at assessing situations, and then adopting a commonsense approach to solving them. This is what you should train yourself to do.

RECOGNISING AND DEALING WITH INAPPROPRIATE CONDUCT

The principles of recognising inappropriate conduct are again identical to role plays. However, there is a significant difference in how you deal with it here. For example, you cannot challenge the person who has made the comments, as they are obviously not in the room with you.

So, how can you deal with inappropriate behaviour, in whatever form you find it? Clearly, the only way you can do this is to bring your high professional standards to the attention of the assessor by building something into your written answer. A typical example could be that within a report you are reading as part of your brief, the member of the public complaining inserts a comment referring to the fact that *'women don't like to lift heavy items in case they ruin their makeup'*. Hopefully you will by now recognise this as a totally unacceptable, sexist remark.

The danger of ignoring comments

Some candidates try to avoid the issue of what to do next by simply ignoring the comment. This is likely to get you a dangerously low mark for diversity, however. You must therefore address it directly. The way to do this is to note it in your response, probably at the end, dependent upon the context. So, in the above example, if the writer of the report containing the sexist comment was a storekeeper in the shopping centre, I would respond at the conclusion of my proposal along the lines of

> *I note Mr Smith makes a sexist comment about female colleagues in his letter. I personally find this remark patronising and unacceptable, and upon seeing Mr Smith next week I will politely but firmly point this out to him, and remind him of company policy regarding inappropriate comments.*

Obviously, the way this is worded depends upon the comment and the scenario. Solve the scenario first, but do not forget to challenge the comment. Remember, unacceptable behaviour certainly covers anything racist, sexist or homophobic, but can also involve poor work standards, etc.

THE PRINCIPLES OF WRITTEN RESPONSES

In the same way as role plays, the written reports have a basic format that should be followed. Effectively, this format can be categorised into the following steps:

- Summarise information.
- Generate options.
- Make decision and recommendation.
- Explain why you have made this recommendation.
- Explain how you intend to put your recommendation into action.

Depending on the exercise, this may need to be varied slightly, but the basic principle will remain the same. Each of these points will now be discussed in more detail.

Summarise information

The skill of summarising information is almost a disappearing one these days. Police officers are required to summarise information accurately and concisely as part of their everyday duties. In this exercise, the candidate is given a relatively large amount of information to read. Remember that the response the candidate has to write is intended for somebody who may not have a full grasp of all the other facts of the issue. In other words, if you have been asked to write a proposal for a manager, you cannot assume that manager will know what the problem is about. At the same time, even in the real world, it would be unreasonable to expect the manager to read through all the correspondence that is attached to the file. Managers want to make decisions based on information, not necessarily to read through every single thing in front of them. This is where the importance of the summary comes in. This exercise examines a candidate's ability to look at several pieces of paper, each containing some information, and to be able to evidence in their answer that they have understood what the problem is about. This is why it is always advisable to start off a written answer with a summary of what has happened so far.

Using a summary effectively

It is important therefore to understand what a summary is. It is most definitely not repeating every single piece of information that has been given to you, but in a slightly different format. In any event, you would not have time to do this. In this context, a summary should simply be a very brief paragraph outlining the situation so far, along with what has been done about it to date (if anything), and the result achieved (again if anything).

Students on courses will often say to me that it is impossible to summarise the information given in the time provided. However, it should be remembered that this exercise will have been piloted by people who are at the level judged to be competent in the role. Therefore the average successful candidate will in fact be able to finish the exercise within the time provided. The real issue is that people fail to realise how brief a summary can be. A summary is defined merely by the length of space or time that one has to spend on it.

Example summary

For example, the Second World War ran from 1939 until 1945. However, if one had to, it could be summarised as 'a conflict started by the Germans, and won by the British'. If it had to be summarised in two words, it could be edited down to 'World War'. The point I have tried to make is simply that an inability to complete a summary in a reasonable time merely indicates an inability to complete summaries. It does not indicate that the original information was too long. It should be possible to summarise the information given in the exercise so that it takes up no more than three or four lines. This has the effect of showing the assessor you are able to take in information and understand its significance. It also shows you can put the information into a readable format that makes sense.

Summaries should not be judgemental, nor should they attempt to suggest options or outcomes. Your summary should not contain any thoughts that you have on the issues – it should simply be the main facts of the briefing information reduced down to one short paragraph.

Identifying the key issues

Having summarised the briefing information, the next part of your proposal should state what you now believe are the key issues in this matter. Look beyond the immediate symptoms or obvious problems and try to find the causes. Be quite clear to the assessors in the way that you identify these key issues. Do not be embarrassed to use the phrase, 'in my opinion the key issues to be addressed are'. Make sure you are quite clear as to what you see as the problems.

Example key issues

If the issue involves a parking problem, look beyond thinking that the cars parking in a specific place is the problem.

The cars may in fact simply be a symptom of the fact that the place where cars should park is being used for something else. To illustrate this further, imagine you are asked to write a proposal to stop people parking illegally outside the shopping centre's information office. Let us assume that you have been told that people constantly abandon their cars outside the centre in spite of the 'no waiting' cones. Let us also imagine that the information goes on to say that in the ordinary course of events, visitors to the information centre would normally park in a small visitors' car park. However, at the moment this is being used for the vehicles of contractors who are working on another part of the building.

The key issue in this case is not so much the fact that people are parking illegally to go into the information centre, but instead the fact that the car park has been given over to another use. Therefore, the solution may well revolve around moving the contractors' vehicles in order that the visitors can park where they are supposed to park. This shows better thinking than just giving out tickets to cars parked where they shouldn't be, although of course you may have to resort to that depending on the circumstances.

If you read a report complaining about people smoking outside the front entrance of the building, consider why they are smoking there to begin with. Perhaps there is nowhere else to go, and the problem could be resolved by providing a suitable space.

Generate options

Having now identified the issues, the next paragraph of your answer should involve coming up with solutions to deal with them. Ideally, you'll come up with at least a couple of possible solutions. This is enough to show the assessors that you are thinking creatively and will get you the required mark. Any more than three or four will not get you any further marks, but will eat into your remaining time.

The problems, and therefore the solutions, will be relatively straightforward. For example, you may be given a task to do with disorder in a particular location. Any aspiring police officer should have read enough of policing issues to immediately be thinking of such basic solutions as CCTV, security guards, wardens, passing police patrols and better street lighting.

If the problem is about parking outside a school as parents drop children off, consider such simple stuff as 'no waiting' cones, wardens, teachers being on the road at key times and so on. Try to involve the complainant in the solution if you can. In the school example, why not consider getting the head teacher to produce a leaflet for parents asking them not to park in advance of the commencement of ticketing the following week?

Being creative with solutions

The above are examples of creativity. However, try not to be over creative or come up with things that simply do not exist. For example, in the case of the town centre trouble spot, you cannot suddenly invent a team of 20 wardens with special powers who have never even been mentioned in the briefing. That would be considered silly. Conversely, in the school example, you cannot suddenly announce that luckily enough the council have just put road calming measures in place which will stop people parking where they should not. You have to be realistic.

The way to develop your ability to create solutions is to read as much about local community policing in your area as you can. You will find forces are very good at publicising ideas they have come up with, and these can be recycled for your assessment with ease. Additionally, if you get a problem at work, try to think what you would do to solve it, irrespective of your rank or grade in the job. If your email account fails at work, instead of just reporting it, try to think what else you can do. Can you use a colleague's computer? Is there an empty office that you can use? Can you get a friend to print out the document and fax it instead?

When stating the options, do not at this stage give any indication of which one you favour. That will come in the next section of the report. You do not wish to give the impression at this stage of being biased until you have fairly assessed the other options. You are merely aiming to gain marks for coming up with a number of workable solutions.

Making your decision and recommendation

Having outlined a number of options, in this paragraph you should now make it clear which specific option you are choosing. Be quite definite about this. It will not usually matter which option you actually pick, provided you are able to justify it. Quite often, there will be no right or wrong answer. The marks are to be gained in making the choice, irrespective of which choice it actually is. The way to lose marks in this section is to try and avoid committing yourself. As a police officer, you will ultimately have to choose certain specific options. If you are dealing with an incident, your choice may be between having to arrest the individual concerned, or not. You will have to choose – you cannot recommend both arresting and not arresting him! So make your decision and state clearly which option it is.

Explain why you have made this decision

Having made your decision, you should now explain why you have picked that option over the others. Clearly, the explanation here depends on the circumstances of each individual exercise. Note that some exercises do not require you to provide a range of options, but merely want you to make recommendations based on those already provided. In this case, if you are making the recommendations, simply say why you're making them over the other choices. If for example, there is an issue where people are struggling to find car parking spaces, although the car park should be large enough to accommodate everyone, if you want to paint allocated spaces on to the tarmac, explain why you're doing it.

If the reason is because there are no painted lines between spaces and you are painting the lines to stop people leaving large gaps thus losing capacity, that will be another probable mark. The assessors are looking for you to be able to justify why you have chosen a particular course of action. Policing is all about accountability. Therefore, it is not unreasonable to expect the candidate to be able to justify why they made a certain decision. The counter argument is, 'If you did not know why you made a certain decision, why did you then make it?' Clearly, this is a very difficult question to answer.

Explain how you intend to put this recommendation into action

Having made a recommendation, finally you should give practical examples of how you intend to put your recommendation into action. Try to evidence how you will take personal responsibility. If possible, try to include yourself in your customer service role into the solution. For example, imagine that there are health and safety issues inside the centre which have been brought to your attention. You may have made various recommendations on how to improve certain aspects of the centre's lighting, emergency exit signs and so on. To achieve maximum marks, it would be sensible and prudent to state that you intended to establish a health and safety committee, which you would be volunteering to chair. At this committee, the members would allocate the things that needed to be done and inspect the work later to ensure it had been done to the correct standard.

COMMON MISTAKES IN WRITTEN REPORTS

Poor time management

Without doubt the biggest mistake when it comes to written reports is, as ever, poor time management. You can only be marked on what you have written. So, assuming the length of the exercises is 20 minutes, if you spend the first 15 minutes reading through the briefing material, and come up with a superbly planned idea of how to formulate your response, you have a maximum of five minutes to put that response on paper. If you only get a quarter of the way through your solutions, the chances are you will fail because no one will ever know how good your original idea was. As has already been stated, you must be ruthless with yourself in your time management. If you think you will struggle to read the material in the time allocated, read more quickly!

Missing out information in the reading stage

This sounds almost contradictory after talking about time management, but it is essential to make sure that you actually read all the documentation. Imagine suggesting that an issue over a shared loading bay can be resolved by giving each company alternate days, only to discover in the last 30 seconds of the exercise that each store is committed to having deliveries every day, therefore making your solution completely unworkable!

Failing to show creativity

Because of the current trend in the police service, in many forces, when you first join you will be assigned to a neighbourhood policing unit. Here, you will probably be given a geographical area to look after, and be directly responsible for solving community issues. Largely because of financial constraints, in order to solve these issues police officers need to be creative. This is the purpose of this section of the exercise. I have discussed creativity previously. If your current job does not require you to come up with 'on the spot' solutions, train yourself by reading newspapers, studying force websites and public relations articles and actively quizzing yourself about how you would solve some minor problems that you have heard about. By doing this, you will start to force yourself to think of ways to resolve situations.

Failure to appreciate underlying issues

Going back to my visitor parking example on page 235, if the candidate's solution was simply to go out and give a fixed penalty notice to every car parked illegally, they would not really be solving the problem. The real issue is the fact that there is nowhere for vehicles to park. Until you solve that issue, you will not solve the problem of parking. Having said that, it is important not to lose sight of the immediate problem. Candidates should ensure that in addition to making good the damage that has already been caused in terms of public relations, for example, they put in place measures to ensure it does not happen again.

Failure to address inappropriate behaviour

It is very likely that in at least one of the written exercises, you will find some form of inappropriate behaviour or conduct which you will be expected to challenge. If you fail to notice it or fail to do anything about it in terms of your response, you will probably get an extremely low mark for diversity. This in itself can result in an automatic fail. You must remember to be extremely politically correct on the day. If you find any behaviour which causes you even the mildest moment of thought, deal with it. Be polite but firm. If you choose not to, the chances are you will fail.

Variations on the themes of written exercises

There are numerous ways of composing written exercises; however, there are a number of main types of format. Although these are superficially different, they all follow the same core principles discussed so far. On the following pages are three slightly different types of exercise. I have broken them down, explaining how each provides 'clues', and have outlined appropriate techniques to use when tackling them. These techniques will be applicable in one way or another to all forms of written exercise.

Using tables of information

In the first exercise, the exam writer has chosen to provide information in table format. The purpose of this is to see whether or not the candidate can take information from a numerical source and use it to solve problems. Again, the form these take will not be all that difficult. If a table is present, then it will have some form of recognisable pattern in the information or some definite conclusions to be drawn from it, otherwise there is no point producing the table in the first place.

The only possible exception to this could be where information contained within the table contradicts the view or perception of another source of information. In this case, you may well find that the writer is making vague, unsubstantiated allegations about some incidents taking place. However, the accompanying table will show that the reality is that these incidents are simply not happening. Your solution therefore would need to take into account the fact that you somehow need to correct the wrong impressions of the person originally complaining.

In Exercise 1, some tables are included. As you read through the exercise, try to identify the underlying issues, as opposed to the obvious problems.

Exercise 1: Complaints of potentially inappropriate conduct

Memorandum

To: Customer Service Officer

From: Customer Service Manager

Subject:

Dear Colleague,

Please can you deal with this matter in my absence? As you will see from the attached tables, I am concerned at the level of complaints arising from inappropriate comments or conduct in some of our departments over the last six months.

Each of the five departments listed on the table is of comparable size, and has the same split of gender, sexuality and all other factors. I am concerned that these high levels of complaints reflect poorly on the centre. Clearly, diversity training is expensive, but not as expensive as being sued by a victim of such behaviour. I would ask therefore that you examine the tables and provide me with some proposals to help us lower the number of complaints.

The first table provided gives a breakdown of the number of complaints from each department. I am at a loss as to why such differences exist. The second table shows the measures put in place by each department with regards to diversity. All have at least taken some form of positive action, or had a stab at it.

Please provide me with your proposals as to how the number of complaints can be reduced, along with any suggestions you yourself may have as to how the centre may reduce complaints further. I did ask your predecessor to do this, but then the silly young girl got herself pregnant. Typical!

M. Stone
Customer Service Manager

Table 1. Types and numbers of complaints by department

Type of complaint / Dept	Unfair treatment	Sexual harassment	Racism	Bullying
Stores	**4**	**3**	**3**	**4**
Administration	**0**	**0**	**0**	**0**
Security	**3**	**2**	**2**	**3**
Cleaning	**4**	**3**	**4**	**3**
Finance	**3**	**3**	**4**	**4**

Table 2. Diversity training measures put in place by each department

Measure in place / Dept	Display posters	Awareness Courses	Supervisors attended diversity management training	Clear departmental policy in place	Guest speakers on diversity topics
Stores	**Y**	**N**	**N**	**N**	**N**
Administration	**Y**	**Y**	**Y**	**Y**	**Y**
Security	**Y**	**N**	**N**	**Y**	**N**
Cleaning	**Y**	**N**	**N**	**N**	**N**
Finance	**Y**	**N**	**N**	**N**	**Y**

N = Yes **N = No**

What is this exercise telling you?

The opening paragraph clearly states that you, the candidate, are expected to provide recommendations to reduce the high level of complaints.

Each department is comparable, so therefore it is fair to assume each department should have similar numbers of complaints. This is a clue for a switched on candidate to be consider – are the complaints really around the same level, and if not, then the candidate should be wondering why not.

Furthermore, although specific figures are not given, you are told the breakdown of minority and gender is also exactly the same. This means that any comparisons will be fair. Obviously, if everyone in one particular department was the same gender, statistically the chances of sexual harassment must be reduced (although, of course not totally eradicated!)

The manager has clearly not made the link between the number of complaints received and the diversity measures that have been put in place in each department.

The manager states that all departments have 'taken a stab' at some form of diversity awareness. This half-hearted reply indicates a real lack of appreciation of the issues on the manager's part. This will clearly need to be addressed.

By asking for your proposals and 'any suggestions', you are being invited as a candidate to come up with your own ideas in addition to solving the immediate problems.

Finally, the manager has ended the report by making a sexist comment about the 'silly pregnant girl' who was your predecessor. Clearly, this will also need to be addressed.

Technique

Firstly, you need to briefly summarise the problem. Next, you need to draw up some form of conclusion from the tables to show that you recognise exactly what they are telling you. In this case, four departments have a broadly similar level of complaints. The administration department, however, stands out from the table with no complaints whatsoever. This is significant as we have already been told that the make-up of the departments is directly comparable. You should immediately be asking yourself why this is so.

Your answer must tell the assessor you have picked up on this. In addition, you also need to highlight the fact that in four of the departments listed in Table 2, the ones with complaints have only utilised part of the diversity training methods available to them. For example, the only diversity awareness action taken by the stores department is to put up a few posters. This hardly shows a commitment to true diversity. Your report should therefore identify this as a very clear issue. The administration department has had zero complaints probably due to the fact that it is very proactive in promoting diversity, using whatever means of awareness training it can.

It needs to be stressed that Table 2 indicates that a positive response to diversity training results in fewer complaints. The lax attitude of the manager, in terms of their reference to 'having a stab' at diversity training, will also need to be addressed in your report, usually at the end. After all, if the manager is not really committed to diversity, this is likely to be picked up on by the department heads (as it appears to be), and they too will not really be interested!

Your answer must provide recommendations to get the administration department's approach applied to every other department. You will need to be specific about how you intend to do this.

Consider how such action can be achieved. You should also be looking to build in some form of role for yourself in order to achieve these actions. Ideally, you may be able to suggest a role for yourself to monitor what actions each department puts in place.

From a creative perspective, as well as suggesting each department applies every element of available diversity training, why not also suggest that the manager of the administration department, who appears to be very proactive in this area, gives a talk on how they have achieved zero complaints to the other unit managers?

Finally, your answer must deal with the inappropriate attitude and comments of the manager, in a firm but polite and respectful way.

Specimen answer

Subject: Reducing complaints of inappropriate behaviour

Dear (Insert name),

I am writing this report in response to a request for proposals to reduce the number of complaints regarding inappropriate behaviour.

Having examined the figures provided, it is clear that four of the five departments have averaged around 14 complaints of inappropriate conduct over the last six months. This is clearly unacceptable. One unit, however, the administration unit, has not had any complaints whatsoever during this time period. As all departments are made up in a similar manner in terms of gender etc., I then examined the second table. This clearly shows that of the five departments assessed, administration is the only one to employ the full range of diversity awareness strategies. The other departments have simply taken smaller measures such as putting diversity message posters on the walls, and done nothing else. This is unacceptable and will have contributed to the high level of complaints within those departments.

I propose the following steps. All departments should immediately begin taking up all diversity training and policies available. This means that in every department, in addition to staff attending diversity awareness courses, supervisors should also be trained. Clear diversity policies should be introduced into each department, and guest speakers invited to address each department on relevant topics.

As suggested in the original report, this will of course have a financial impact upon the organisation. However, from a financial perspective, this will still be more cost-effective in the long run than being sued by a member of staff who feels they been discriminated against. In addition, as a responsible employer, we should in any case be striving to achieve a diverse workforce free from inappropriate conduct.

I recommend that a monitoring system be put in place to assess how these plans are implemented, along with their effectiveness. I would be happy to volunteer for this position if you consider it appropriate. In addition, I suggest that as an immediate measure, the manager of the administration department is invited to provide a presentation to the other managers as to how they have achieved zero complaints from their staff members.

I also wish to raise the following point. It appears from your report that you have been happy in the past to allow departments simply to make a token attempt to comply with diversity. I respectfully suggest that a more robust approach needs to be taken. In addition, I would also point out that your final comments in your report regarding my predecessor could be construed at best as patronising, and at worst as a sexist comment. It certainly provides a poor example in terms of setting the appropriate standards to staff members, and may even lead to a disregard for appropriate behaviour. I would ask therefore that you reconsider your views and form of words in future.

With thanks

Customer Service Officer

Exercise 2: The parking problem

From: Property Manager, Peter Jenkins
To: Customer Service Officer

Subject: Traffic congestion ideas at the centre's nursery

Dear Colleague,

An issue has arisen I would like your help with. You will be aware that the centre runs a drop-in nursery for people attending the centre. People leave their children at the centre nursery whilst they pop in and do some shopping. It is also extremely popular with members of staff who work at the centre during the day. Recently, however, an issue has arisen regarding a problem with parents dropping off and picking up children at peak hours in the early morning and late afternoon. The road outside the nursery is only just wide enough for two vehicles to pass. If a vehicle stops by the nursery, and a wide vehicle is coming the other way, a traffic blockage occurs. Apart from delays, this means that there is effectively no emergency access during the time that the vehicles are in place. We have warned parents before about this, but have found the situation gets better for only a few weeks, then returns to unacceptable levels again.

The road cannot be widened due to building restrictions. There are no road markings in place at present, although as the area is private land we can put down whatever road markings we wish. Again, as we own the land, enforcement by private traffic wardens is possible and we have the staff to do this. However, I would not wish to upset our staff until other options have been explored.

As it happens, parking is available about 50 yards away from the nursery. This is a space that was formerly reserved for senior management, and it does in fact have enough space to cater for the normal number of vehicles dropping children off. Few parents realise they can park there, however, because it is still signposted for senior managers only. In fact, the senior managers allocated that space have now moved to a different office and it is no longer used.

I am very concerned about this problem, and have asked the parents and staff committee who help run the nursery for ideas, but they have been unable to come up with any. I believe if the situation continues, an incident will take place where someone is involved in an accident or else an emergency vehicle attending an incident will be unable to get past.

Can you provide a report not to me, but to the Customer Service Manager, M. Stone, with some ideas as to how you would propose to remedy this issue? I personally feel it is these dizzy blonde women driving people carriers that are too big for them who are the problem, but that's just my own view!

Peter Jenkins
Property Manager

What is this exercise telling you?

Before thinking about the answer to this, remember what the whole purpose of the written exercise actually is. It is there to test your abilities to:

- summarise information;
- generate options;
- make decision and recommendation;
- explain why you have made this recommendation;
- explain how you intend to put your recommendation into action.

A poor candidate will view this as an exercise purely to stop people blocking the road, and therefore deal with it at that level. A strong candidate will understand the whole problem. In this case, the underlying problem is that people using the nursery have nowhere to stop when they drop their children off. The real problem therefore is the lack of parking, and it will continue to exist whilst there is a lack of appropriate parking facilities. This is why the short-term measure referred to in the report concerning the parent groups did not work for more than a few weeks.

Consider again what the exercise is actually telling you about the issues and symptoms:

- Parents dropping children off are causing dangerous blockages in the road.
- The road cannot be widened.
- Previous solutions had only short-term benefits, which is not good enough.
- There are no road markings in place, the implication being you can arrange for some to be painted in the road.
- Enforcement of parking regulations is possible, ideally though only after other measures have been tried.
- There is in fact nearby parking but few people are aware of it and think they're not allowed to use it.

- The property manager has used an inappropriate phrase regarding women drivers which will need to be challenged in your response. (Note that your reply is to another manager, which will impact on the manner in which you report this comment.)

Technique

The problem needs to be resolved by providing a realistic solution in terms of allowing parents to drop off their children. Ideally, this will involve a period of education followed by a period of enforcement for those who do not get the message you try to convey.

So, you should be considering the following in relation to the points highlighted in the briefing document:

- The dropping off problem is a symptom of the fact that no parking exists. Therefore, it is not sufficient for the candidate to come up with a solution to stop people parking, i.e. putting bollards in the road. You need to ensure the solution means people can easily get to the nursery.
- As the road cannot be widened, the assessors are blocking off an easy solution. This is meant to make the candidate think more broadly in terms of answers.
- By stating previous solutions have had no long-term benefits, the examiners are prompting you to include in your answer some form of long-term planning and monitoring.
- The fact that there are no road markings provides a clear opportunity to promote a partial solution. It would clearly be sensible to get some road markings painted, and some signs provided, but will people realistically take notice of them if there is no alternative for them to do anything other than park outside the nursery? Road markings are part of the solution, but only part. This piece of information also offers some other prompts for the candidate, however. If you're going to put up signs, do not limit your thinking just to a sign saying that parking is not allowed. It makes sense, if you're going to have an alternative parking space, to take the opportunity to direct people to that particular place.

It is probable that a weak candidate will take an easy way out in terms of solutions, and simply arrange for parking fines to be handed out. However, issuing vast amounts of tickets on one day will serve no long-term purpose. A truly creative solution will use the fine enforcement option as part of an overall package of educating people as to where they should in fact park, and then enforcing penalties against them if they fail to comply.

There is in fact a suitable car-park 50 yards away from the nursery which would be ideal. The briefing sheet gives a plausible reason as to why it is not used and so, clearly, any solution should involve using that particular area.

The exercise is looking for a long-term solution, so it is desirable to be creative. Any solution should deal not just with the existing problems, but also aim to stop them occurring again. In addition an ideal solution will have the candidate again volunteer to set up some form of liaison and monitoring committee.

Utilising all these elements therefore, it is possible to come up with a high scoring answer.

Specimen answer

Memorandum

From: Customer Service Officer
To: Customer Service Manager

Subject: Parking issue outside children's nursery

Dear Mr/Ms Stone,

This report is in response to a request from the property manager for proposals to deal with the parking issues outside the centre nursery. As I understand it, the problem is that parents are stopping for short periods of time directly outside the nursery entrance. Because of the narrow width of the road at that point, other vehicles are prevented from passing, with potential issues for access and emergency vehicles. The purpose of this report therefore is to suggest some proposals to deal with this.

There appear to be a number of causes which have led to this problem. As the road is not wide enough, parents must somehow be stopped from parking outside the nursery. The obvious solution would be to widen the road, but it would appear this is not physically possible. Previous solutions to do with enforcement and requesting people not to park there have had only temporary success. I believe that the real issue is not the fact that people are parking as such, but rather the fact that there is nowhere else for them to park at present. Parents need to be able to drop children off, and until an alternative is provided, no matter what short-term solutions are offered, the problem will not be solved.

I note that there are no road markings in place outside the nursery. I recommend that 'no parking' signs be erected or placed there in order to inform people they should not park there.

I also recommend that leaflets be sent out to all parents using the nursery, explaining that by parking outside they are causing a danger to their own children and those of others. I further recommend that once these leaflets have been distributed, the next stage should be to arrange for the parking wardens to place warning leaflets on offending vehicles, rather than issuing tickets straight away. I suggest each one of these phases lasts for a week. Following the second phase, I suggest that we actually start issuing parking tickets.

However, as I have already said, I believe that this by itself will not solve the problem. Instead it will only deal with the immediate consequences. I note that there is an unused senior management car park a short distance away. I therefore recommend that the use of this car park be changed so that it is reserved for the use of people attending the nursery. It has the capacity to deal with this. However, at present parents believe they are not allowed to use it. I therefore recommend that at the same time as telling people they must not park outside the nursery, we also inform them of the location of the new car park. So, the three phases will be to inform people via leaflets and a meeting that they must not park outside the nursery, to put extra signs up to this effect, whilst at the same time using each of these opportunities to tell them that there is another car park that they should use. Once this has been done, parking tickets can then be issued which should not cause any ill-feeling as we have provided a reasonable alternative for people to use.

I would also recommend that a parking group be established to put all these actions into place and to monitor the issue. I'll be happy to volunteer to do this if you think it appropriate.

Finally, I would note in the initial report, the property manager Mr Jenkins has used an inappropriate phrase regarding female drivers. I find this remark to be sexist and personally offensive. I will write to him myself pointing this out politely but firmly, but also ask you to note it.

Customer Service Officer

Exercise 3: Health and safety inspection of the centre kitchens

Memorandum

To: Customer Service Officer

From: Customer Service Manager

Subject: Health and safety inspection of kitchens

Dear Colleague,

I require you to look at the following report and provide me with a solution to the issues raised.

Last month, the kitchen areas at the centre were visited unannounced by Health and Safety Executive hygiene inspectors. Their report was extremely critical of the state of our food preparation areas. A number of problems were identified. Uncooked food was stored in fridges above cooked food, so risking contamination. The dishwasher needed servicing and cleaning. The areas behind the cookers were dirty. The kitchen signs, such as those for emergency exits, 'wash your hands now' and directions for fire blankets, were missing or obscured. When questioned by the health and safety inspectors, none of the staff knew what the emergency procedures were for the kitchen area, and this included the head chef. There was no system for ensuring food was used in rotation, so a risk existed that out of date food might be used.

In short, standards have clearly slipped over a long period of time. The inspectors are due to return in four weeks' time, and stated that if the kitchens are not up to the required standards, they will be closed down. This would clearly be extremely embarrassing, in terms of organisational credibility for ourselves, as well as costing us a great deal of money in loss of income.

I require you to submit to me certain proposals detailing how the situation can be rectified, together with any ideas you may have to prevent such an occurrence happening again.

Customer Service Manager

SOME GENERAL POINTS ON THIS TYPE OF EXERCISE

This is the classic format for a proposal exercise. It outlines a problem, and is looking for the candidate to deal with the issues raised. Typically, the candidate is being given the opportunity to rectify all the problems before the next occasion (or in this case, the health and safety inspectors' next visit). However, you should also be aware as a good candidate that the assessors will be looking to ensure the problems do not arise again. Although it does not happen in this particular exercise, sometimes you may find that on the first visit or occasion, there were certainly lessons to be learnt. However, it may be that not all of those lessons will be applicable to the second visit. For example, the report may be about a political rally in a local park where the Prime Minister recently gave a speech. Perhaps at that speech, certain things were not done in terms of providing facilities. Usually, the candidate is expected to suggest recommendations that will stop such things happening again the next time there is a visit by another politician. The twist in the exercise could be to make the second visit that of a local councillor. This means that whilst the candidate may still need to apply some of the lessons learnt for the Prime Minister's visit, not all of them may be applicable to the councillor's talk. By way of illustration, if you did not have enough stewards for the thousands of people who turned up for the Prime Minister, whilst you may still need some for the councillor, you may not need as many.

What is this exercise telling you?

- Initially, the customer service manager is reminding you that you need to solve the problem raised.
- The inspection by the health and safety inspectors has been extremely critical and the issues raised must be dealt with.
- There are specific failings in the management of the kitchens which must be addressed.
- Staff are unaware of key procedures and this includes the head chef. This is going to need rectifying.

- Reference is made to the fact that there is no system in place for ensuring that food is used by its 'use by' date order to ensure freshness. This is an opportunity for you as a candidate to be thinking of installing systems which will stop this happening again, and also an opportunity to tell the assessors you intend to set up such a system.
- Standards have slipped over time. This is a management issue in many ways and part of the solution must include dealing with this.
- The kitchens are said to be important as their closure would cause great embarrassment to the centre and impact on income. It is logical to suggest that the centre spend some money therefore to get the kitchens clean and safeguard this income. There is nothing in the note to say that you cannot spend money, so it is permissible to justify spending a relatively small amount.
- In addition to telling you again that your answer must contain proposals for dealing with the issues, it gives another prompt to come up with your own ideas.

Technique

As ever, you first need to summarise the situation. This should take no more than a few lines. Your answer should recognise that the state of the kitchens is a symptom of a larger problem. This larger problem, which amounts to mismanagement, needs to be dealt with. In addition but just as importantly, the lack of training also needs to be tackled.

Being a stronger candidate

Even a poor candidate will deal with the obvious cleaning issues. However, the stronger ones will also identify and, more importantly, rectify the issues over such lack of training.

There are numerous opportunities in this exercise to display creative thinking. The issue of training is one, and it can involve the use of courses or seminars to increase staff awareness of key information.

The kitchens generate income, so it is not unreasonable to spend a little bit of money to ensure their income is not lost. Show the assessors you realise the importance of the financial implications of such a loss.

Specimen answer

Subject: The kitchen inspection

Sir,

The purpose of this report is to provide recommendations to ensure the issues surrounding the cleanliness of the kitchens in the centre are rectified. At its conclusion, I will provide recommendations for your consideration.

The situation is as follows. The kitchens have been inspected by the Health and Safety Inspectorate, and a number of faults found concerning hygiene and labelling standards. In addition, staff awareness of such issues seems to have declined over time. The inspectors are due to return in four weeks, and if standards have not improved, the kitchens will be closed down. Such a closure will cause great embarrassment and loss of income to the centre.

In order to assure that the inspection is passed, certain actions need to be taken immediately. Clear labelling must be introduced for food fridges and shelves, so to ensure for example that cooked and uncooked food are not stored together. I would in fact recommend the purchase of another fridge to separate cooked and uncooked items. The dishwasher requires servicing, and a regular cleaning programme put in place. This again needs to be arranged as a matter of urgency. The area behind the cookers needs thorough cleaning. There are a number of signs in the kitchen that need replacing or renewing, particularly those relating to emergency procedures. In addition, the inspection found that no members of staff, including the head chef, knew what emergency procedures should be in place. A training programme must be put in place at once to bring knowledge levels back up to the required standard. A food rotation system must also be introduced, in order to ensure that food does not go past its use-by date.

Whilst these recommendations will solve the short-term issues, there are also some longer-term ones that require attention. The staff are quite clearly in need of training on the issues highlighted, as is the head chef. I recommend some form of day release course to ensure this knowledge is brought up to date, and to ensure standards do not slip again.

With regard to the cleaning issue, bearing in mind that the reinspection is to take place in four weeks' time, and that a closure would impact on revenue, I suggest a professional cleaning company be brought in to start the new regime. If this company can do an excellent job on the kitchen, it will set a standard for staff to aspire to.

I also believe it will be beneficial to have a dedicated member of staff to liaise between the kitchen staff and management team. The role of this individual would be to monitor the training programme and ensure that standards are maintained at a level to ensure future compliance. I would be happy to take on this role in addition to my other duties

Customer Service Officer

SUMMARY OF WRITTEN REPORTS

A written report or proposal is simply a role play in a paper format. It conforms to the same rules. Ensure you are dealing with the original cause of the problem, and not just the symptoms. As well as stopping the current behaviour, if possible repair the damage already done, and put a strategy in place to stop it happening again. If your strategy can involve you, so much the better.

Be conscious of any inappropriate behaviour and deal with it at the most logical part of your proposal, which will probably be at the end. Finally, as ever, be very conscious of your time management.

By way of practice, once you have finished the role plays in this book, use them as practice exercises to write a report summarising what you think the key issues are and how you intend to deal with them.

10

Preparing for the assessment centre

PREPARATION TECHNIQUES

The police service would have you believe that you cannot prepare for or be taught techniques for assessment centres. The advice that is most often given is simply to 'be yourself'. This is because the assessors really want to see you 'act naturally'. If they can see you in this unprepared state, then the theory is that they are choosing their candidates from a level playing field. As I have already explained, this is totally unrealistic. If a candidate's current job is that of a salesperson, they will probably have undergone role-play training and will naturally have an advantage in that part of the assessment. If another candidate is a personnel manager and therefore skilled at interviewing, they will clearly have an advantage in the structured interview. So the police theory that everybody starts equally is unrealistic.

Developmental training

The service also ignores the fact that most forces run some form of developmental training for officers seeking promotion to the ranks of sergeant and inspector, with the aim of helping them to pass the role play section of the exam. The role plays in the recruit assessment are simply a low-level version of the promotion examinations. If serving police officers seeking promotion are told by the service to develop in order to pass those examinations, it is clearly illogical for forces to say that recruits cannot. In any event, do a quick search of the internet and you will find numerous colleges and universities producing articles advising their students on how to prepare for assessment centres when seeking employment. In my opinion, if a university careers department is advising a student to prepare for assessment centres, clearly working on the basis that preparation can help to pass, that is good enough for me.

Preparing for the role-play exercises

The only effective way to prepare for the role play section of the examination is practice. By practice, I mean getting hold of as many role plays as you possibly can, and then acting them out with a friend or member of your family taking the role actor position. Practise planning using the CAR method, making sure you do not overrun on time. Use the time pressure as an incentive to be decisive in creating your plan and ensure that you can create a reasonable blueprint to use in the interactive stage. Train yourself to listen to the small voice in the back of your head that will begin nagging when you read a certain sentence that does not appear to be quite right. Learn to trust your instincts. If something in the documentation doesn't ring quite true, or seems to beg a further question, then do something about it!

Practising role-plays

Most of us need to practise the way we deliver certain phrases, especially with regard to challenging people. Devise a form of words as a challenge you are happy with and incorporate it into your practice exercises. If you role-play with a friend, ask them to change the scenario slightly each time you do it. Perhaps they can add some more details to make you ask more questions – this will stop you assuming that you know what the role play is about. Another good practice method is to tape record yourself. Listening to yourself on tape can be a revealing, if sometimes uncomfortable, exercise.

Use of language

Many candidates have grown into bad habits in the way they speak to people. There may be nothing wrong with some phrases that we use in the normal context of our lives, but they may well be unsuitable for a police assessment centre. Depending on your geographical background, for example, you may well use such phrases as 'love', 'pet', or 'mate'. These kinds of names can be considered patronising or inappropriate in a role play. If you use such phrases in your normal everyday speech, the chances are that under pressure you will do so in your assessment centre. Now is the time to start mentally correcting yourself, so that by the time you arrive at your assessment centre you are no longer using them.

Be especially careful in the way you refer to various communities. Research on the internet will indicate what phrases are acceptable.

Listening

Many of us are poor listeners. We have a conversation but we fail to pick up on the 'clues' people give us with regard to what they're really thinking. A common example is when we casually ask someone how they are today, and they reply along the lines of, 'Yeah, I suppose I'm OK', in an unenthusiastic voice. Think about the last time someone replied to you in this tone of voice, and what you did about it. The chances are you didn't do anything. However, in the assessment centre world, this would be a sure sign that the individual is anything but fine, and should prompt you to ask questions as to why this is the case.

Develop your listening skills

When you are with friends, every now and then sit back from the conversation. Listen carefully to what people are saying and you'll often see that whilst people may be exchanging words, they fail to understand exactly what is being said. The significance here is that you need to be able to pick up on the subtleties of what people say to one another. This is because you will need to act on these subtleties to ask the right questions of the role actor. This is an essential skill for police or police community support officers, and if you can learn it at an early stage, you will be better at your job.

Questioning

When speaking to friends, or reading a newspaper, try to get yourself into the habit of thinking about what you may be unaware of concerning the information you have just gained. Practise generating questions. For example, if a friend tells you that they have just bought a new car, don't settle for this small piece of information. Most of us would probably just ask our friend what kind of car they had chosen, and settle for the answer of it being, for example, a Volkswagen Golf. Train yourself to start thinking along the lines of further questions to ask such as:

- What colour is it?
- What specification is it?
- What does the specification include?
- How much did they pay?
- Where did they get it from?
- What was the sales person like?

Use everyday situations to develop evidence

Be aware of the interactions that take place around you every day. If you know your manager is about to speak to an angry customer, ask if you can listen in. Get yourself involved in situations – for example, where a customer may be unhappy with the level of service they have received, or times when you need to display team working, respecting diversity or working under pressure. Start keeping a log of these examples, otherwise when you come to prepare answers you will have forgotten what you really did.

If you see inappropriate conduct, do something positive about it at the time. The whole assessment centre process is based on a candidate providing evidence. If you can't provide it, you will fail. So start preparing now.

Do unto others...

Get into the habit of treating the people you come across in the way you yourself would expect to be treated. Think about levels of service you have received when in a shop or bank, especially when you have complained about something. Consider what elements made you feel good or bad. Customer service is not always about giving the customer everything they want; instead it is about improving communication, so that people understand the reasons why things have happened. Treat people, including the role actor, as you yourself would wish to be treated.

Interviews

Whilst preparation for every exercise is vital, its importance with regard to interviews cannot be stressed too much. Quite simply, if you do not consider your examples in advance, you are really going to struggle to speak for five minutes in the interview. As a candidate, you will know the main areas and the competencies you will be questioned about. You effectively have from now to the day of your assessment to prepare answers. If you choose not to do this, you are severely damaging your chances of passing the interview. Look at the question areas and prepare specific answers. Get a friend to listen to your answers, and have them tick off the individual behaviours as you are talking. Don't let your friend be soft on your answers. If the evidence is not there for a specific point, then you need them to tell you. It is better to be told an answer is not very good, and have the chance to rectify it, than have your friend instil a completely false sense of confidence in you.

By the time you get to your assessment, you should have written out draft examples of your answers dozens of times. Your answers on the day of the assessment should be almost automatic.

Written reports

Start reading a decent daily newspaper. Reading a quality newspaper will develop your skill of rapidly reading through articles and your ability to pick out relevant facts. Having read through a story, try thinking about how you would summarise it into a few lines.

Timing the exercise

When completing a practice exercise, be aware of the timing. Note when you stop reading and the point at which you start writing within the allocated time period. In this way you can work out how long it will take you to read documents of various lengths and therefore you can work out a comfortable reading and writing balance for yourself.

Spelling and grammar

Be careful of your spelling and grammar. Don't use words or phrases unless you are certain you know how to spell them correctly. If you're not very good at spelling, do something positive to improve it now before you let yourself down at assessment centre.

Getting value from the exercises

As a way of getting more value from the practice exercises, when you have finished the role plays, use them as a basis to write reports on the issues they contain. Observe how other people deal with conflict or problems. Try to identify solutions yourself, and consider what you would do if the problem was really yours to solve.

Finding out what is in the assessment centre exercises in advance

If you have understood the principles of this book, you will already know the general outline of what will happen at your assessment centre. However, in the age of the internet, finding out the specific content of the exercises is also quite easy. They have even been known to pop up on YouTube. This is particularly likely given the fact that the role plays are theoretically changed only twice a year at the time of writing, and that anything up to 7,000 people will go through them within a six-month period. Finding out advance information is therefore easy. Remember, that for a six-month period, the interview questions, role plays and written exercises are identical, word for word, no matter where in England or Wales you take the assessment. (In fact, although the police wish to change the examples every six months, they are running them for 12 months.)

There are two schools of thought as to whether having advance knowledge of the specific scenarios in exercises actually helps or not. These two arguments can be summarised as follows:

Advantages of knowing the exercise content in advance:

- You have time to consider what issues may be coming up.
- You have time to consider various ways in which the exercise may go.
- You have the ability to partially pre-plan.
- You have the ability to consider various alternative responses.
- Issues may be flagged up to you that you may miss under pressure on the day.
- The fact certain points are known to you can enable you to ask the correct questions.

Disadvantages of knowing the exercise content in advance:

- You are working from someone else's perception of what the exercise was about. They may well be wrong.
- Just as the perception of your informant may be wrong, your information about what the issues or facts are may also be wrong. There is a danger therefore you will be misled, either accidentally or deliberately.
- If you think you know what the issues are, there is a danger you may miss out on some other issues that your informant did not notice.
- It is very easy if you think you know the answers, and perhaps the solution, to forget to ask relevant questions. There is a danger therefore you could find yourself solving the problem, but fail the assessment centre because you do not ask relevant questions.
- It may be obvious to the assessors that you have been 'contaminated' by advance knowledge. Whilst they cannot technically fail you on this, they can always find something else to mark you down on, and you will never know.

Checking the facts

If you do obtain information, use it simply to enable you to think about various ways such a scenario may go. Do not assume that you have the full picture or that the person who told you the information got the answer correct. Check facts yourself, and most importantly, only deal with the information you're presented with on the day. Go with what you find in the exercise, not what somebody else has told you.

11
The marking guide

EXPLAINING THE MARKING GUIDE

The marking guide is far more complex than you may think. The following description is vastly simplified and takes a few liberties with explanations for the sake of making life simple. However, it will suffice for our purposes. Candidates' marks for each exercise are fed into a computer. The computer then adds up all the grades awarded and produces a result arrived at by a sophisticated scoring system. It is not necessary for candidates to understand this, but it is still worthwhile having an appreciation of the marking process.

Passing or failing

The first thing to understand is that with the exception of the written exercises, candidates do not pass or fail on a single exercise. Each competency is tested a number of times throughout the day but not in every exercise – the exception being the competency of diversity. This is in fact tested in every single exercise, which illustrates its importance in the eyes of the service. So, for any given exercise, there will be a number of competencies being tested and a number that will not. On average, each exercise will probably test between three and five of the seven competencies.

The average mark

At the end of the assessment the grades awarded for each competency are fed into the computer. It then examines how candidates have performed on average across the day in all the competencies and a grade is then awarded for each single competency. For any competency it is the average mark that counts. So, if you do poorly in team working in one particular exercise, you can make up your average grade by performing well in team working in another exercise. Again, the only exception to this is diversity. A single grade D in diversity is an automatic fail.

Achieving a pass grade

Every competency is then awarded an overall grade. To be successful, you must achieve the pass grade in all seven competencies. This is why people cannot understand how they managed to achieve a grade A in almost everything, but failed overall. Inevitably, such candidates will have underperformed in admittedly a small number of areas, but they were usually in the same competency. Therefore, whilst they may have a good percentage of the available marks, they have failed to display all seven of the required competencies and are therefore unsuccessful. The logic for this is that if all seven competencies are required to be a successful officer, then not having one means that you are not yet ready to perform the role.

A simplified marking guide

A simplified version of a marking guide is shown in Table 9. The competencies are listed down one side of the table, and the exercises listed across the top of the page. For the purposes of illustration, you will see that in this particular case the candidate has done extremely well in six of the competencies. However, in community and customer needs, they have done poorly on a number of occasions. This would mean that they have failed to reach the required standard in this competency, and would therefore fail the entire assessment centre, irrespective of the high marks they achieved in the other competencies.

Table 9. An example marking guide.

COMPETENCY	Role play 1	Role play 2	Role play 3	Role play 4	Written 1	Written 2	I/V	Verbal test	Number test	Result
Respect for values of others	B	B	A	A	C	B	C			Pass
Team working	B				B	B	C			Pass
Customer and community needs	C		D	D						Fail
Effective communication		B	C	B	B	B				Pass
Verbal communication	A	A	A	A			B			Pass
Written communication					A	C		B		Pass
Overcoming problems	B	B	B	B	C	B	C		B	Pass
Taking responsibility		B		B			B			Pass
Working under pressure	B	B	B							Pass

Note: Communication is split into two sub areas, written and verbal. This particular candidate has achieved a pass in every competency except customer and community needs. This means they would fail irrespective of how well they did in the other areas.

12

The final word: IQ and fitness tests

THE IQ TEST

On the day of your assessment, you will undertake two IQ tests, one verbal and one numerical. You will be sent practice questions several weeks before your assessment date. You will therefore have an idea of the kinds of questions that you will be expected to answer. It is an accepted fact in the academic world that the more IQ tests you complete, the better you will become. They are a specialist area in terms of designing and writing. I have not provided specimen questions in this book as there are numerous other books written by specialists in that particular field. A search of the internet will provide recommended books to buy. However, I will provide some basic advice on general techniques.

Answering the questions

To begin with, there is no negative marking in the police system. This means you do not get marks deducted for getting an answer wrong. At the start of the tests, you will be told by the assessors not to guess at answers. However, it is good exam technique to watch the clock closely, and as you get to the last 30 seconds of your time, just tick any box on the remaining questions. If you have five questions which you were not going to finish in the time allowed, statistically by guessing you should get at least one right.

Watching the time

Keep track of the time yourself. Always be conscious of how long you are spending on each question. The key issue here is self discipline. Divide the number of questions you have to complete by the time allowed, which will give you an amount of time you can spend on any one question. For example, if you have 30 seconds per question, make sure you stick to that time. There will always be the odd question that you cannot see the answer to under pressure. It will not be that the question is too difficult, it's just that under pressure we can all have mental blockages. If you cannot work out the answer within a few seconds, move on to the next question. You can always go back if you have time. Wasting excessive time trying to work out a single question will really damage your total score, as you may miss out on answering several easier questions.

Expect to feel pressured

Remember that you are not necessarily expected to complete all the questions. Part of the purpose of the IQ tests is to put you under a little bit of pressure. By putting in more questions than it is possible for a reasonable candidate to complete, the assessors are achieving this. Do not get overly concerned if you do not complete the paper in the time allowed – chances are nobody else in the room will be finishing all the questions either!

THE FITNESS TESTS

The police service fitness test varies slightly from force to force and from role to role. It is not the place of this book to prepare you for it as it is not connected to the assessment centre as such. However, to find out further information on it, I would suggest that you search the internet. Several forces have downloadable leaflets on the exercises you will need to do, and tips on how to prepare. It's not as hard as many people think so don't be discouraged if you are perhaps an older applicant or have not exercised for a while.

Prepare for the fitness test

My one comment would be this: from the moment you apply to join the service, you know you will have to do a fitness test. Therefore, start to prepare for it now. Even if it takes you a long time to get through the assessment, you will benefit by being fitter and so help yourself to live longer! It irritates me when people say things like, 'I have just found out I have passed the assessment, and only have a week to prepare for my physical'. I often find that people have submitted their application forms some six months previously, yet have done nothing to prepare fitness-wise since then. This can only be described as foolishness, or lack of self motivation. Make sure it does not happen to you. It is a shame to put all of the effort into passing the assessment only to be rejected on a physical.

The final word

By now, you will (hopefully!) have a far greater understanding and appreciation of the police and PCSO recruitment system. I have tried to explain as fully as possible the techniques required for each stage of the process. It is without doubt a difficult process. This should not put you off applying, however. If you can understand the principles contained within this book, you are in a far better position to succeed at the process than the average candidate. Remember, most of your competitors will simply turn up on the day having put little if any thought into their preparation.

Preparation is the key to success. It will all be worth while when you get your acceptance letter.

If I see you on a course, please feel free to tell me what you thought of this book!

Good luck.

John McTaggart MBA BA (Hons)

13

Example role-play exercises

GENERAL INSTRUCTIONS

On the following pages you will find the candidate's instructions for the named exercises below, as you would get them on the assessment day. As in the real role play, each one has its own title page and also lists the documents attached to the individual exercise. Following on from the exercises are the briefing sheets that a candidate would not see, i.e. the role actor's instructions and marking guide. I have also included a specimen plan for the sake of completeness.

The example exercises are:

- Abbot;
- Byrnes;
- Charles;
- Deane.

Notes on gender of role actors

All of these exercises are deliberately written so that the role actor can be male or female. Do not worry therefore when the text refers to people by last names or makes use of general phrases like 'they' when good English would suggest 'he' or 'she' should be used.

Candidate's instructions

Abbot

Contents

- Memo from Customer Service Manager.
- Letter from Abbot.

Memorandum

To: Customer Service Officer
From: Customer Service Manager

Subject: Local minor offender rehabilitation scheme

Dear Colleague,

Please can you deal with this matter in my absence. I have received a letter from a local resident, called Abbot. This individual is complaining about the above scheme. As a new employee, you may not be aware of this scheme. When a young offender is sentenced by the courts, if appropriate they are offered the chance of doing good work in the community rather than going to prison. In essence, the centre offers up to ten young offenders the chance to complete their community service in the centre workshop.

As part of our scheme, offenders make toys for disadvantaged children such as those living in places like Chernobyl, the town in Russia affected by a nuclear accident. In addition, we often take supervised groups of visiting children to meet the offenders in the workshop, so both groups get the chance to understand the other's lives and personal circumstances.

The scheme has proven to be a great success. There is the obvious benefit of the fact that the children are getting toys provided for them. However, research has shown that the offenders are often shocked by the children's stories, to such an extent that many of them become involved in charity work in some way and do not reoffend.

Despite what Abbot appears to think, or the rumours they may have heard, all of the offenders have committed very minor level crimes, and have no previous backgrounds of violence or of offences against children. Clearly, if they did we would never let them work here.

There is no additional risk to the public as all of the offenders are carefully supervised. Crime, by the way, has fallen at the centre by 5 per cent.

Reoffending rates are 20 per cent lower for this scheme than for other forms of sentence, and the scheme costs far less than prison. All visits are carefully supervised and monitored. A parent's permission is given before any meetings.

In short, this scheme is extremely worth while, and everyone benefits from it. The community especially is safer as there are fewer offences committed by offenders who have completed the scheme.

Please meet Abbot and resolve the issues they raise if possible. I would like to know how the meeting goes.

Regards

S. Bailey
(Customer Service Manager)

6 The Quarry
Newtown
England

Dear Sir or Madam

I am writing to express my concern at the new scheme I believe you have introduced allowing dangerous criminals to work in the centre. I believe that you have allowed a large number of hardened criminals to work in your centre, under some alleged rehabilitation scheme. I regularly visit the centre with my young family, and am extremely concerned at this. I have heard rumours about the kinds of crimes that these people have committed, and as a result I and many others are most alarmed at the thought of these animals running amok unsupervised.

I have evidence that the number of crimes committed in the centre has gone up, and it must surely be obvious even to you why this is so. Many of my friends are also concerned, and in fact I have asked for the subject to be brought up at a monthly local community group I attend.

As if this was not alarming enough, I am also told that these animals are working with children as well!

This seems to me just another expensive scheme from well-intentioned social workers. I believe that these people should be in prison, which no doubt would be cheaper and give them a proper lesson to stop them committing crime in the future!

I look forward to meeting you and getting your assurance that this scheme will be stopped in its tracks.

Yours sincerely

J. Abbot

Candidate's Instructions

Byrnes

Contents

- Letter of complaint from Byrnes
- Memo from Customer Service Manager

Memorandum

To: Customer Service Officer
From: Customer Service Manager

Subject: letter of complaint from G Peters

Dear Colleague,

As I have to attend a meeting today, can you please sort this out for me? I have enclosed a letter of complaint from G Peters. You will see for yourself why the customer is unhappy.

I have asked Cleaning Attendant Byrnes to see you in your office shortly. As far as I am aware, this individual was on duty that day and so is probably the member of staff involved. Byrnes has worked at the centre for some years, and has an excellent work record. Byrnes has a very old fashioned attitude sometimes, but keeps the areas of the centre very well managed. Take whatever action you feel appropriate against Byrnes, however – if indeed any is required.

I am unsure if Byrnes has been on one of the new customer service courses that we have just started running.

I am sure you will be able to resolve this matter to Mr/Ms Peters' satisfaction.

Thanks for your help.

Customer Service Manager

12 Glenside
Newtown

Dear Sir or Madam,

I am writing to complain about the manner in which I was dealt with recently by one of your staff. I had parked my car for only a minute whilst I went into the kiosk near to the car park entrance to buy a drink. As I got out of the car, I admit I foolishly emptied my car ashtray onto the car park floor. Upon leaving the shop, I saw one of your cleaning control staff standing next to my car. I realise you have the power to hand out litter tickets on centre property, and so prepared myself to receive one.

What I did not expect was what happened. Upon my walking up to the car, the warden started making comments to me about my level of personal hygiene. Initially, they were being extremely sarcastic, criticising my ability to walk, and then commenting that my car was nice and tidy for an unhygienic person, which of course I am not. They then started talking about my ability to read 'no litter' signs, and questioned whether I had learned to read or not yet. I found this extremely annoying, not to mention embarrassing as other people were present.

I had to stand there for several minutes and listen to this person criticise me in a sarcastic manner, before telling me I was free to go.

The attitude of this staff member portrays an extremely poor picture of your facility, and I will think twice before attending there again.

I do not wish to make a formal complaint, but do think I was extremely badly treated. I would not like to think of this individual treating other members of my family like this. I would have been happy to accept a litter ticket, even for this one-off thoughtless offence. It was totally out of character, and I deserved a ticket. What I was not happy about were the sarcastic comments.

I would like you to deal with this matter, and look forward to you informing me of the outcome.

Yours sincerely,

G. Peters

Candidate's Instructions

Charles

Contents

- Memo from Customer Service Manager
- Report from Security Supervisor

Memorandum

To: Customer Service Officer
From: Customer Service Manager

Subject: Allegation of inappropriate conduct against Security Guard Charles

Dear Colleague,

Please deal with this matter for me and take any steps you feel necessary to resolve the issue. I have attached to this document a report from the security supervisor concerning this individual.

Security Guard Charles has been a good worker at the centre for the last five years. They have always been good at their work, and been punctual and well turned out. It is disappointing that this specific issue has arisen. It is even more surprising given that it has also revealed that their performance appears to have dropped significantly, beginning three months ago.

Use of company information technology systems for personal use, and shopping in company time is obviously a gross breach of company policy.

In any event, such conduct is unacceptable, in terms of individual performance as well as the negative effect it would have on the staff. We simply cannot afford to have people who are turning up late for work, nor to employ people who are carrying out personal activities on company time. If you feel disciplinary action, further training or welfare assistance is required, please arrange it and I will support your decision.

Please update me on the actions you have taken.

Customer Service Manager

Report from J. Goldsmith: Security Supervisor

Subject: Incident and background concerning Security Guard Charles

Sir/Madam,

The purpose of this report is to notify you of an incident that took place last week concerning the above individual. Charles has worked at the centre for five years, and up until three months ago was a model worker. They were conscientious, totally reliable and trusted implicitly to work unsupervised. Charles was particularly good at dealing with youngsters in the centre, probably because of the fact they have a young family themselves. Charles works on the standard rotating shift pattern, so performs night and late evening cover.

Suddenly, however, three months ago, the performance of Charles suddenly dropped. Since then, they are constantly late, and they often appear to be scruffy. For example, often their shirt is not ironed, nor their shoes polished.

I have emailed Charles about this decline in work standards, and told them in no uncertain manner it was unacceptable. I have not had a chance unfortunately to speak to them in person.

The matter has now come to a head. Yesterday, I was in the staff room when I saw Charles using one of the company computer terminals that has internet access. I happened to look over their shoulder, and saw they were obviously doing an online shopping order from one of the large online supermarkets. Security Guard Charles had clearly been shopping online whilst on duty, as it was in the middle of the shift. This is against company policy, in terms of both the use of the computer for personal purposes, and also the fact they were doing this shopping on company time.

I was about to go and speak to them when I was called away, and am now off on leave for a week. Please can a member of the management team speak to them regarding this matter? Such conduct damages the rest of the department if not dealt with.

J. Goldsmith
Security Supervisor

Candidate's Instructions

Deane

Contents

- Memo from Customer Service Manager
- Report from Storeperson Deane

Memorandum

From: Customer Service Manager
To: Customer Service Officer

Subject: Staff report from storeperson Deane

Dear Colleague,

In my absence could you please deal with this issue for me? Deane is a storeperson in our warehouse section. They are an extremely competent worker, and well liked. However, they clearly have an issue with our policy aimed at increasing the number of females in work areas traditionally dominated by males.

Attached is a report that Deane has submitted complaining about a forthcoming 'open day' that the stores department is having. As an equal opportunities organisation, we wish to open up all areas of employment to both genders. We are traditionally under-represented in the area of fork lift drivers, in that of 20 drivers, none is female. The purpose of the open day Deane refers to is to encourage females to have a look around the department, and drive the trucks, with no pressure, in a supportive environment. Indeed, our latest trucks even have such driver aids as power steering. Whilst the day is open only to females, this does not mean that they will be given any form of favourable treatment at selection. All candidates will be judged on the same criteria, and applications will be accepted from both genders. There is no quota for either gender. Selection will be purely on merit.

This is perfectly legal under equality at work regulations. We have found in the past that if we hold general open days, females are reluctant to attend as the days become male dominated events. I do not wish any males to attend this event for that reason.

Deane has also apparently made some unhelpful comments regarding the process to Debbie Ferguson, which you may wish to discuss with them. Deane has applied on previous occasions to be a fork lift driver but been unsuccessful.

Please take any action you see fit to deal with the matter.

Customer Service Manager

Memorandum

From: Storeperson Jay Deane
To: Customer Service Manager

Subject: Forthcoming 'open day' for potential fork lift truck drivers

Sir,

This report is intended to highlight my concerns at the above planned event. I have worked as a storeperson at the centre for two years. I have always wanted to get trained up to drive the fork lifts, which would attract a better salary than my current one. I found out recently that there was to be a recruitment campaign for the post, which would involve an open day, where potential applicants could meet existing staff, ask questions, and actually have a go at driving a fork lift. This I thought was a great idea.

Upon asking for an invitation, however, I have been informed by my supervisor that the event is for female staff only. This is blatantly unfair on any male workers, and will give the impression of favouritism. Clearly, any female who attends the event will have a better chance of passing the interview due to the knowledge they will gain.

In any event, doubtless if the organisation is after female candidates, then irrespective of how the males do, then the females will get the posts.

This is completely unfair, and I am sure illegal.

All of the girls who I know are going on the open day are simply not suited to the job.

I would like to meet with you to get your assurance that males can also attend on the open day. That way, everyone who gets the job will know they did so on merit. Fair is fair.

Regards

Jay Deane

14

Role-play specimen plans, role actor's instructions and marking guides

- Abbot
- Byrnes
- Charles
- Deane

The information on the following pages is for the person taking the part of the role actor.

ABBOT: Specimen Plan

Circumstances

Explain purpose of meeting, letter and the fact asked by manager to meet with Abbot.
Get their concerns from them again summarised.
State manager wishes me to give results of meeting to them on their return.

Actions

Why Abbot concerned?
Why alarmed?
What do THEY mean by unsupervised?
Why concerned offenders working with children?
Have they any evidence for concerns?
Would they wish to visit scheme?
Will they let me talk to community group?
What do they mean by phrase 'animals running amok'?
Challenge politely 'animals' comment.

Results

Correct by reassurance Abbot's inaccurate view of scheme.
Point out low reoffending rates.
Point out purpose of scheme.
Explain low level crime background of offenders and screening process.
Explain how community is safer.
Ask if Abbot wants to visit scheme.
Ask if I can attend their community meeting to explain scheme to the other concerned people Abbot refers to.
Point out inappropriate phrase re 'animals' comment.

ABBOT: Role Actor Instructions

You are Abbot, a local resident who lives near to, and shops at, the centre. You have a couple of young children.

You have heard via rumours that there are dangerous criminals and offenders against children being allowed to work with children in the centre. You have *no* evidence to support these rumours. Initially be quite outraged at the perception you have about offenders being allowed into the centre.

You have written the enclosed letter to the centre management in order to complain. You believe that the offenders are a risk to children, and that prison is a much more effective way of dealing with offenders. You again have no evidence to back this up if the candidate asks.

Refer several times to the fact that 'these animals are running amok', which is an inappropriate remark that should be challenged by the candidate.

The candidate should ask you for evidence for your views, but you have none. They should then persuade you gradually that in actual fact, the scheme is a success, quoting figures where possible to you.

They should ask you about the local group you attend, and should ask/offer to attend your community meeting and explain the reality of the situation. If they do, invite them along. The candidate should also ask if you would like to visit the scheme. If so, reluctantly agree.

Do not immediately give in to the arguments of the candidate. Allow yourself to be reluctantly persuaded if they give reasons that are worth while.

Remember the concerns that you raised in the letter you wrote. The candidate should address all of your concerns, after first checking if you have any evidence for feeling that way.

Basically, your views are due to your lack of knowledge, and your inaccurate perception of the scheme. If the candidate does their job properly by informing you of the facts in a reassuring manner, whilst acknowledging your concerns, allow yourself to be reluctantly persuaded the scheme is OK.

ABBOT: Marking Guide

- Explains purpose of meeting. ☐
- Clarifies concerns from Abbot. ☐
- Clarifies what rumours Abbot has heard. ☐
- Offers clarification that these rumours are incorrect. ☐
- Challenges phrase 'animals running amok'. (Says why unacceptable.) ☐
- Explains crime figures. ☐
- Explains how crime has not in fact gone up. ☐
- Points out no reason for people to be alarmed. ☐
- Points out that all participants will be vetted and risk assessed. ☐
- Points out crime levels will be monitored. ☐
- Points out participants are trusties, who are doing charitable work. ☐
- Points out scheme reoffending rates are lower and it is more cost effective than prison. ☐
- Offers Abbot chance to visit scheme. ☐
- Informs Abbot scheme will be continuing. ☐
- Volunteers to take responsibility to attend community meeting and explain scheme. ☐

BYRNES: Specimen Plan

Circumstances

Explain letter from Peters complaining about recent cleaning issue.
Compliment Byrnes on work record.
Will report back to customer services manager on outcome.
Explain issue re allegation of sarcasm re litter offence.
Brief summary of letter.

Actions

Get Byrne's version of story.
Ask what litter offence (if any).
Ask if Byrnes actually issued ticket?
Ask what comments made (exactly).
What sarcasm? If so, challenge!
Why was Byrnes sarcastic (any excuses)?
Was there problem with Peters' reading ability/legs, possibly verbal abuse by Byrnes? (Probably not!)
Is Byrnes willing to apologise?
Has Byrnes been on customer service course? If so, when?

Results

Point out unacceptable conduct.
Make decision re disciplining Byrnes.
Monitor future Byrnes behaviour.
Point out negative effects of sarcasm.
Arrange apology if possible from Byrnes to Peters.
Send Byrnes on customer course or refresher.
Inform Peters of outcome.

BYRNES: Role Actor Instructions

You are Byrnes, a cleaning attendant at the Hapsford centre. You have been there for several years, and have a good reputation for keeping the areas around the centre clean. You do have the power to issue cleaning tickets for those who are littering under certain circumstances. You have been called to see the customer service officer, but do not know why.

They want to see you regarding an incident last week. This should be pointed out to you, but do not admit it was you until the candidate actually confirms with you that it was indeed yourself involved.

At this incident, you saw a car parked. As the driver got out, they threw the contents of the ashtray onto the ground, an area you had just cleaned. The driver went into a shop, and after a few minutes came out of the shop with a canned drink. You pointed out to them the cleaning offence, then started to make some sarcastic comments along the lines of 'Can't you read the no litter signs?' and 'Are your legs that bad you could not walk to a bin?'

You were indeed rude and sarcastic, and admit this happily if it is pointed out. Your view is that the person deserved it for littering there. Anyway, although you did have the power to issue a ticket, you decided that the sarcasm was enough. It is your view that the driver should consider themselves lucky as they did not get a ticket. The candidate should ask you to admit the remarks you made to the driver, and when you do so take the view you have done nothing wrong. If the candidate challenges you on your attitude, pointing out that it is unacceptable *with reasons*, then accept it.

You have not been on a customer service course, but are happy to go on one.

If the candidate suggests it, on reflection you would be willing to apologise to the driver.

If the candidate points out that it is not your role to be sarcastic, just to enforce your job fairly and firmly, agree not to be sarcastic in the future. If the candidate suggests that you would not like someone from your family to be spoken to in this sarcastic manner, slowly begin to admit that you were wrong. Go along with any punishment you are given, i.e. written warnings.

BYRNES: Marking Guide

- Compliments Byrnes on good work reputation. ☐
- Clarifies that Byrnes was member of staff concerned. ☐
- Clarifies purpose of meeting. ☐
- Explains letter of complaint has been received. ☐
- Clarifies exact comments made. ☐
- States comments unacceptable. ☐
- Clarifies if Byrnes gave out littering ticket. ☐
- Points out use of sarcasm unacceptable. ☐
- Asks how Byrnes would feel if someone was sarcastic to them. ☐
- Makes decision regarding discipline over comment. ☐
- Asks if Byrnes has been on customer contact course. ☐
- Sends Byrnes on customer contact course. ☐
- Checks if prepared to apologise to motorist. ☐
- States will monitor future behaviour. ☐
- States will update Peters re outcome of meeting. ☐

CHARLES: Specimen Plan

Circumstances

Explain purpose of meeting.
Comment on prior good work.
Explain allegations.
Point out poor performance over last three months.
Point out allegation of shopping.
Point out shopping against company policy including use of computer.

Actions

Confirm facts re shopping – e.g. on duty, it was shopping, and no good reason.
Get explanation of event.
Get confirmation that they admit their performance was poor.
Ask what happened three months ago.
Ask why performance dropped.
Do they realise behaviour is unacceptable?
Are they aware not supposed to shop/use company computers inappropriately?
Check reasons for why Charles behaving like this.
(WHY ONLY IN LAST THREE MONTHS?)
DID ANYTHING HAPPEN THREE MONTHS AGO TO START THIS OFF?
WHY IS THE SHIFT PATTERN MENTIONED?

Results

Point out unacceptable conduct.
Make decision re disciplining Charles.
Monitor Charles' future behaviour.
Inform manager of outcome.
Stop poor performance happening again.
IF THERE IS PROBLEM AFFECTING CHARLES' PERFORMANCE, SOLVE IT, OR AT LEAST HELP!

CHARLES: Role Actor Instructions

You are Mr/Ms Charles, a security guard at the centre. You have worked there for five years, during which time you have been very good at your job and this is recognised by your colleagues and managers. You are very proud of your role.

Three months ago, however, you received some bad news. You are very close to your family. Your partner had to have an operation on their spine, which makes it very hard for them to do much around the house. They cannot therefore do a great deal to look after the house and children. You are therefore having to look after them and your three children on your own. This takes up every spare moment of your time, as the children are only young. You get in from work, and have to spend every minute caring for them, picking them up from activities and so on.

This is the reason that you have been falling down in your performance at work. You do not have time to iron shirts or polish shoes, as you are genuinely stretched coping with the demands of your family.

You are unable to go shopping when off duty, as you have no one to help with the children. You have no home internet access, as you cannot afford it. You have no family in the area, apart from a cousin who can only help on certain days. The main problem you have is the shift pattern.

Therefore, when things are quiet at work, you sometimes use the company computers to quickly order your groceries via an online supermarket and get in your shopping. You genuinely have no other time sometimes, and no internet at home. You cannot physically go shopping as you have no babysitter.

This is what you were seen doing yesterday. You know it was wrong and against policy, but feel trapped by circumstances. You are very sorry for your performance and really are desperate for help.

Ideally, the candidate will realise this, and offer you some form of referral to the welfare unit. They should also offer to help you change shifts. If your shifts were more flexible, your babysitter is prepared to do more, the pressure on you would be relieved.

Do not offer information easily, make them work for it. Your overall attitude should be that of a good worker who is faced with pressures they cannot deal with without help. Do *not* reveal them though unless the candidate realises why you were doing personal tasks in work time.

CHARLES: Marking Guide

Explains purpose of meeting. ☐

Acknowledges previous good work. ☐

Outlines allegations. ☐

Asks for explanation. ☐

Ascertains reasons why Charles using internet. ☐

Points out shopping is unacceptable. ☐

Clarifies reasons for shopping in work time. ☐

Points out performance issues (late/untidy, etc.). ☐

Explains poor performance unacceptable. ☐

Clarifies reasons for this performance (i.e. family related). ☐

Makes decision re discipline. ☐

Asks how centre can provide help. ☐

Provides suggestions re time problems with school (shift change, etc.). ☐

Offers to refer to welfare department. ☐

States will monitor future behaviour. ☐

DEANE: Specimen Plan

Circumstances

Compliment Deane on their past work record.
Outline purpose of meeting to discuss concerns raised in Deane's report AND to address some comments made that appear to be unacceptable.
Clarify what Deane wants and their objections.

Actions

Why are they unhappy? Any complaints they are making?
What comments re Ferguson? Are they unacceptable, if so deal!
Why has Deane failed to get truck driver job before?
What do they mean 'all girls I know not suited to job'?

Results

Explain purpose of open day.
Deal with any unacceptable comments.
Help Deane to develop for next interview, or at least ask.
Correct any impressions amongst other people that process unfair.
Explain selection will be based on merit.
Explain why males will *not* be allowed to attend.
Explain why action is *not* illegal.

DEANE: Role Actor instructions

This role play can be played by either a male or female. If you are female, your view throughout is that you want the job on merit and not because there have been any allowances made for you as you are female.

You are Jay Deane. You have worked for two years as a storeperson at the centre. You have tried three times to get a better job as a fork lift truck driver which is also better paid; however, each time, your interview technique has let you down. You know this from your interview feedback and accept it. Do not tell the candidate this unless specifically asked, however. Drop a hint you know why you have failed if you have to.

You have learnt that there are more fork lift driver posts coming up, and that an open day is to be held where people will get the chance to drive the vehicles and have a go at loading pallets. When you asked to go, however, you were furious to find that it was for females only. You feel this is extremely unfair, and against the law (although it is not). You believe that the open day will give females an unfair advantage, and also that they will simply be given the jobs at the interview to fill some kind of quota.

You have made comments to Debbie Ferguson, another potential candidate, that women should not be allowed to do the job unless they have strong enough arms to steer the old fashioned trucks (in your opinion). Debbie has reported these comments to her manager. This is also your reason for saying that all of the girls you know who are applying for the job are not suited to it. You think they are not physically strong enough to do it.

The candidate should explain that the process is fair, and that selection will be on merit. Reluctantly accept this. The candidate should probe to find out why you failed before, and offer some support to develop you. If offered help with interview preparation by candidate, accept it.

Drop into the conversation a comment stating that many males feel the same way. The candidate should pick up on it and undertake to speak to the group concerned to point out that it is unacceptable.

You should be challenged on your own views and if you are, agree that there is a need for more females, but not at the expense of fairness.

If the candidate explains the fairness issue sufficiently, accept it reluctantly. If you yourself are female, the exercise is still valid. Take the attitude that as a female you do not want any preferential treatment and want to get the job on 'your own merit'.

DEANE: Marking Guide

- Explains purpose of meeting. ☐
- Explains reason for open day (to avoid male domination). ☐
- Asks why Deane feels they are unfair. ☐
- Explains no gender quota. ☐
- Explains not unlawful. ☐
- Clarifies why Deane has failed before to get fork lift truck job. ☐
- Offers preparation/development help to Deane for next interview. ☐
- Explains that selection will be on merit. ☐
- Clarifies comment 'girls are not suited to the job'. ☐
- Points out unacceptable sexist attitudes. ☐
- Explains Deane will not be allowed on open day. ☐
- Arranges to hold meeting with staff to fully explain purpose of open day. ☐

Index

application forms
  competency questions, 46–52
  forms, 10, 41–5
  motivation/perception questions, 53–7
asking questions
  about asking questions, 91–3, 107–8, 128
  being intrusive with questions, 141
  failure to ask questions, 162
  using 5WH, 124
assessment centres
  background, 6
  change of formats, 7
  finding out information in advance, 261–2
  preparation, 4–6
  typical assessment centre format, 59

CAR system
  purpose and importance, 63–8, 107–10, 184–6, 189–93
core competencies,
  definitions, 30–6
  how they developed, 26
  types of, 27
  using as an answer to a question, 56

fitness tests, 268–9

inappropriate behaviour
  background, 17, 61–3
  challenging, 24
  dealing with, 23, 101–2, 155, 157, 158–61, 231
  inappropriate language, 24, 90
  inside knowledge, 138
  recognising, 129, 156–7
  scalars, 161
  trapdoors, 141
interviews
  competency-based interview, 60
  competency question types, 194–212
  good interview evidence, 186, 187
  length of answers, 181, 193
  local in-force interview, 215–23
  using the CAR system, 184–6, 189–93
IQ tests, 267

marking guide
  role play plan relationship, 121

role plays
  ascertaining facts, 91
  conflicting information, 82
  inside knowledge, 138
  making decisions, 94–5, 154
  preparing for the exercise, 69, 71, 75, 103–4, 107–11
  purpose of the role play exercise, 96
  realism, 73
  role actors, 70, 74, 88, 89, 171–2
  signposts, hooks and blocks, 83–8, 125–7
  solutions, 97–101, 151–2, 165
  taking personal responsibility, 78
  time management, 76, 77
  timings, 144
  understand perspective, 80–1, 106–7
  using the preparation material, 82
  what are role plays?, 69, 96

welcome pack
  familiarity, 68
  introduction, 63
written reports,
  common mistakes, 238–9
  format, 227
  length of answers, 230
  principles, 232
  summarising, 232
  technique, 248–9
  using tables, 240
  what is being looked for, 229